POWER
PLAYS

—

JOHN O. WHITNEY
and
TINA PACKER

POWER PLAYS

—

*Shakespeare's Lessons
in Leadership and Management*

ILLUSTRATIONS by STEVE NOBLE

Macmillan

First published 2000 by Simon & Schuster Inc., Rockefeller Center,
1230 Avenue of the Americas, New York, NY 10020

First published in Great Britain 2000 by Macmillan
an imprint of Macmillan Publishers Ltd
25 Eccleston Place, London SW1W 9NF
Basingstoke and Oxford
Associated companies throughout the world
www.macmillan.co.uk

ISBN 0 333 78155 4

3 5 7 9 8 6 4 2

A CIP catalogue record for this book is available from
the British Library.

Printed and bound in Great Britain by
Mackays of Chatham plc, Chatham, Kent

to Mr. W. S.
from
two adventurers
setting forth

Contents

Contents

POWER
PLAYS

—

Prologue

WILLIAM Shakespeare as a management consultant? "Nonsense," you say? Not so fast. Shakespeare wrote one hundred fifty-four sonnets, several long poems, and thirty-nine plays. No other writer in the history of literature has displayed such a combination of industry and genius. Shakespeare wrote twenty-seven of his plays in one ten-year period; he finished the masterpieces *King Lear, Macbeth,* and *Antony and Cleopatra* in fourteen months. There is hardly a topic under the sun that he did not explore. Brilliantly. Good and evil, love and hatred, justice and mercy, pride and humility, guilt and innocence, war and peace. But the one subject he returns to again and again is leadership.

Successful CEOs are great leaders, and William Shakespeare probed more deeply into the problems of leadership than anyone before him and most who came after. Presidents and prime ministers still use Shakespeare's words to stir their people. So do revolutionaries. And no wonder: Shakespeare is our language's greatest writer; he is arguably the Western tradition's greatest thinker and student of human psychology. James Joyce once said that after God, Shakespeare has created most. The eminent Yale literary critic Harold Bloom has long argued that Shakespeare's plays can be taken as a kind of secular Bible of modern consciousness. According to Professor Bloom, an unabashed proselytizer of Bardolatry, his plays "remain the outward limit of human achievement." Bloom even goes so far as to argue in his most recent book, *Shakespeare: The Invention of the Human,* that by inventing so many deep and diverse characters that have entertained playgoers and readers for almost half a millennium, Shakespeare has, in effect, *invented us.*

I will leave the defense of those claims to Professor Bloom. Yet I, too, believe that if you look into Shakespeare's mirror, you will see yourself. If you read his plays carefully, the power of his language, his characters, and the situations he puts them in are bound to make you stop and wonder: What would I have done? Shakespeare has something to say to everyone, but Tina Packer and I genuinely believe he can be especially helpful to modern business leaders at every level of the game.

Profits sagging, business flat? Then you'd better rally the troops, just as Shakespeare's King Henry V did before the Battle of Agincourt, when the weary, damaged English forces were outnumbered by the French five to one. If you have received a promotion that colleagues do not think you deserve, *King Henry IV* could instruct you in how to deal with the backlash. How will the person you beat out for the job respond? *Othello*'s Iago, one of the greatest villains in dramatic literature, could offer some clues that you ignore only at your peril. You're in a new job and facing a building full of hostile employees. Mark Antony's brilliant funeral oration on behalf of Julius Caesar is a textbook on how to win over an angry crowd.

How do you deal with an unreasonable boss? When is it time to stick it out, when to move on? *King Lear* has the answers. This great Shakespearean tragedy is, in fact, a treasure trove of business models: managing succession in family companies, the dangers of flattery, and the folly of co–chief executives, not to mention the penalty of disregarding the advice of loyal employees.

And then there's *Hamlet*.

Have you ever wondered about your own reluctance (or inability) to make a decision and then act? Scholars disagree on many of the causes of Hamlet's analysis-paralysis, but most agree that one of the causes was certainly the conflict in what we business school professors call his "external decision models."

What about your own decision models? Are they in conflict? Do they still reflect your business realities? Where does intellectual capital stand on your balance sheet? Does the current accounts balance mean the same thing in the year 2000 as it did in 1980? How do you measure gross domestic product with the accounting methods used by global enterprises? Business leaders who do not know whether those apparent anomalies are temporary or enduring, independent or interdependent or just plain illusory, will find that Hamlet's paralysis can be contagious.

Sixteenth-century England was fascinated by and preoccupied

with leaders. Throughout the Middle Ages, England had seen too many flawed monarchs. Richard II, vain, profligate, and indecisive, died in prison in 1399. His usurper, Henry IV, was an effective crisis manager; trouble was, the rebellions he gained fame for suppressing were the result of his overthrowing Richard. Henry's son, Henry V (Shakespeare's "Prince Hal"), was an effective and popular leader who consolidated his position with a questionable war (a political device not unfamiliar to twentieth-century leaders). And so it went. Indeed, after Henry V's death in 1422, serious leadership and succession problems persisted in England for the next 136 years, until the coronation of Elizabeth I, whose forty-five-year reign took England through one of its greatest eras. The "Virgin Queen" was a constant source of fascination and inspiration for her loyal subject William Shakespeare. (Happily for Shakespeare and us, Elizabeth was a great fan of the theater.)

That was four hundred years ago, of course, and things have certainly changed. But the psychology and practice of leading large numbers of people in a hard-knuckled world is not one of them. How leaders emerge at any level of society has a pattern. No matter how different cultures are, the ways of power appear as a constant, whether in medieval England, in tribal Africa, in Communist China, or in corporate America. The pivotal people may bear different titles—king, emperor, chief, duke, consul, president, CEO, chairman of the board. But the powers that they hold, their influence over other people's lives, the new ground they break, the good that they can do, and the harm that they can cause—all these have parallels in every society throughout history.

How alliances are created and acts of loyalty are rewarded, how dissenters are punished, how leaders are toppled, how grand designs lose the name of action—these are the pathways to power, which have been going on for centuries and doubtless will continue for centuries to come. Literary or moral genius is not progressive. In the same way that the Old and New Testaments of the Bible, written thousands of years ago, still speak to us, so does Shakespeare. Relations between a nation's major vested interests (in other words, the dukedoms, churches, important families, political party factions) and the governments that Shakespeare lived through in the reigns of Elizabeth I and James I generated power players familiar to us in the Age of Globalization: advisers, courtiers, lobbyists, old-boy networks, party hacks, secret lovers, masons, kith and kin. Nor are we strangers to the efforts of outsiders to step onto the ladders of power. We too are familiar with the glass ceiling of discrimination that seems to hover over women and minorities. And what business leader today has not faced the challenge of balancing career and family?

When you are in the midst of such maelstroms, it is very difficult to pause and reflect on who has been there before. The aim of this book is to point out that wherever you are in your career or private life, Shakespeare has been there already, and he has much to teach us. He has certainly helped Tina Packer and me on our very different ways in life. Tina is the founder and CEO of Shakespeare & Company, a thriving classical theater in Massachusetts. She is a Brit by birth and a pragmatic political radical by choice. I am a professor of business at Columbia University and a former CEO who for twenty-five years specialized in corporate turnarounds. I am from Oklahoma and politically conservative.

But Tina and I share a passion for Shakespeare, a passion for life, and a passion for getting things done. (We also are inclined to agree that, in the end, such passions are what's most important anyway.) Over the years, we have both used the plays of Shakespeare as a source of inspiration in our professional lives. As the woman who has directed probably more productions of Shakespeare's plays than any other in the world, Tina lives with Shakespeare all the time. She can scarcely make a move without seeing the parallel in Shakespeare's universe.

I first met Shakespeare as a student and have kept a copy of one of his plays in my back pocket ever since. Most of us have one unforgettable teacher in our lives, and mine was Franklin Ikenberry, a professor of English at Tulsa University. In Ikenberry's classes, Shakespeare's lessons in leadership sprang to life for me. My student days at Tulsa were lived in Hamlet's tortured dilemmas, and my first job working for someone else was full of Hotspur's impatience. And when I quit that job to create my own advertising agency in Tulsa, Oklahoma, with $3,600, most of it borrowed, I had a wife, two kids, no clients. When I was exhausted and ready to pack it in, I remembered the heroic example of Shakespeare's Coriolanus, who entered the enemy's gates alone and single-handedly defeated the enemy.

In 1972, I was recruited from my position as associate dean of the Harvard Business School to help turn around Pathmark, one of the nation's biggest supermarket chains. Layoffs were feared; morale was low. But I knew exactly what to do because I had listened to the incomparable Falstaff when he taught Prince Hal in *King Henry IV, Part 1* that if he was going to lead people he needed to enter their world. I immediately visited Pathmark's stores and warehouses. And, like Henry V before the Battle of Agincourt, I rallied the troops. In the face of opposition from the people I was working for, I stuck to my guns because I had learned from *Macbeth* the risks of abandoning your principles. *Julius Caesar* had also taught me that the rigid, dogmatic leader risks getting it in the neck; and from *King Henry IV* I learned how important it is for a leader to create a strategy and stick with it. Of course, I had enemies eager to see me fail, but what they didn't know was that I had been instructed in malicious deceit by Iago. On more than one occasion, I avoided being dispatched into oblivion by recalling *King Lear.*

I now teach a course called "In Search of the Perfect Prince" on Shakespeare and Leadership at Columbia Business School (a course Tina has now taken over). I also conduct seminars for diverse groups of business leaders. The first thing I do is break down the intimidating barrier between them and what they perceive as "Great Literature." Shakespeare is undeniably great, but a student's anxiety about understanding a poet who lived four hundred years back in history disappears immediately once I persuade them that they and Shakespeare have a lot in common. For starters, Shakespeare was from a business family, the son of a glove merchant and butcher who did a stint as mayor of a thriving market town. Shakespeare was a poet, an actor, and a playwright, of course; but he was also a businessman, shareholder in the most successful theater company of his time, a servant of the king, and, by the end of his life, one of the wealthiest men in his hometown of

Stratford-on-Avon. (In his early thirties, Shakespeare bought the second-biggest house in town.) He was certainly no stranger to money, debt, business plans, or profit-and-loss statements, and his plays reflect this knowledge.

Shakespeare, contrary to our modern stereotypes of ivory-tower intellectuals and of poets who will not descend to the world of commerce, was a true man of the world. He hung out in the pubs and understood the lives of ordinary people as well as the political and social intrigues of the courts of Elizabeth and James I. Shakespeare was well versed in the uses and abuses of power; he took the great wealth of information pouring off the new printing presses—the historical chronicles, the great classical writers of Greece and Rome, fairy stories and folk tales, the Bible—and made his plays. *Playwright* means literally "maker of plays," in the same way that the cartwright was a maker of carts or a wheelwright made wheels. Each artisan took the materials he needed and crafted them into something that worked, that people could use. Shakespeare's materials were ideas, stories, words. Like his fellow Elizabethan writers, Shakespeare had no qualms about plagiarism. He lifted great swaths of text from his predecessors, altered a few words here and there to make them more to his own taste, and thus made new cloth out of old geniuses.

The people flocked to hear his work, and, according to recent box office numbers, they still do. It is the premise of this book that Shakespeare's genius in exploring the motivations of men and women, great and small, his uncanny insight into what is obvious but we cannot see, is a huge resource for any businessperson. We hope you find him as inspiring as we have, and just as useful.

This book is organized around three major themes in Shakespeare's plays that resonate as clearly in today's business world as they did in Elizabethan days:

Part I deals with power. Shakespeare understood that while leaders have power by virtue of their position, subordinates can also have enormous influence on how their leaders exercise power. We'll reveal what Shakespeare has to teach about how a leader can use power well, how executives can manage the natural tension between them and the people who report to them, and how business leaders and their trusted lieutenants can maintain their focus on the business at hand, making money and growing a company.

Part II turns to the crucial business skills of effective communication and persuasion. Leadership is theater. To be in charge is to act the part. "All the world's a stage," Shakespeare wrote, and no writer has a deeper grasp of the power of performance. Nor is anyone more instructive on what it takes for a leader to gain the support of followers to achieve his objectives. Tina and I analyze what Shakespeare teaches us about the use of ceremony, symbols, and oratory to signal a commitment to your people without having to compromise your ability to make decisions, even occasionally unpopular ones.

Part III deals with values and how to reconcile what we believe in as moral agents with what we need to do as leaders with responsibilities to bosses, boards, stockholders, and employees. After all, that is the definition of a moral dilemma—two goals in conflict (for example, my personal concern about the environment versus my fiduciary responsibility to my board and stockholders). When is it appropriate to deceive someone? When is it not? How can you avoid becoming a Hamlet—so self-conscious about your beliefs that you are unable to act? We at the top of the power pyramid tend to take ourselves very seriously. Shakespeare has an antidote for every organization: his name is Falstaff.

Every chapter will combine anecdotes from our own business experiences and Shakespearean parallels and analogies. In business schools, we learn a lot from real-life "cases" drawn from the corporate world. In the chapters that follow, I point out events in the marketplace where some players are so talented, so much "bigger than life," and so tragic that the only word that does their exploits justice is *Shakespearean*. I examine Jack Welch, the exemplary leader of General Electric for twenty years, as a foil to Shakespeare's most incompetent leader, Richard II. We look at Al Dunlap, whose lean, mean style earned him the nickname "Chainsaw Al," through the story of Coriolanus, the rigid Roman general of Shakespeare's tragedy of that name.

Tina Packer has reminded me that one reason Shakespeare

wrote so much about kings and queens and power was that they represent the human psyche magnified. His audience could see immediately a particular character grappling with one dilemma or another, and then Shakespeare shows that each individual action has immense repercussions in the outside world. We see Macbeth agonizing over the desires of his "vaulting ambition" to be king, versus his good conscience's warning against becoming a murderer. When he chooses to be a killing machine, others' lives are doomed. His wife, who encourages him to assassinate the king, eventually goes mad with guilt. Richard III's unbridled ambition not only turns England's politics upside down, it ruins his own life. Today, businesses are limited only by the size of the globe. The biggest corporations are genuine "empires." What Jack Welch does at General Electric can affect his direct reports, all of GE's thousands of employees and their families, not to mention the lives of millions of GE's customers. (And when you add the fact that GE also owns the television network NBC, the numbers multiply by the tens of millions.)

And thus Shakespeare does not seem so old-fashioned after all. Tina also points out that in Shakespeare's day, art, new ideas, and business acumen collaborated in a way that changed the world forever. (The Renaissance, which began in Italy in the fourteenth century and spread throughout the rest of Europe over the next two hundred years, literally means "rebirth.") It was not unusual for a great man to accomplish great things in many arenas. Leonardo da Vinci, the Italian painter, sculptor, architect, engineer, scientist, and musician, is the prototypical Renaissance genius. In Shakespeare's England, Sir Walter Raleigh was a poet, an alchemist, an explorer of the New World, a favorite of Queen Elizabeth. (He was executed for treason by her successor, James I.) Another English Renaissance man was Sir Francis Bacon, the philosopher, scientist, and essayist, who ran afoul of Elizabeth but fared better under James, serving as attorney general and then lord chancellor. (Bacon, one of Thomas Jefferson's intellectual heroes, was such an extraordinary figure that some have claimed that in his spare time he was really the author of Shakespeare's thirty-nine plays.)

As a new century begins, Tina and I see signs that the creativity of artists and the practicality of businesspeople may, once again, become allies. We would like this book to be a small contribution to that collaboration. On a more workaday level, we hope that after reading *Power Plays: Shakespeare's Lessons in Leadership and Management,* you will head out on your next business assignment, as Tina and I do, with Shakespeare at your side.

So let's begin, or, as Shakespeare says in his play *King Richard II:*

> For God's sake let us sit upon the ground
> And tell sad stories of the death of kings:
> How some have been depos'd, some slain in war,
> Some haunted by the ghosts they have deposed,
> Some poisoned by their wives, some sleeping kill'd,
> All murthered—for within the hollow crown
> That rounds the mortal temples of a king
> Keeps Death his court, and there the antic sits,
> Scoffing his state and grinning at his pomp . . .
> KING RICHARD II (3.2, 155–63)

Part I

POWER

For Good and for Evil

———

1

Power Is a Freighted Idea

Understand It Before You Use It

> How sweet a thing it is to wear a crown . . .
>
> Richard in KING HENRY VI, PART 3 (1.2, 29)

Power! Shakespeare! Few would put these two words together. For if you want to understand power—how to get it, how to keep it, what to do when you have it, and how you lose it—then Shakespeare is your man. Power is a central theme in many of his plays. No writer ever portrayed the ambiguities, trappings, dangers, and blessings of power better than Shakespeare. He shows us how power is passed down through the generations. For instance, Harry Bolingbroke knocks Richard II off the throne and ends up causing the Wars of the Roses, a hundred-year strife between the

House of York and the House of Lancaster. Shakespeare shows how power slips away. Henry V builds an empire, but his son Henry VI makes so many mistakes that he ends up wandering around the countryside, alone, yearning to be a humble shepherd. Shakespeare shows the seduction of power. In *Hamlet* Gertrude marries the man who has annihilated her husband, Rosencrantz and Guildenstern betray their classmate, and Polonius sacrifices his daughter, all because they want to stay close to the seat of power. Shakespeare shows the abuse of power. Richard Plantagenet (ultimately Richard III) exults in the act of evil, not interested in the complexities and responsibilities of power. It takes him twenty-three years to get his crown, but only two to lose it. Richard III wants power so badly that he literally kills for it. As does Macbeth. Of course, no sane CEO sets out to be Richard III or Macbeth. To hear them tell it, every CEO is in business to make the world a better place. But too many successful business leaders, despite their good intentions, end up believing their press releases, perceive power as an end rather than a means, and get distracted from their real jobs: growing their companies, making money for their shareholders, and, in the process, serving their employees, customers, communities, and society at large. And too many CEOs, like Julius Caesar, hang on to power, don't see that times have changed and that it's time to go, before they are pushed.

The proper exercise of power is one of the most persistent challenges facing us in our work lives. Some of us, like Shakespeare's Richard II, the man Bolingbroke pushed off the throne, do not understand it at all; and like him we lose it. Others of us might understand it but then fail to use it; and, like Prince Hamlet, we lose it. Understanding power—its strengths and limitations—and knowing when and how to use it are critical to success in the business world, as well as in our personal lives.

Our age is the age of power. Incredible power. World power. Media power. Technological power. Money power. Power that can alter things so quickly, a shift has occurred before most of the world's population knows anything about it. Power to lift up and throw down like a great tornado. And if you are a young executive who wants power, well, you're going to have to fight for it every bit as fiercely as Shakespeare's medieval knights hacking each other down in battle. But you are going to need more than courage and brute strength. You are going to need self-knowledge, know your strengths and weaknesses, have stamina and intelligence, know when to speak out, when to keep quiet, know how to inspire, how to apologize, when to act alone, when to support someone else, when to seize leadership, how to learn from mistakes, how to keep focused when everyone else around you is screaming, and how to balance personal life and professional life—and, above all, how to retain passion, compassion, and commitment in the face of unending complications and seemingly insuperable barriers.

The desire for power can be satisfied in ways other than a cavernous corner office overlooking Central Park—for example, in organizing thousands of people for public service or leading the best-known R&D department. Some of the perks of power are tempting—the corporate jet, the car and driver, the corner office and executive secretary. But be forewarned: the symbols of power are not power; they are only symbols. Because I spent most of my business life running start-ups and turnarounds, it would have been counterproductive to be seen enjoying these kinds of perks, although they looked good to me. Now, as a corporate board member and guest speaker, I get to use these symbols of power from time to time. They're fun, but they're certainly not what power is all about. They are just the trappings. And like despotic rulers— Richard III and Macbeth—they have given power a bad name, causing many people to believe that power, by its nature, is evil.

Several years ago, I delivered a sermon at my church in which I simply referred to the notion of power. Afterward two women scolded me severely for bringing up such a vulgar issue in church. I stuttered some polite reply. Today, I would advise them that power is not necessarily an evil thing. Power is a freighted idea, filled with shifting cargo: power to build, power to tear down; power to hasten, power to delay; power to inspire, power to frighten; power to give, power to withhold; power to love, power to hurt; power to do good, power to do evil. The two church ladies, like Richard Plantagenet and Macbeth, did not understand power.

POWER: UNDERSTAND IT OR LOSE IT

What is the reach of power? Will a given action radiate beyond its intended scope? Will there be other unintended consequences? Should limits be put on power? What should you use it for? How far can you take it? How often can you use it? How will you know if it is effective? What will be your response if it is ignored? Above all, you must understand its target. For whom, or at what, is it directed?

There are always complex answers to these questions. What works for one person or group might not work for another. What works today might not work tomorrow. Shakespeare certainly doesn't provide absolute answers, but he poses questions so provocatively that our understanding is enriched as we contemplate the problems he presents.

POWER IS RELATIVE, NOT ABSOLUTE

Power is relative to time, place, person, and situation. I have seen managers who, because they have power on their own home turf, assume they are powerful everywhere. And what about the young investment banker glowing over his first six-figure bonus, who becomes an overnight expert on economics, political science, and the weather? Money is powerful only in certain contexts: if knowledge or compassion is what is needed to understand something, money may not help.

Ask the people at IBM, Motorola, or Eastman Kodak whether power is relative or absolute. Then ask them if in the 1980s they had an understanding of the sources of their power. If at that time they had been able to acknowledge that what goes up can come down, ask them what they would have done differently. Answer: just about everything. These companies are so large that their fortunes and misfortunes are well chronicled. But many of the analyses miss the real story: these leaders and managers did *not* know the sources of their power, and they thought that the elevators ran only one way—up.

Fortunately, what goes down can also go up. So as we start the new millennium, IBM is back on top once again, Motorola is clawing its way back up the success ladder, but Eastman Kodak is still struggling. We will be looking more closely at these companies later, but wherever they are—and more importantly to you, wherever you are on the ladder of success—don't ever lose sight of your real sources of power. Where does your power come from? And don't let today's success lull you into thinking that tomorrow will always be like today.

A brilliant exposition of how power shifts with time and circumstance is found in one of Shakespeare's lesser-known plays. In *Coriolanus*, Caius Martius is an experienced, powerful Roman warrior. After his superb military leadership at the siege of Corioli against the Volscians, Martius is rewarded with the name Coriolanus and encouraged to stand for consul, one of Rome's most powerful jobs. But Coriolanus, whose arrogance matches his ego, thinks he should be made consul without going through the steps necessary for elected office. He feels that the "politicking" he must do to be elected consul is beneath him. So his first error is to think that being a great warrior automatically qualifies him to be a politician. Second, he fails to recognize that Rome's tribunes, the city's middle managers, are out to destroy him politically. And because their tactics are unlike a soldier's, Coriolanus has no idea of or desire to counteract their activities, and they succeed in getting him banished from Rome. The indignant Coriolanus seeks revenge. Dressed in rags, with no weapons, he makes his way to the Volscian camp and seeks out his old adversary, Aufidius. This time he makes a masterful move and in a gesture of humility offers his naked throat to Aufidius:

> . . . and present
> My throat to thee and to thy ancient malice;
> Which not to cut would show thee but a fool . . .
>
> CORIOLANUS (4.5, 98–100)[1]

You can see that Coriolanus has undergone two major power shifts: from Roman noble to battle hero to failed politician. And now he undergoes a third: to bum. He is a supplicant, like a fallen corporate hero once "master of the universe" whose company faces bankruptcy, pleading with bankers for more time and more money. However, this time Coriolanus's actions pay off—probably because he understands his enemy and fellow warrior, Aufidius, better than he did the tribunes. "Go to someone you know and who knows you" is probably not bad advice. Aufidius, appreciative of Coriolanus's prowess in battle, knows that with Coriolanus's help, he, Aufidius, can achieve his lifelong dream, the conquest of Rome. So he assigns half of the Volscian army to Coriolanus's command:

> . . . take
> Th' one half of my commission [soldiers], and set down
> As best thou art experienc'd, since thou know'st
> Thy country's strength and weakness . . .
>
> CORIOLANUS (4.5, 140–43)

So the power shifts again. And Coriolanus is on his way back up, and he's back with people he understands: soldiers. Like General MacArthur's men, ordinary troops idolize him. Aufidius's lieutenant reports a potential problem to him—Coriolanus's relationship with half of Aufidius's army:

> I do not know what witchcraft's in him, but
> Your soldiers use him as the grace 'fore meat,
> Their talk at table and their thanks at end;
> And you are darken'd in this action, sir,
> Even by your own.
>
> CORIOLANUS (4.7, 2–6)

Although Aufidius realizes he is losing the loyalty of his own men, he ruefully replies:

> I cannot help it now,
> Unless, by using means, I lame the foot
> Of our design [to conquer Rome].
>
> CORIOLANUS (4.7, 7–9)

Aufidius is so eager to report a profit next quarter that he ignores the fact that it could be dangerous to have Coriolanus leading his troops. He has turned over half his company to an ambitious vice president, who promises results even though his credentials are questionable. And for a short while it looks as if Aufidius's gamble is going to pay off. But just before Coriolanus is about to attack Rome (and both sides are convinced he will succeed), his strong-willed mother talks him out of sacking and burning his hometown, convincing him to seek an armistice instead. Because Aufidius has given up so much of his power to Coriolanus, Coriolanus can do this. But when Coriolanus completes the peace negotiations and Rome is saved, Aufidius is so humiliated that he and a group of conspirators assassinate him.

In today's world, this scenario of shifting power is all too familiar. Once, not long ago, the jobs of senior executives were seen as sinecures. If you made it to CEO, vice president, or division manager, you could count on having a smooth ride to age sixty-five, collecting your gold watch, and living comfortably on your pension. No more. And probably not ever again. The competitive landscape is changing too fast, and stockholders expect near-perfect performance. Still, many executives I have known have let themselves be lulled into thinking that today's success will be repeated automatically and forever. I don't counsel paranoia, but in the first four chapters of this book we'll demonstrate some of the pitfalls—and pratfalls—lurking for leaders who believe that power is absolute. Let us be clear: it is not absolute, it is relative to time and place, person and function.

———

POWER FOR POWER'S SAKE IS POWER LOST

If we believe or act as if power is for power's sake alone, we are sure to lose it. One of Shakespeare's first protagonists, the man who would be Richard III, originally appears in two early plays, *King Henry VI, Part 2* and *Part 3*, dreaming about "how sweet a thing it is to wear a crown." By the time of his own play, *King Richard III,* an older if not wiser Richard has become a single-minded terrorist who slaughters his way to the throne. He has his own brother stabbed and then drowned in a barrel of wine, his nephews smothered to death, his wife poisoned, his in-laws executed.

Richard has the great business leader's ambition and determination, no question about it. His rise is proof of the power of power, not to mention its addictive properties. Richard does not seem to have any goal other than to be king. After a brief reign (his two years on the throne are reduced to about two weeks by Shakespeare), when he tries to escape death in battle, he is more than willing to give up the throne he murdered eleven people for, to save his own neck. "A horse, a horse, my kingdom for a horse!" he exclaims for generations who will repeat his phrase. A desperate trade, but appropriate for one who wants power only for power's sake.

Macbeth, too, wanted to be king without knowing exactly what to do with the power once he was crowned. He, too, was willing to kill for power. But while Richard III is the kind of monster that even the most aggressive executive will have trouble recognizing in the mirror, Macbeth is like us. He wants power, but he also feels guilty about what he's willing to do to get it. A brave and loyal servant of a good king, the warrior Macbeth learns from the three witches he meets in the third scene of the play that he is destined to be king. Immediately, Macbeth can see himself on the throne; worse, he realizes that he is willing to consider assassinating King Duncan to achieve this destiny. When he tells his wife about the three witches' prediction, Lady Macbeth encourages him to go for it even though she's confided to the audience earlier that he's "too full o' the milk of human kindness." But what executive (or his wife) has not dreamed of making the boss disappear? Macbeth, like us, resists his urge, for a moment anyway. He has a conscience. He knows Duncan is a "gracious" man. However, when he tells his wife of his qualms, she lets him have it: "When you durst do it, then you were a man." She also puts their relationship on the line: "From this time forth, such I account thy love." It's all Macbeth needs to get him over the moral hump. He sets out to kill King Duncan.

The appeal of Macbeth to the audience, as many critics have noted, is that we can empathize with him. While his murders might

appall us, his desire to get rid of the opposition hooks us. In spite
of knowing what he ought to do, he does otherwise. Do we see ourselves here? As he says:

> . . . why do I yield to that suggestion [of murdering Duncan]
> Whose horrid image doth unfix my hair,
> And make my seated heart knock at my ribs,
> Against the use of nature?
>
> MACBETH (1.3, 134–37)

We understand the temptation he faces because we, too, aspire
to the big job. We also have been fed the fallacy that great leaders
need to be "killers." We have heard Lady Macbeth question our
manhood. And who in the business world does not understand the
power of what Macbeth calls his "vaulting ambition"?

But what does Macbeth accomplish once he wears the crown?
He becomes a serial killer. To secure his power, Macbeth orders
the deaths of his best friend, Banquo, Fleance, his best friend's
son, anyone who is against him, even Macduff's children. A noble
warrior, he seems never to have thought about the necessities of
politics or the good of the people he is leading. He is interested
only in power for power's sake. And therein lies the seed of
Macbeth's tragedy. In the characters of both Richard III and Macbeth, Shakespeare shows us the most dangerous temptation of
power; namely, that we think it is a good in itself. Might is right.

Beginning in the 1960s, many successful chief executives began
to grow their companies for the sake of growth only. Every healthy
organization requires growth. But sound growth is one thing, unbridled growth quite another. The early conglomerates were often
cobbled together under no grand strategy other than "Bigger is
Better." James Ling was at the forefront of this movement. At the
start of the decade he acquired several firms to create Ling-Temco-
Voight (LTV), an aircraft and electronics manufacturing corporation. At the end of the 1960s he went on a tear, acquiring other
conglomerates in sporting goods, foods, pharmaceuticals, airlines, and car rental companies. But when he bought Jones &
Laughton Steel, the debt forced him to divest many of his other

holdings. In the late 1970s he renewed his quest, buying a sheet and tubing firm, a steamship line, a maker of military vehicles, and finally another steel company, Republic. By 1986, LTV was bankrupt. It emerged from court protection only in 1993—as a debt-ridden producer of flat-rolled steel.

During this same period Charles Bluhdorn, the swashbuckling chief executive of Gulf + Western, acquired a very successful Hollywood movie and TV studio, Paramount, and then added the country's leading book publisher, Simon & Schuster, as well as an array of consumer and industrial products firms. Within three years after Bluhdorn's death in a plane accident in 1983, his successor, Martin Davis, had sold sixty of these companies, reducing its workforce by two thirds and its sales by half, finally giving it a new focus and vigor. The studio and publishing arms were renamed Paramount Communications. Ten years later it was sold to Sumner Redstone's Viacom and functioned effectively as part of a large entertainment corporation. While Paramount and Simon & Schuster flourished, Gulf + Western no longer existed.

More recently, the investment banking firm Drexel Burnham Lambert went down for the count for the same fundamental reason. During the junk-bond craze, DBL issued ever more risky debt for companies no one else would finance. When these firms foundered, DBL lost its credibility and financial clout. It declared bankruptcy.

The U.S. economy has been excellent the last few years, so the dramatic unraveling has not been quite so dramatic. However, the current wave of spin-offs does show that executives today might have learned something from the 1970s and 1980s and that they are more wary than their predecessors. The acquisition frenzy of the 1970s and 1980s only proves a point that Shakespeare was making four hundred years ago: Power sought for its own sake is bound to be power lost. No matter what level you're playing at, the manager who is interested in power only to acquire "more" is in business for the wrong reason. When you are reveling in your "killer instinct," you may want to think about how Macbeth and Richard III (and Jimmy Ling and too many others), the most powerful men in their realms, each met, as Shakespeare says of Richard, "his piteous and unpitied end" (*Richard III*, 4.4, 74).

Over and over again, Shakespeare advises us that the best leaders seek power in order to accomplish something.

POWER FROM THE PEOPLE: A CONUNDRUM

The leader must understand the source of his power, and he must also understand that pandering to that source will ultimately defeat him. On the one hand, we all know that the authority to lead is derived from those who are led. A good leader hears the people he is leading and lets them know they are being heard. However, when he or she has to make a judgment call about the course of action, it may not be the popular one. The people may not even have thought of the action that the leader is preparing to take! And the person remains a leader only if the people will be led. Making people do things because you can is not a very good way of leading— for power alone, ultimately, cannot protect power. Even dictators, though the army and the secret police might support them, can be deposed. Hitler died in his bunker; Mussolini was hanged by his heels. "Baby Doc" Duvalier was banished. Even those dictators who died in bed will eventually be discredited; Mao, Stalin, and Lenin are now seen for what they were—ruthless murderers, not compassionate servants of the people.

And yet, perceiving that even the most entrenched leaders can be deposed, some leaders, in their desire to hold on to power, will do anything to keep the people happy. On the political scene, we see polls and pandering being used as the very foundation of leadership. In the corporate world, we see leaders who are afraid to take a principled stand, leaning toward powerful but unrepresentative shareholder factions, bending for public interest groups (which may or may not have the public interest in mind but do make a lot of noise) and aggressive minorities. It is true that a political leader needs the information that polls provide; a business leader needs information from marketing research, financial advisers, public relations polling, and employee surveys. But how important is that information? How should it be used?

If the leader gains insights from the resources listed above, should he or she devise a course of action that at least will please the majority? First he must ask, "Which majority?" Perhaps a majority agrees about one destination, but each individual wants to take a different route. However, if a different destination were offered, a different majority might materialize in its favor. Even if these problems were solvable, what about the minority and its many permutations? We may need their support, too, if we are to reach the destination.

None of this is new to leaders, managers—or followers. The newly appointed manager learns the first day on the job that he or she cannot please everyone all the time. Some elected leaders have learned, to their sorrow, that a preoccupation with polls is a prescription for failure. Would that more leaders in government or business had read, understood, and had the courage to act on Edmund Burke's advice: "Your representative owes you not his industry only, but his judgment; and he betrays, instead of serving you, if he sacrifices it to your opinion."[2] Perhaps Burke was advised by Coriolanus, who, flawed as he was, knew some tenets of leadership. Coriolanus urges his fellow senators to see that by yielding to popular demands,

> . . . Thus we debase
> The nature of our seats, and make the rabble
> Call our cares fears . . .
>
> CORIOLANUS (3.1, 135–37)

He goes on to say,

> . . . Your dishonour
> Mangles true judgement, and bereaves the state
> Of that integrity which should becom't . . .
>
> CORIOLANUS (3.1, 157–59)

Leaders are not sponges to soak up and then squeeze out the same muddy water. Leaders are not conduits merely, but creators.

And great leaders are great creators. Someone else would have discovered America if Christopher Columbus had been required to put his proposition to a vote.[3] Would General Electric be as successful as it is if, twenty years ago, Jack Welch had sought to please his hierarchy of comfortable vice presidents—senior vice presidents and group vice presidents—and asked them to approve his sometimes draconian measures? Franklin Roosevelt and Ronald Reagan were elected by the people, but had they been required to put to vote every action they deemed necessary in order to create the New Deal or to win the Cold War, the country could have taken years to recover from the Depression and the Cold War might have gone on forever.

A leader must understand the capabilities of his followers, not as they exist today, but as they would exist if they were stretched. The leader's job is not to seek what is comfortable, but what is possible and what will ultimately serve the purpose. Yes, the leader must also understand the mood of those he is leading, but not in order to pander; rather, to know where to place the ladder, so that he and his followers can climb together. And ultimately a leader must convince her followers, through action, example, and argument, that this is the way to go and together they can do it.

POWER IS A TOOL

When we understand that power is a tool—and can be used as a tool for good—we begin to unlock its potential. Tina Packer began her career in the theater with a prejudice against power. Raised in England in a family with deep attachments to the working class, Tina, who went to school in the 1960s, believed that the rich and powerful were always out to exploit the poor and the weak. Then, as she entered the workforce as an actress, she began to think more deeply about power. She was a member of England's legendary Royal Shakespeare Company: a small cog in a large organization. Soon she conceded to herself that she wanted power. "Because I had none," she recalls. But Tina, unlike Macbeth or Richard, did not want power only for the sake of having it. Let her explain:

I wanted power because I couldn't bear not having a voice. As a mere actor in the theater world, you have no voice. You're cast based only on what you look like, and you begin to lose all sense of who you really are. I knew if I wasn't to lose myself, I had to start doing the kind of theater I thought was important. Even though at that time I was working with the best theater directors in the English-speaking world, I still felt as if I was of no consequence because what they were saying was not what I wanted to say. Mind you, at that time I didn't really know what I wanted to say. But I had to step out and start saying what I thought I thought; otherwise I would remain voiceless. I had to start making my own mistakes in order to define who I was. If I can generalize for a moment, I think that's true for a lot of women. Often we feel that we're powerless, at least in the ways that the world currently defines power. One of the joys I look forward to is the ways in which women can influence the way power is manifested. I wanted to articulate what I thought would make a great theater company, and I wanted to run it in a way that would include everyone's creativity.

So Tina, a born critic of the powerful, realized the only way she could find out whether she could do a better job than the people she was working for was not to sit on the sidelines and criticize but to try to get her own vision working. And that meant leading and being willing to step out and create a different kind of theater. And she found that she could do it. She didn't want power for power's sake. But she did want to get something done. She was, if you will, called to power.

POWER — USE IT WISELY OR LOSE IT

Action without thought is foolish, but thought without action is fruitless. There comes a time to decide, then act. You might not have all the information you need (in fact, you never have *enough* information), but if you wait too long, the opportunity will pass you by. In the turnarounds that I have led, I have rarely had all the information I wanted; but when I weighed the consequences of delay, there was no contest. If a company is already in crisis, there is little left to lose but much to gain. In that respect, turnaround decisions are less complex than decisions in stable business enterprises. Ironically, however, the context of stability can lead to inaction, and then once great or near-great companies themselves become candidates for a turnaround. General Motors, in the 1960s and 1970s, was hopelessly ensnarled in stability: its market share plummeted from a high of 50 percent to under 30 percent today. The Japanese, who not only understood quality but acted to improve it, stole the market. But quality alone cannot sustain an economy. Now bureaucratic stagnation has helped turn the Japanese economic miracle into an economic mess. I have consulted in Japan for many years, and, as much as I enjoy the people I work with, I am dismayed by their inability to act quickly and decisively. I spent years encouraging middle management to offer ideas to their bosses, terrific ideas, ideas that would have made a real difference to the company—only to have them quashed simply because they came from someone below the status of executive! This lack of openness is death to a vital organization. The exceptions are there, of course—Toyota, Sony, Shisheda, and Kao clearly demonstrate that they can compete globally; but even those companies are having troubles in their domestic market that have diverted their attention away from developing effective global strategies.

STRATEGIES — POWER FOCUSED

In Chapter 11 we argue that every person and every enterprise has a strategy of some sort. It might not be obvious; it might be submerged in a muddle of an unconscious mind; it might change from moment to moment; it might be contradictory or fuzzy; but whether or not we can articulate it clearly, our actions are always dictated by some kind of strategy. However, before we comfort ourselves with the notion that we are strategists, we need to realize that strategies with the characteristics described above are rarely effective. A strategy should be well crafted, well articulated, and relatively consistent, and should have criteria by which its success or failure can be measured. We'll talk more specifically about strategy in Chapter 11; but it goes almost without saying that with no plan or criteria to measure your performance, you might stumble into success—but then, you might also win the Irish Sweepstakes.

In the plays *King Richard II* and *King Henry IV, Part 1* and *Part 2*, we see a man who has thought carefully about both his personal and political strategies. We first meet Harry Bolingbroke (who is to become King Henry IV) in *King Richard II*. Richard is a self-absorbed, profligate ruler who makes a suicidal mistake: after the death of one of the kingdom's most powerful nobles, Bolingbroke's father, John of Gaunt, Richard cuts off Bolingbroke as his father's heir and confiscates Gaunt's lands and possessions. He commits one of the major sins of a leader: he doesn't protect the rights of his people, he exploits them, thereby enraging not only Bolingbroke but also all the other nobles in the land. He creates an opposition to himself. "If it can happen to Bolingbroke, it can happen to me." Shortly before John of Gaunt's death, Richard, in an attempt to settle a quarrel between the Earl of Mowbray and Bolingbroke, banished Mowbray for life and Bolingbroke for six years. On hearing of the confiscation of his inheritance, Bolingbroke stole back to England, organized other nobles, and with relatively little opposition not only reclaimed his inheritance but deposed Richard and assumed the throne as King Henry IV. Scholars disagree whether it was Bolingbroke's strategy all along to become king, but most agree that once he assumed the throne, though he did not always continue to be clever about aligning the nobility to his cause, he was an effective strategist both politically and personally.

In a lecture to his wayward son, the drinking, whoring, ne'er-do-well Prince Hal, Henry IV describes how while he was still Harry Bolingbroke, he inspired the people, even when Richard was present:

> And then I stole all courtesy from heaven,
> And dress'd myself in such humility
> That I did pluck allegiance from men's hearts,

Loud shouts and salutations from their mouths,
Even in the presence of the crowned King.

KING HENRY IV, PART 1 (3.2, 50–54)

He then reveals that this persona he projected—the modest, courteous person—was in fact a strategy. In contrast to Richard II—described as the skipping king—Bolingbroke was seen little, and when he was seen, he was seen to great effect:

. . . and so my state,
Seldom, but sumptuous, show'd like a feast,
And wan [won] by rareness such solemnity.

KING HENRY IV, PART 1 (3.2, 57–59)

He states his strategy simply: "Thus did I keep my person fresh and new." Richard II, on the other hand, was about the silliest strategist ever written about. He thought he deserved to be king simply because he was king. He vacillates, changes his mind, has favorites, dramatizes every situation, but doesn't act. Bolingbroke relies on his own decisiveness and strength. He is a king, fit for the task rather than merely born to it. He is also a king with a political strategy. And he needs one, because his usurpation of the throne and his subsequent summary dismissal of his former allies foster rebellion against him. Henry knows that to preserve order in the kingdom, he must put down armed rebellion swiftly and efficiently, no matter how justifiable the cause may seem. This is the simple and straightforward strategy that drives him through his fourteen-year reign. When he smells rebellion, he acts quickly to quell it. He says to his son, Prince Hal (also nicknamed Harry):[4]

The Earl of Westmoreland set forth today,
With him my son, Lord John of Lancaster . . .
On Wednesday next, Harry, you shall set forward,
On Thursday we ourselves will march . . .
Our hands are full of business, let's away,
Advantage feeds him fat while men delay.

KING HENRY IV, PART 1 (3.2, 170–80)

Even on his deathbed, Henry proves himself a strategic thinker, advising his son and successor, Prince Hal, that the best way to prevent further civil war is to find an overseas battle to fight. An outside enemy will unite the people. They will forget the wrongs of the past because of the danger in the present.

> . . . Therefore, my Harry,
> Be it thy course to busy giddy minds
> With foreign quarrels, that action hence borne out
> May waste the memory of the former days.
>
> KING HENRY IV, PART 2 (4.5, 212–15)

The lessons of how to use power effectively are all here: develop the right strategy—the right "course"—and communicate it effectively to your people. Then execute it. Even though consistency is important, you should also be prepared to improvise. What if you make a mistake? Be thankful! You've learned something. Strategies sometimes have to change. But you will want to measure every move, assess its implications, and thus, over time, figure out what works and what doesn't. (You will never know if you don't try.)

My first business was a woefully undercapitalized advertising agency. The firm I had been working for would take on any client, large or small, trade, industrial, consumer, financial. It was not only a hodgepodge, it was an inefficient hodgepodge. Our big clients were unhappy because our work was late; we were late because we couldn't hire enough people to do the work; and we couldn't hire people because we were losing money on most of our clients. After eight years, I finally quit to strike out on my own. My father-in-law, concerned about the well-being of his beloved daughter and our family, asked me, "What if you fail?" I replied: "My new agency might fail, but I won't. I know where I'm going, and one way or another, I'll get there."

I did not fail. In fact, we prospered. *Because we had a strategy.* I set five criteria for selecting clients:

• The client would have to agree to sign our "Belief Relationship," a document that described the professional relationship the firm would have with all its clients. We would not bribe clients with tickets to shows or ball games; they would pick up the tab for lunch.

• We would select clients willing to take chances, who wanted creative solutions to their problems, not stand-on-your-head creative, but penetrating, thoughtful work that would differentiate the client from its competitors.

• We would represent clients only in the consumer product business. I turned down the first two businesses that came to me because they would take us in a different direction than where I planned to go—even though I was nearly broke. By sticking to my strategy of consumer product clients, I was able to attract other clients in that same business. Soon, we were viewed as the pros in consumer product advertising.

• The client had to be big enough to deserve the attention of our best and brightest. We did make a few exceptions for personal reasons, including a small Chinese restaurant because we liked the owner. We lost our shirts on that account, of course, but we made a good friend and had some great Chinese food.

• We would not work for the customary 15 percent commission if that amount did not add up to a decent profit.

Soon we began to attract the best writers and art directors in the business, a few even willing to take pay cuts to work in our shop because they wanted to stand for something. What made me so cocky? I had read *King Richard II* and knew that he lost power because he did not use it. I also had remembered that Henry IV, who takes away Richard's power, creates a strategy to use his power to protect his enterprise and eventually dies in bed. Listen to the directness of these two lines. On being informed that the rebels are fifty thousand strong, Henry says:

> Are these things then necessities?
> Then let us meet them like necessities . . .
> KING HENRY IV, PART 2 (3.1, 92–93)

That should be the motto of every business executive.

CORPORATIONS ARE NOT DEMOCRACIES

We acknowledged earlier that authority to lead is derived from those who are led. Without followers, you cannot be a leader. But sometimes you have to make a judgment call, and your decision may not be the obvious one. What if your people disagree? You've listened, but no successful leader makes decisions by consensus. You can't lead according to the polls. You can lead only by acting upon the course you think is right.

When I took over the job of turning around Pathmark, for the first time in the company's history its sales were less than they had been in comparable periods for the previous year. The sales of some stores were down substantially, and margins were slipping across the board. It looked as if the company would be reporting a substantial operating loss. Worse, its stock price plunged from the mid-twenties to under three dollars a share. I had to move fast. Our competitors had slashed prices, but we recognized that in our precarious financial situation, cutting prices would be suicidal. Due to high fixed costs and a precipitous slide in our sales volume, cost cuts wouldn't get us back into the black.

The way to go, I decided, was marketing. Our store managers may have lacked discipline, but, on the whole, they were aggressive and flexible. Before my arrival, the company had been considering an innovative proposal to keep stores open twenty-four hours a day. I backed the idea, as did the CEO, but two of the company's founders were worried about the fact that we would be the first supermarket chain in a large metropolitan area to stay open all night. Did we know how to pull it off? The logistical problems would be horrendous. The vice chairman of the company thought we were crazy and was so upset he had to leave the country for three months. "I can't stand it," he said. "You're going to ruin the stores." I fought for keeping the stores open around the clock, we did it, and the gods were smiling. The results were electrifying, capturing the imaginations of the press and customers. Pathmark's revolutionary twenty-four-hours-a-day campaign increased our sales by $170 million at the end of its first full year. Instead of reporting a huge loss for the year, we reported a small profit. And from that success, I was able to build the next strategy.

Sometimes, of course, you do make mistakes. But I believe that the biggest mistake any leader can make is to sit there and do nothing. When I was running my advertising agency, on my return from a long business trip, my key people greeted me with a great big paddle and said: "Stir it up again!"

I will confess that during my business career, I loved shaking things up. That's the way the most *profitable* breakthroughs are made.

POWER AND TOUGH DECISIONS GO TOGETHER

In 1998, Gary Wendt's GE Capital raked in 41 percent of General Electric's profits. But before the year was out, GE's chairman, Jack Welch, had accepted Wendt's resignation. One Sunday afternoon in October 1998, Sandy Weill and John Reed, co-CEOs of Citigroup, fired Jamie Dimon, the dynamic, effective, and popular forty-two-year-old president of the financial services giant created when John Reed's Citicorp merged with Sandy Weill's Travelers in 1997. In 1994, Joseph Volpe, the general manager of the Metropolitan Opera, stunned the music world when he fired the talented soprano Kathleen Battle, a major box-office draw in opera-mad New York.

Jamie Dimon and Gary Wendt are incredibly talented executives who are bound to surface again. Kathleen Battle's career remains huge, even without the Met. But successful companies must stand for something. The beautiful Battle had been playing too well the role of the spoiled diva; she had canceled appointments, indulged in fits of arrogance, and antagonized other singers. The Metropolitan Opera, Volpe argued, was larger than one soprano, no matter how talented or profitable. GE watchers on Wall Street had detected tensions between Welch and Wendt, whose impressive success at GE Capital seemed to make him forget one of Welch's cardinal rules of management: everyone is a team player. Wendt also did not share his boss's passion for cost cutting; worse, he was prone to playing the role of the imperial CEO. (According to one widespread story, when Wendt was bored in a meeting, he would just get up and leave.)

Jamie Dimon was widely believed to be the heir apparent at Citigroup. For the previous fifteen years, he had been Sandy Weill's trusted lieutenant and top analyst. And though he had reportedly expressed reservations about trying to combine Travelers and Citicorp too hastily, he wanted to preside over the union. It was a rocky tenure. Dimon also was cool about Weill's acquisition of Salomon Smith Barney. The investment banking unit racked up hundreds of millions of trading losses in the third quarter of 1998. Dimon, however, was in no position to gloat; he was co-supervisor of the unit. According to *The New York Times,* he was requesting to be named president of the unit. Perhaps most divisive of all was the fact that Dimon had become a darling of Wall Street, and Weill, sixty-five, reportedly resented the attention his young protégé was getting. What had once been called a "father-son relationship" was clearly breaking up over differences in long-term strategy, accelerated perhaps by the press. Citigroup was supposed to be a new kind of supermarket of financial services for the new era of global capitalism. Dimon seemed to have his doubts, and, if so, Weill and Reed were right to send him packing. (Even if Dimon was right.) The freight in Jamie Dimon's hull was shifting.

Anyone unwilling to serve the grand design of the enterprise must leave one way or another. That does not mean that there is no room for mavericks. As we shall see in Chapter 10, mavericks make the world go round and the profits go up. But once the direction is set, mavericks cannot undermine the cause. The mission of the company must be paramount—more important than short-term profits and bigger certainly than any one person, no matter how effective or popular that person might be. A good leader has to make tough decisions.

Remember Aufidius? He did not make the tough decision. When his lieutenant warned him that Coriolanus was gaining power to the detriment of Aufidius, the Volscian leader should have changed his strategy. Instead, he equivocated. Like so many of us, he said, "I cannot help it now." Nonsense. He could help it. He was still in command. It would have been tough to fire Coriolanus, but not impossible. I think he should never have hired Coriolanus in the first place; but if he did, he should have gone to the gates of Rome with Coriolanus, then fired him the moment he started to negotiate the peace, then attacked Rome himself. You might say that Aufidius won out in the end: he had Coriolanus killed. But Coriolanus was not the objective, Rome was. Aufidius lost his opportunity to take Rome, and he lost his reputation with the Volscian leaders.

TIMING ISN'T EVERYTHING, BUT IT MIGHT BE EVERYTHING ELSE

When Bolingbroke was beginning to form his coalition of disgruntled nobles, Richard II decided it was time to prance off and fight some Irish wars. His timing was lousy. Not only did Richard give Bolingbroke the opportunity to consolidate support, he lost his prime ally, his uncle, the Duke of York. By the time Richard got back to England, the best he could do was "sit upon the ground and tell sad stories of the death of kings." He could not possibly win an armed conflict; his only hope was to negotiate—at which, as we will see later, he was equally inept. "I wasted time, and now doth time waste me," he admits to the audience in the last act.

There is a marvelous statement in *Julius Caesar* about the importance of timing when Brutus counsels Cassius:

> There is a tide in the affairs of men,
> Which, taken at the flood, leads on to fortune;
> Omitted, all the voyage of their life
> Is bound in shallows and in miseries.
> On such a full sea are we now afloat,
> And we must take the current when it serves,
> Or lose our ventures.
>
> JULIUS CAESAR (4.3, 217–23)

Ironically, Brutus's speech is better than his next move. Brutus wants to attack Antony's and Octavius's armies right away. Cassius wants to wait. Cassius was right. Brutus's premise was right, but his action was wrong. Overriding Cassius, they attack and lose the war.

Nevertheless, timing often makes the difference between winning and losing. General Motors was late to the SUV (sport utility vehicle) market. The Ford Explorer got a great head start on the General Motors Bravado, and Lincoln's Navigator has left the Cadillac Esplanade to eat its dust. If General Motors ever catches up, it will take years to do it. On the other hand, you can rush to market too soon—either before the demand can be established or before your product or service is right. In 1956, Ford rushed its Mercury Cruiser to dealers so fast that instructions were included on how to fix the defects that had not been corrected at the plant. It was a disaster—and one it certainly learned from. In fairness to Ford, its unseemly rush was caused more by an ambitious vice president than by policy. The lesson, however, remains.[5]

How does one know when the "time and tide" are right? I have found that the best answer is rigorous analysis followed by insight and intuition. There are, of course, the great intuitive leaders, whose gut feelings are better than a conference room full of market researchers. But, when you scratch these so-called intuitive leaders deeply enough, you'll find both experience and analysis there. I would not trust my intuition to solve a problem in Boolean algebra, but I would trust it to time a supermarket promotion or the introduction of a new consumer product. Intuition that is not backed up by experience and hours of internal debate is worthless.

However, I don't want to make the choice of the right moment sound like a one-man or one-woman band. When I have had to make timing decisions without the benefit of experience, here's the process that has served me well. I fill a conference room with market researchers and, just as important, people who are close to what I call "the point of contact"—people close to the work (production) and those close to the customers (salespeople). We engage in a vigorous debate—no holds barred—everyone has a voice. I enter the debate from time to time, but I try to listen more than talk. I thank the people for their hard work and insights, then I go fishing, play golf, read a Shakespeare play, or take a walk—anything that will let my subconscious take over, sort out conflicting viewpoints, synthesize other viewpoints. When I'm lucky, the answer will come to me, uninvited, within a few days. If that doesn't happen, I take the initiative. My timing has not always been right, but on those occasions when I have been wrong, the early analysis and debate then helped me correct my course.

Henry IV didn't know Brutus (except, of course, in the imagination of William Shakespeare, a man whose timing was impeccable), but Henry did know that "there was a tide in the affairs of men." He used time to his advantage in deposing Richard II. He also considered the counsel of others, such as Northumberland, Westmoreland, and Sir Walter Blunt, but throughout his reign the decisions and the timing were his.

Earlier, we referred to the speech when Henry was deploying his forces for the battle of Shrewsbury. The line I will never forget is: "Advantage feeds him fat while men delay" (*King Henry IV, Part 1* [3.2, 180]).

Henry IV understood power and he used it. He also understood that he was in an ideological battle.

IDEOLOGIES — THE GREAT DIVIDE

In the business world, most differences of opinion can be accommodated through negotiation and compromise. However, occasionally they cannot. It is important to understand when they can and when they cannot. When they cannot, it is usually because of ideological differences. Some people might say that the term *ideological* applies only to religious and political differences—it is too strong to describe business. Having spent half a century in the business trenches, I disagree. Business issues can become as polarized as the Serbs and the ethnic Albanians in Yugoslavia. The arguments at IBM—mainframes versus all the other alternatives—and the old arguments at Apple Computer over whether the operating system should be proprietary or open became as hotly contested as the clashes between liberal and conservative politicians—or as those between the Yorkists and the Lancastrians in the Wars of the Roses. I imagine that the arguments at Motorola were similar. Not too many years ago, Motorola controlled 60 percent of the cellular phone market, using analog technology. Then came the upstarts, led by Nokia, using digital technology. Technology choices often create divides; choice of technology becomes ideological. Once a commitment is made, it is hard to back down, hard to mobilize the resources to change direction. Nokia swept the market. Ironically, Motorola had always had a presence in digital radios, satellites, and the communications infrastructure, but not in the cell phones themselves. When the retail market suddenly turned toward digital, Motorola had not invested adequate resources and struggled for two years to catch up.

Eastman Kodak is in the same boat. Once the world leader in silver halide technology, it is now facing the new world of digital photography. But that is not the only ideological battle that was being fought in this once great company. There were those who believed that the mystique of the yellow box (Kodak) was so strong that those "foreigners" with the green box (Fuji) could never unseat them. Armed with this arrogance, Kodak kept its prices so high and trade practices so rigid that it unwittingly issued Fuji an engraved invitation to enter the U.S. market.

One need only take a cursory look at the business pages for further confirmation of how damaging ideological conflicts can be, particularly if they are not dealt with quickly or forcefully. In addition to IBM, Motorola, and Eastman Kodak, consider these:

- Goldman Sachs' internecine struggle over whether the firm should remain private or be taken public.
- Compaq's acquisition of Digital—a decidedly different and a troubled company. Mixing Digital's engineers with Compaq's go-go guys was like mixing matches and gasoline.
- Chrysler management felt they should conserve their cash for a rainy day, while Kirk Kerkorian wanted the cash distributed immediately. This disagreement will seem like child's play compared with the ideological differences between Chrysler's American-style management and the buttoned-down style of the German managers at Daimler-Benz. These differences are not just cultural.

Indeed, mergers and acquisitions are breeding grounds for ideological differences. It would be a joy to believe that not only could these ideological differences be resolved, but that a richer, more satisfying culture could come forth out of opposing mind-sets. Tina Packer swears that creative processes are most potent when opposite truths are held in one moment and you step forward. She says a different answer, one you haven't thought of, appears. Tina's approach is certainly worth a try. I embrace it but at the same time offer this caution: The debate—rather than the action—can become the goal. Why waste time? When the debate goes on too long, the enterprise falls into a hopeless tangle. In the end, when the cultures are widely divergent, efforts to solve pressing issues with discussion and debate usually fall victim to the side with the most power. When the dominant entity recognizes that the issues are ideological and widely divergent, it should take charge and call the tune. If it doesn't, there is a real danger that the enterprise will lose focus and collapse in hopeless wrangling.

When Ideologies Are Intractable

Blinkered leaders often do not understand ideological opposition; do not understand that on the other side of the argument, there is another general who has beliefs as fierce and deeply held. He too has followers. And if the opponent loses a battle, he too will be prepared to retreat and regroup so he can fight again. If the battle is already joined, the military analogy is instructive. First, the general looks to his army: Are his soldiers trained? Do they have physical stamina? Do they have the emotional stamina to advance in the face of hostile fire? Is the army big enough? If not, recruiters must be trained who can enlist others into the cause. As the army is being consolidated, the leader recruits resistance groups behind the lines; and his first barrage is not bombs or bullets, but broadcasts and leaflets. Psychological warfare is engaged, not necessarily to sway officers or the opposition, but to sow doubts and fear in the foot soldiers and those who are wavering. When Octavius Caesar is preparing for the decisive battle against Mark Antony (in *Antony and Cleopatra*, the follow-up to *Julius Caesar*), he puts the soldiers who have defected from Mark Antony in the front lines, so that Antony's men can see that already they have lost great numbers of their comrades. When the psychological battle is being won, only then does the army advance. With luck, the general will find some weak spots, win a few fast skirmishes, give the troops a taste of victory, and sow further doubts in the opposition's ranks. He'll recruit as many defectors as he can and seek to neutralize others who are wavering.

Then, as he mounts the first major battle, he must be prepared for both victory or defeat. If he wins the battle, he will know his next move. If the battle goes against him, he must know how his retreat will happen so he can quickly regroup to fight again.

Is the military analogy too strong for comparison with conflicts at Compaq and Digital, or among the executives at Goldman Sachs, Apple, IBM, Motorola, or Eastman Kodak? The correct course of action is usually apparent long before action is taken. In business there is never a guarantee that you will be right. But there is an overwhelming probability that the enterprise will suffer if the debate goes on too long. I have talked to many deposed leaders who admitted that they *did* know what to do, but they failed to take decisive action quickly enough. So I'm not saying here that people should not have ideals or should always agree. As we shall see in subsequent chapters, ideas do not need to be congruent. Indeed, a strong case can be made for supporting mavericks in every organization. And everyone needs to know what he or she stands for. But when differences become so widely divergent that discussion ends and emotional positions take over, the differences are rarely reconcilable in a short span of time.

Then the military analogy holds true. This is particularly true when those who have power hold divergent opinions—and are cunning enough to conceal their true intentions.

When Ideological Differences Are Not Readily Apparent
It's not always easy to see ideological differences. A leader must be eternally vigilant—should never be lulled into the belief that always and forever, he or she will know the location and strength of opposition. Coriolanus reluctantly agreed to address the Roman

populace to seek approval for his election as a consul of Rome. He won that approval from the plebeians, only to lose it later because the tribunes—middle managers—feared and hated him. The tribunes reconvened the meeting, salting the crowd with other dissenters—who were told what to say and when to say it. Ultimately, the populace disavowed their earlier support and banished their former hero from Rome. Coriolanus was a great warrior but a naive politician. He did not fully understand the strength of the opposition. Nor did he fully understand the consequences of profound ideological differences. The Romans with great cost had recently deposed a tyrant king, Tarquin the Proud, and established a republic. When the tribunes hinted that the autocratic Coriolanus was acting like Tarquin, the people became convinced that their republic would be in danger if an arrogant, patrician warrior were elected a consul of Rome. And Coriolanus confirmed their fears by refusing to understand their concerns. His behavior played into the ideologues' hands—and the battle lines were drawn.

Julius Caesar had a similar problem. He had held power over the army for years. He was the leading general and the leader of the Senate. Rome was in a state of great unrest. Many leaders and ordinary people thought Rome would be better off under the tight rule of a king. They were pressing Julius Caesar to accept the office. This action by the people together with the fact that Caesar was not clearly opposing it—indeed seemed at times to be considering it—was all that Cassius, Brutus, and the other conspirators needed in order to act swiftly for their own ideological position: Rome must always remain a republic. They decided to kill Caesar. Caesar himself had a clear sense of mission about himself as leader of Rome and deeply held core values:

> But I am constant as the northern star . . .
> And men are flesh and blood, and apprehensive;
> Yet in the number I do know but one
> That unassailable holds on his rank
> Unshak'd of motion; and that I am he . . .
>
> JULIUS CAESAR (3.1, 60–70)

Brave, thrilling words! Chilling words, also, for only seconds after uttering them, this unassailable star had fallen from the sky. If Caesar could speak from the grave, he well might ask us to consider "when is constancy not a virtue, but a vice?"

What went wrong? Brutus, the chief conspirator who kills Caesar, is not evil. Indeed, he is an "honorable man"—and he was Caesar's friend. But between them, as Caesar rose in power, a deep ideological gulf appeared. The Romans had fought for almost five hundred years—since before Coriolanus's time—for their hard-won republic. Brutus's father-in-law, Cato, had undoubtedly made an indelible impression on Brutus's already deeply held beliefs. Several years earlier, when Cato, a staunch conservative and fierce defender of the republic, had faced imminent defeat by Caesar in civil war, he had had two choices: to surrender and abjectly receive Caesar's magnanimous offer of pardon, or to die. After debating through the night with his family about the nature of freedom, he decided that one could be truly free only in death; he killed himself the next morning. That is a man who stands by his ideals! And he's also dead, like Caesar.

Brutus, Cassius, and the other conspirators, in their fear that Caesar will turn the republic back into a monarchy with Caesar wearing the crown, decide not to debate the issue but act. *After* the death Brutus defends the assassination on ideological grounds— that Caesar was ambitious. He says to the crowd:

> . . . not that I loved Caesar less, but that I loved Rome more. Had
> you rather Caesar were living, and die all slaves, than that Caesar
> were dead, to live all free men? As Caesar loved me, I weep for him;
> as he was fortunate, I rejoice at it; as he was valiant, I honour him;
> but, as he was ambitious, I slew him.
>
> JULIUS CAESAR (3.2, 21–27)

So, even though Caesar was "constant as the northern star" and had a clear sense of mission and deeply held core values, he, like Coriolanus, did not fully understand the source and strength of the opposition. Indeed, Caesar had come to believe that the adulation he received from the crowds and foreign potentates was universally given. His dying words, as Brutus stabs him, "Et tu, Brute?" are spoken in profound disbelief.

Ideological Differences—Preventive Maintenance

Be careful. Shakespeare reveals another secret of successful and enduring leadership: Be strong in your convictions, but not so rigid that you don't understand the arguments on the other side. On some occasions, accommodations can be made that will forestall any need for the warfare we have just described.

Great leaders understand the enemy. Coriolanus, as a leader, was great in understanding Aufidius, great in understanding soldiers, terrible in understanding civilians. Coriolanus recognized his own prowess, but he failed to see that the people had power too. Instead of fighting back politically or understanding the fears of the Roman people, Coriolanus spewed insults at them:

> You common cry of curs! whose breath I hate
> As reek o' th' rotten fens, whose loves I prize
> As the dead carcasses of unburied men
> That do corrupt my air: I banish you!
>
> CORIOLANUS (3.3, 120–24)

And thus, instead of allaying their suspicions, he only confirms them. His own mother warns him, "You are too absolute." She even points out to him that he aligns strategy and honor when he's in battle—why can't he do it in peace?

> . . . I have heard you say,
> Honour and policy, like unsever'd friends,
> I' th' war do grow together: grant that, and tell me,
> In peace what each of them by th'other lose,
> That they combine not there.
>
> CORIOLANUS (3.2, 41–45)

Your enemies might be telling you the thing you need to know. Instead of going into ideological opposition, see if you think there is any merit to their argument. If there is, use it. It pulls the teeth of their argument. Yet every day, modern business leaders fall from grace because they lock their minds too soon. As we said earlier, if after careful thought you truly believe that you are right and others are wrong, you have few options other than using your persuasion or power to change their minds. And not everything is right or wrong. An open mind before a debate begins can work wonders. Yes, it is difficult to recognize that others are as strong in their beliefs as we are in ours. However, being "constant as the northern star" is the sole property of no one. If you rush to turn strong principles into dogma, you have lost flexibility and you might have forgotten that power is relative.

Finally, there is another danger in living in constant polarization. Say that you win one battle, and then another and another. If you're not careful, the rush of battle replaces the mission. You begin to enjoy power for power's sake, seeing whom you can knock over. You are entering *King Richard III* and *Macbeth* territory here. In Chapter 11 we will see how good leaders can "reframe" issues, not only for others, but also for themselves, to avoid that irreparable damage of polarization.

2

Uneasy Lies the Head
That Wears a Crown

Promoted? Transferred? New Hire?
Tips from the Master

> . . . God knows, my son,
> By what by-paths and indirect crook'd ways
> I met this crown, and I myself know well
> How troublesome it sat upon my head.
>
> Henry in KING HENRY IV, PART 2 (4.5, 183–86)

WHEN I arrived at Pathmark in 1972 to be the new COO, I found a company in crisis. Once a darling of Wall Street with its stock at twenty-four dollars, Pathmark now languished at under three dollars a share. They were losing money both in their supermarkets and in their department stores. Debt was high. The main competitor, A&P, had started a price war that had driven down everyone's prices. The board of directors had pushed the company's three co-founders into bringing in an outsider who could turn things around. At the time I was an associate dean at the Harvard Business School, where I had written cases and articles about supermarket advertising and marketing (my own area of expertise as a former adman) for the *Harvard Business Review*. During their salad days, management at Pathmark had asked me to do some consulting for them, so they knew me.

I was under the gun. But there were some ideas already in the works, including a scheme to stay open twenty-four hours a day, which had been tried out West in some small stores with success. Coincidentally, I had been doing some research on the twenty-four-hour-a-day experiments and thought it was a smart move for supermarkets. But it had never been tried in big metropolitan areas like New York, New Jersey, and Connecticut. One of the founders and executives at Pathmark thought that keeping the stores open all night was too risky. Another was neutral, but the CEO was all for it. So we did it. And it worked. That was in May. In September, I launched a program to post prices in our pharmacies. Pricing in pharmacies was unheard of at that time. But the public loved it, and it immediately affected sales. By the end of the year, we did the "double-your-money-back-if-you-are-not-satisfied-with-the-freshness-of-our-meat" campaign. Another triumph. My strategy was to initiate something new every three or four months and keep the organization supercharged. Within six months of my arrival, profits, though slim, were back, cash flow was positive, and employee morale was on the rise. Best of all, customers were happy. And for the next two years, things kept getting better.

Or so I thought. I hesitate even to raise my experience at Pathmark again. For me, frankly, it's ancient history, another war story from another COO. But Shakespeare has taught me that you can learn a lot from old war stories. Here's what you can learn from mine: I saw myself as the savior. But in fact, I was an interloper.

Three years into my job as COO, I was still naive enough to think I had a line on the CEO position. After all, I had been the catalyst in the turnaround; and the company was now asking me to work with their department stores too.

I was foolish—and blind, to boot. What I never understood was that many of my colleagues in the company viewed me as an outsider. To the couple of senior management people who also had an eye on the CEO's job, as the new operations boss I had usurped a position that they believed was theirs by divine right. So they certainly weren't going to support my elevation any further. Worse still, my presence was an embarrassment to the company's co-founders, who had been forced to call in an outsider to rescue them. They after all were supermarket pros, and here was a Harvard Business School lecturer and former adman from Oklahoma running the business that they had started and nourished.

It took me almost four years to realize that I was in a dead-end situation. I didn't get fired, but I was feeling the push, and it was neither subtle nor gentle. I finally headed for the exit on my own accord. After years of thinking about this experience, I realize that I had been so focused on creating new initiatives, making decisions, riding high on the successes, that I didn't think about my fellow executives. But King Henry IV could have seen what I was blind to. With the help of the Percy family he had successfully usurped Richard II's crown and was the new king. Now what was his relationship with his kingmakers? He didn't trust them. But he was also insecure about his throne, because the people of England knew that he had stolen it—even if he was a better ruler than Richard II. He was always on his guard. There were several attempts to topple him, and civil strife, occasionally breaking out in open rebellion, marked most of Henry IV's fourteen-year reign. And yes, he made quite a few mistakes in his dealings with those kingmakers, the Percy family. But he was never blind to them, as I was at Pathmark.

Shakespeare makes it very clear that a usurper's life is never easy. The founders of Pathmark had invited me into their organization, but I was still the interloper who had to prove his worth every moment, and the very people who had helped me to my job were also the people looking to push me out again.

In my innocent enthusiasm to work some magic at Pathmark, I failed to understand that anyone who has been promoted, transferred, or brought aboard to do a job can be perceived as a usurper by those who think the job ought to be theirs. Even someone inside the organization, who has earned the job over a period of years, will be viewed by some colleagues as an interloper. Whether you like it or not, the new boss is a foreign substance injected into a living organism. He or she is the grain of sand in the oyster—will either be rejected or will cause a pearl to be made. After all, the company has been there for years; most employees and many executives have had their jobs for years. Unless they are in a desperate, near-death mess, they will not see you as their savior. More likely it will feel to them as if you are disrupting communication channels, power relationships, and traditional loyalties as well as organizational structure and processes.

Keep remembering Henry IV's rueful observation: "Uneasy lies the head that wears a crown."

Tina Packer has reminded me that any time you assume the role of a leader, something happens to you, whether you like it or not. People project thoughts and feelings onto you that may have nothing to do with you. People will assume things about you that may or may not be true. Says Tina:

> I found it one of the hardest things to learn—namely, what I thought about myself was not necessarily how other people saw me. I would say something innocuous, which then got interpreted a different way. As a theater director, I work very closely with the actors. As a manager, I'm more distant but am still fairly dominant. Because I span all aspects of the organization and we are very close-knit, I become the parent of the organization. The human psyche, of course, is always looking for a pattern it can react to, and as our relationship to our mothers is the first one in our lives, it is the one most likely to come up when there's a problem. Then it's only a step to interpreting my actions with the mother's motive. And then it's Mother's fault!

Tina does not take credit for this psychological insight. Shakespeare already had it. Henry V says the night before the Battle of Agincourt:

Upon the King! 'Let us our lives, our souls,
Our debts, our careful wives,
Our children and our sins lay on the King!'

KING HENRY V (4.1, 226–28)

And you do have power over other people's lives if you are the boss. You are not responsible for everything that happens to them or how they respond to life. But your actions affect their private and public lives and in turn those of their families. So people talk about you, your motives, your manners, your ambitions, your style, your clothes, how you handle people. They may blame you or blindly give you too much credit. A leader is like one of the Roman gods: a focus point for the attention of many people. But everybody, including interlopers, is responsible for his or her own actions.

So what does it take for the interloper to succeed? A mild case of paranoia and the ability to make a lot of clever moves. Then there are several other things that you can do that will make wearing a crown a lot easier.

CREATE YOUR OWN TEAM OF LOYALISTS

When you take over any new position, everyone in the organization—or kingdom—will be watching and waiting. Some will actually want you to succeed. Treat these people as your friends. Embrace them when you find them. Others will want you to succeed, but they are also sitting on the fence to see what will happen. Then there are the players who want the job you "stole" from them; these characters will be jealous, secretly or openly, and will probably do everything possible to undermine you. Finally there will be others who know about countermoves going on in the organization against you but who will keep their own counsel. And they, too, will be watching, waiting.

It's a tough situation. You are a moving target. It is important to take the focus off yourself and your accession. At Pathmark, I kept creating new "campaigns." With a real problem to solve, everyone can focus more on work than politics. Tina offers a Shakespearean parallel in *King Henry IV, Part 2* (4.5, 212–13), where the king instructs his son and successor to unite the factions at home by finding a foreign enemy, and thus by an outside threat keep the kingdom together: "Busy giddy minds / With foreign quarrels." Politicians use this device so regularly that we are automatically suspicious. The film *Wag the Dog* was a marvelous satire on this theme. Hal, as soon as he becomes Henry V, declares war against France and does indeed unite England once more.

Another way to keep yourself out of the gun sights of your enemies is to create your own team of loyalists. Shakespeare learned from his knowledge of history and, I'm sure, from his reading of Machiavelli's *The Prince*, which was completed in 1517 and was a best-seller in Elizabethan England. A new leader often has to clean house and bring in people who will be loyal to him. However, the executives reporting to me at Pathmark were close friends of the founders. It seemed to me unwise to fire them. I was wrong. I should have done it and done it early, while I had the clout. Machiavelli, much of whose advice is no longer valid though very interesting, made another pertinent observation. While the leader's best job insurance is to enlist the support of the people, that alone is not enough: watch out for the nobles. The masses don't aspire to your position, but the nobles do. Here are some things about picking your own team I learned from subsequent turnarounds.

The first challenge, of course, is to pick the right people. You can't do that with your office door closed. When I run a company, I make it a practice never to be in my office more than two days a week. Anything you learn in the office has come up through the bureaucratic hierarchy, massaged, filtered, and positioned. As important as the pyramid of authority can be to a business, it does not necessarily reveal what you ought to know; more often it reveals what other people want you to know. Hierarchy, in this instance, can be a short circuit. So I get out of the office. And employees, particularly those farthest from your inner circle, appreciate some attention from the boss. During one of my inspection trips to a Pathmark store after we began staying open all night, I met an assistant produce manager at 4 A.M. "Mr. Whitney," he said, "you're the first suit I've seen in four years. Even if you came here to chew me out, I'd be happy to see you."

The way to assess people's skills, commitment, and future loyalty is to work with them, closely. The best thing about Prince Hal's hanging out on the streets and in the taverns of Eastcheap, an ancient and disreputable commercial district in London, was that he got to know his people in a way his father never did. While Henry IV has trouble assessing the loyalty of his lieutenants, Hal never does. He experiences the ways of common men, and even puts himself into a highway robbery in order to understand real life (and himself). "And when I am King of England, I shall command all the good lads in Eastcheap," he says in *King Henry IV, Part 1* (2.4, 13–14). Hal was right: You must watch your people in action and see how they respond to others (and to you), especially under stress. If you find out they are not straightforward with their colleagues, they are not likely to be giving you an unvarnished picture of what is going on either.

The worst thing you can do is to gather the wrong people around you. Richard II, as Henry later puts it, "mingled his royalty with capering fools." The very names of Richard's friends—Bushy, Bagot, and Green—reflect their inadequacy for the task of advising the boss. Bolingbroke refers to them as the "caterpillars" whose influence on Richard has been disastrous for England. (Historical figures with those names did exist and were associated with Richard, and one can't help thinking that Shakespeare reveled in using their descriptive names to fit their roles as Richard's insects.) Once the trio realizes that a Bolingbroke victory is bound to cloud their futures, they flee, but to no avail.

Shakespeare tells the tale of bad friends and advisers in many plays. Timon of Athens is a man with such a sunny view of humankind that he thinks everyone is his closest friend. When he is finally bankrupted by his generosity toward these hangers-on, they abandon him. Enraged and maddened, Timon withdraws from society and kills himself, leaving behind a curse for mankind. This is a lose-lose situation.

In *Julius Caesar*, Octavius, Caesar's heir, is the right ally for Antony in his fight against Brutus and Cassius. Shakespeare portrays Octavius as a cool, efficient leader. Antony is astute enough to know that he and Octavius together can overcome Brutus and Cassius. (The historical Caius Julius Caesar Octavianus—known to historians as "Octavian"—became the emperor Augustus, whose political genius turned the Roman Senate into servants for his imperial goals. The literary critic Harold Bloom calls Octavian the "world's first CEO.") The alliance between Antony and Octavius was a powerful one. It took many years for them to become each other's enemy—why did they fall apart? Does having two equal bosses ever work? Yes, but only in special circumstances, as we discuss later.

REWARD YOUR PEOPLE — HANDSOMELY

I might be accused of trying to buy loyalty (which I believe is impossible), but I insist on paying my team enough (in money, stock options, and recognition) so I won't have to worry about losing them to the competition. Shortsighted executives forget that there are two aspects of the reward system: what you pay for, and what you get. Stingy CEOs usually get what they pay for—and deserve it.

But monetary rewards, important as they are, are not enough to keep people enthusiastic and committed. They want a piece of the intellectual action, too. Give them tougher and tougher challenges and give them the room and resources to do the job; then, when they succeed, reward them with recognition as well as cash. Bring them into your confidence; listen with respect to their ideas on strategy as well as operations. All this sounds right and good—and it is. However, you will find that some very effective people are simply not cut out to be team members, and others whom neither money nor recognition can make part of the team. I have found this to be especially true of those people who helped you to your present position. Richard II calls Northumberland, one of the nobles who helped Bolingbroke to the throne, "thou ladder wherewithal the mounting Bolingbroke ascends my throne" and then goes on to point out

> . . . thou shalt think,
> Though he divide the realm and give thee half,
> It is too little, helping him to all . . .
>
> KING RICHARD II (5.1, 59–61)

It was my experience time and time again to have previously helpful people wane in their support. Was it something I had done? Did I underneath suspect they could pull me down because they had helped me up? Richard goes on:

> He shall think that thou, which knowest the way
> To plant unrightful kings, wilt know again,
> Being ne'er so little urg'd, another way
> To pluck him headlong from the usurped throne.
> The love of wicked men converts to fear,
> That fear to hate, and hate turns one or both
> To worthy danger and deserved death.
>
> KING RICHARD II (5.1, 62–68)

To avoid surprises like being plucked headlong, stay in touch, stay involved, and reward your people as their merit deserves. And however important it is to reward your inner circle, don't forget the people who do the daily work. Even though their contribution is on a smaller scale, their motives, desires, and needs are the same as those of the nobles in your court.

By now you must be thinking, "What's wrong with Whitney? Isn't this a turnaround? In a turnaround, you have to cut costs." Right! Usually I cut costs. But I also add some cost. I'm turning around. In some turnarounds, I have raised average pay by 15 percent, reduced head count by 30 percent, and improved profits astronomically. Robert Lear, my colleague at Columbia and former turnaround practitioner, has made a pithy statement: "Hire four to do the work of six and pay them like they were five." The math works. You get what you pay for.

―――

Clean House if You Must — but with Care and Caution

Picking those you want in your inner circle means that you are, by necessity, excluding others. Too often, a new boss steps into his position forgetting that there is a preexisting hierarchy already in place. No matter how talented or experienced you may be, there is usually someone already at the top of the house who thinks he should've gotten the job you were hired for. You will probably have to depose some potential pretenders to the crown. How you handle this is crucial to the company's future—and your own.

Henry IV, the former Bolingbroke, is, as we have argued, an effective crisis manager over his fourteen-year reign: he puts down rebellion after rebellion and dies in bed. He also has a good sense of which players he can make disappear with impunity. Demanding the execution of Richard's "caterpillars," Bushy, Bagot, and Green, raises no opposition. But Henry IV makes one big personnel mistake that we all can learn from. And he makes it with the Percy family—Northumberland, his son, Hotspur, and his brother Worcester—the family that helped him seize the crown. About a year after Henry IV assumes the throne, Hotspur captures several rebels, including the Earl of Douglas, an equally hot-tempered leader of the rebellious Scottish army. Douglas, renowned for his military prowess, is worth a sizable ransom to his captors. The king demands that the prisoners be turned over to the crown. Hotspur refuses. The king then summons Hotspur, his father, Northumberland, and his uncle, the Earl of Worcester, to the palace.

You have to know that at this point everyone is trying to outmaneuver everyone else without seeming to do so. Hotspur is trying to force the king to release his, Hotspur's, brother-in-law, held prisoner in Wales. The king doesn't want to do it because Mortimer, the brother-in-law, has a claim to the throne. But no one is saying that. When Worcester reminds the king that the Percy family helped him to depose Richard II, the king says he sees "danger and disobedience" in his eyes and, before Worcester can reply, orders him to leave the court with Shakespeare's version of "Don't call us, we'll call you":

> You have good leave to leave us; when we need
> Your use and counsel we shall send for you.
>
> KING HENRY IV, PART 1 (1.3, 19–20)

He is the king, of course, and when he commands, others are supposed to obey. But making an enemy of the Percy family is a mistake. With rebels opposing him in Scotland and Wales, Henry does not need any more enemies. It is folly to antagonize allies who have proven their loyalty in the past and whose territories lie on the border of Scotland. But Henry is not rational around the Percys. He overdoes his arrogance when he says to Worcester, a man older than he, who a year earlier led him to the throne,

> O sir, your presence is too bold and peremptory,
> And majesty might never yet endure
> The moody frontier of a servant brow.
>
> KING HENRY IV, PART 1 (1.3, 16–18)

To label Worcester a "servant" is a huge tactical mistake and proves to be the spark that triggers the rebellion already brewing against the king. After the king leaves the room, Hotspur is furious over the king's disdain toward the Percys. Worcester, however, prefers to get even rather than get mad. The Percys decide on the following plan: release Douglas and the other Scottish prisoners without ransom, and enlist them in a rebellion against the king. Meantime, Worcester will hook up with Mortimer, who is held by the Welsh rebels, and when the time is right, all three forces will join against the king. Worcester is a more formidable foe than Bushy, Bagot, or Green. Firing him was bound to have repercussions. A new manager has a small window of opportunity when she first arrives. If she can identify those in the organization who are likely to make trouble and are not well respected, she should let them go immediately. In the turnarounds that I have led, I have dispatched many Bushys, Bagots, and Greens without remorse or repercussions. However, in one turnaround, I had two Worcesters. Both wanted my job. Both were good at their jobs, but neither was ready to be COO. One was skilled at operations, but he didn't know a balance sheet from a blueprint. The other was terrific at marketing and equally ingenious at turning off other people. He had no political or social skills. My spies reported that these two executives were critical of me—bitterly, openly, and so, stupidly. On the surface, they did nothing to harm the company. However, hundreds of employees reported to them, and by bad-mouthing my leadership they were indirectly hurting the company. The gulf between us was so wide that when I confronted them and tried to talk things over, it brought no results.

I should have fired them. But I didn't. Why didn't I? Two reasons, closely connected: (1) they were friends of the king; (2) I was COO, not CEO. (Mark Twain once said that the difference between the president and the vice president was the difference between lightning and a lightning bug. The analogy also sums up the CEO-to-COO power ratio.) Firing the boss's friend is like firing his son. Sometimes, it must be done. But you must be aware of the consequences. You might not notice any problems until bonus time or the next promotion opportunity. On reflection, however, I should have fired both my Worcesters.

Tina Packer solved her problem about whom to fire in an innovative way: she fired everyone! She was in the third year of running Shakespeare & Company, and there were about forty people in the company. Because money was tight, many people had done many things on a volunteer basis. Tina would reward them for their efforts in various ways, but the quid pro quos were becoming overwhelming. The moment the company hit a pocket of money, everyone wanted to cash in their past favors for a piece of pie, in the form of pay raises or good parts in the plays. She says:

> There was no way I could do that. It would have crippled the company. I had to pay off the debt. And some of the people with the most chips were the least talented. The group was a mess. I decided to put us out of the misery and fired everyone—even those I wasn't paying. Then I announced that if anyone wanted to return to the

company with a clean slate, no more quid pro quos, they should discuss it with me on Monday. The shock broke the tension, and some of us started again. And I learned a lot about volunteerism.

———

A DUKE NEVER UPSTAGES A KING

The marketing campaign at Pathmark was wildly successful. Not only did it bring more customers into the stores, it generated some much-needed good publicity for us in the trade press and, more important, the mainstream media. We got radio and TV coverage, a story in *The Wall Street Journal,* and another in *The New York Times,* accompanied by a three-column front-page photo in the business section. I did not personally invent all the marketing programs; I approved and promoted them. Also, I was the new COO, not the chief executive. On several occasions, I invited the CEO to take the bows. He demurred. So I took the lead and got too much publicity.

I was dozing. I should have *insisted* that the CEO talk to the press more, that he and his people get more credit. Instead, the coverage presented me as the conquering hero—and thus painted a huge target on my back. From day one, the gulf between me and the head office was problematic, and it got wider after all the publicity, no matter how much good it did the organization. A duke never upstages a king: if he does, he'd better watch his head.

All that publicity made it look as if the company's COO was in charge. Worse, because the press is always eager to find a hero, the coverage made it seem as if I had improved the company's fortunes single-handedly. It was not true. A business, like any other kingdom, is a complex system of interrelated elements. Yes, exceptional individuals can produce exceptional results. Only rarely, however, do they do it alone. All the elements must work together; they need to be orchestrated, then conducted.

What would have been the smart thing to do? To have talked about the leadership of the CEO in interviews, given the press only photographs of the boss, the employees, and the stores. I should have taken a tip from the White House and played the role of press secretary for the president.

ACTION, YES! SUPPORTING RELATIONSHIPS, ABSOLUTELY!

Shakespeare often acknowledges the leader's need for the support of others. This is never more true than in a time of crisis. Henry V's stirring speech to his troops the night before the Battle of Agincourt strikes a responsive chord in everyone who hears it. The English troops are outnumbered by the French five to one. Their small number, Henry argues, will be to their heroic advantage, for they will be brothers in glory. And they go into battle on a special day, the feast day of St. Crispin:

> This story shall the good man teach his son,
> And Crispin Crispian shall ne'er go by
> From this day to the ending of the world
> But we in it shall be remembered,
> We few, we happy few, we band of brothers.
>
> KING HENRY V (4.3, 56–60)

In fewer than fifty lines, Henry delivers a speech that would send us all into battle. No wonder these words have become a warhorse of patriotic speeches in the English-speaking world. Winston Churchill used Henry's words, which were familiar to most of his audience, to stir the English people in their battle against Hitler in World War II. (We will return with a more detailed analysis of the speech in Chapter 7.) Never lose an opportunity to rally the troops. Look for support and give support.

The most famous appeal for support in Shakespeare is Mark Antony's funeral oration for Caesar. Antony turned the mob's hostility away from Caesar and onto his murderers. Few executives are eager to incite people to riot, but knowing how to win over a hostile audience separates a great leader from the good ones, and in a later chapter, we examine Antony's speech as a textbook case in skilled communication.

No leader can do it alone. You need backup. If you are feeling doubtful and think it will undermine the company to voice your fears to your colleagues either in public or private, then find someone outside the company to talk to. It's useful to have a secret support system, an old friend, a spouse—someone you can go to outside the company for frank advice, no strings attached. The act of talking it through often clarifies the dilemma. The decision of what to do has to be yours, but articulating the dilemma can be the step you need to take to make the decision.

A LEADER CONTEMPLATES HIS SUCCESSOR WITH THE SAME ENTHUSIASM THAT HE CONTEMPLATES DEATH

Looking back, I now believe that the greatest impediment to my future at Pathmark was speculation in a major trade journal that I was the heir apparent. My protestation to the editor was as fruitless as my assurances to the sitting CEO that replacing him was not my goal. Invitations to join him, his wife, and their friends for dinner at their home vanished. Obviously, the man did not want to give up his job, and he didn't much like my presence around anymore either.

Who can blame him? I confess that I felt the same way years later, as chairman and CEO of a public company. Even when I announced my departure date, it still galled me to think that someone else would be running "my company." I have met few retired CEOs who don't miss the power and its trappings. We all have withdrawal symptoms. The thrill of figuring out how to operate your new home fax machine hardly stacks up to the buzz of commanding thousands of employees and overseeing an operations budget with nine figures in it.

But just as power has its rewards, it also comes with a couple of inevitable, nagging questions: How long can I keep my throne? Who will succeed me? Will my successor's reign honor or discredit mine? Succession has been a major issue since the beginning of civilization. Kings and tyrants went to war to keep their crown; they built pyramids and temples; and they read the stars, the sun, the moon and created religions to justify their power. The Greeks and Romans struggled to formalize tenure and succession, but the hard-won Roman Republic fell eventually to Octavius Caesar's ambition.

The men who killed Julius Caesar to stop him becoming king were in turn defeated by Antony and Octavius, prompting them to commit suicide. Octavius then defeated Antony and became emperor (renaming the month in which he had defeated Cleopatra "August" after the honorific that the Senate had granted him). And then the emperor decided who should succeed him. In the Middle Ages, kings claimed divine right from God to succession and had everyone in the country swearing fealty to them. So they were supposed to be secure. But that was not enough to stop many of them from being violently deposed.

Shakespeare lived in an era of one of the greatest monarchs in English history, Elizabeth I, who ascended to the throne at a time of bloody religious conflict in England. When she died forty-four and a half years later, England had enjoyed decades of civil peace and had become a world power. Fascinated by English history and well aware of the drama of royal power, Shakespeare probed the problems of succession. The age-old requirements of leadership—strength, resourcefulness, guile, knowledge, wisdom, empathy, energy, courage, curiosity, constancy, persuasion, and vision—have never been repealed. They exist today. The hero can never rest. The halo must not tarnish; the crown must be defended.

No sooner is Macbeth crowned than he is worrying about who will succeed him. He and his wife are childless. He recalls that the witches who predicted his crown also informed his friend Banquo that "thou shalt get kings, though thou shalt not be one." Macbeth allows his imagination to run with the implications of that prophecy:

> They hail'd him father to a line of kings:
> Upon my head they plac'd a fruitless crown,
> And put a barren sceptre in my gripe [grip],
> Thence to be wrench'd with an unlineal hand,
> No son of mine succeeding. If't be so,

> For Banquo's issue have I fil'd my mind;
> For them the gracious Duncan have I murther'd;
> Put rancours in the vessel of my peace,
> Only for them; and mine eternal jewel
> Given to the common Enemy of man,
> To make them kings, the seed of Banquo kings!
>
> MACBETH (3.1, 64–69)

And so Macbeth wonders how worthwhile is the guilt that he has incurred by killing a king to be king, if another man's son is to succeed him on the throne.

King Claudius arranges for Prince Hamlet (his stepson and heir to the throne) to take a trip to England—for his own "safety." Of course, the audience knows that Claudius had already made arrangements in England to have the young prince killed. How many chief executives have buried strong contenders for their job by dispatching them to remote outposts for "the opportunity to further develop their leadership skills"? People with power are not inclined to give it up.

In fact, leaders contemplate succession with the same enthusiasm that they contemplate death. If you are next in line to a boss, particularly one whose persona is identified with the company, he will worry about you, even if he is only a year or six months away from retirement. There are exceptions, to be sure, but by and large, few leaders can bear the thought of giving up power and its perks.

CEOs are forever bringing in people as "partners" or to groom them as successors. Watch out! Henry IV does not want to die, not because he fears death itself, but because he does not believe that his son is up to the job: "Thou seekest the greatness that will overwhelm thee" (*King Henry IV, Part 2* [4.5, 97]). As a usurper, Henry IV knows he has enemies, and that, after his death, civil war may become an even bigger threat for his successor. Like every leader, Henry worries about his legacy:

> O my poor kingdom, sick with civil blows!
> When that my care could not withhold thy riots,

What wilt thou do when riot is thy care?
O, thou wilt be a wilderness again,
Peopled with wolves, thy old inhabitants!

KING HENRY IV, PART 2 (4.5, 133–37)

The men and women who rise to the top of the power pyramid and remain there usually believe that no one else can do the job better than they can. Why should they change their minds at the end of their careers? Chief executives know they need a successor; boards encourage them to groom a "partner" or a COO to take over. But consider this statistic: The average tenure of a COO under a sitting CEO is eighteen months. If you have been hired to step into the top job, you'd better keep that statistic in mind when you're negotiating your deal.

If you are a chief executive looking in the mirror and telling yourself you really want a successor, you should also look in Shakespeare's mirror and see Henry IV worrying about succession. He had reason to worry. After he forced Richard II to step down, he then had him killed in prison rather than reign in his shadow. Imagine what energy, not to mention bad publicity and tens of millions of dollars, Disney chairman Michael Eisner might have saved if he had looked into Shakespeare's mirror before he brought his old friend, celebrated Hollywood power broker Michael Ovitz, into the company as a potential successor. Eisner, who had recently had a heart bypass operation, had been criticized for years for not grooming a successor. Not long before, his trusted president, Frank Wells, had died in a tragic helicopter accident. Eisner turned to Ovitz, a friend since childhood. But no sooner was Ovitz in his new office on the Disney lot than he realized he had no power. Eisner, like Bolingbroke, could not bring himself to share his power. Within eighteen months, Ovitz was back on the street, albeit with a severance package that cost Disney some $90 million! Yet Ovitz probably would have paid as much to avoid the public humiliation that this *danse macabre* at Disney created in the press. And it seems to be a pattern. Chairman Eisner acts as if he is terrified by succession and as eager to waste his successors as Macbeth. In

1999, he settled a suit brought by Jeffrey Katzenberg, a former production chief at Disney, who quit when it became clear to him that Eisner would not give him the president's job after Wells's death. Katzenberg claimed that Disney owed him at least $200 million in bonuses that were contractually due to him as a result of his contributions to Disney's profits during his tenure. And how many seconds in command did William Paley appoint during his waning years at CBS?

Yet a truly confident leader can create successors and hand over power to them. GE's Jack Welch has generated double-digit growth since taking over as chief executive in 1981. But the big story around GE is who will succeed Welch, who will retire in April 2001 with nothing else to prove. Welch has often claimed to be unconcerned about succession, but he and a special committee of GE board members have been evaluating several top executives in the company, posted in various divisions throughout the GE empire. And you can bet that whoever does get the job will want to be very clear about Welch's postretirement relationship to the enterprise, so identified is he with GE.

In the summer of 1999, Mark Willes, the chief executive of the Los Angeles Times-Mirror Company, who nineteen months before had appointed himself publisher of the company's struggling flagship newspaper, the *Los Angeles Times,* turned over the publisher's job to the paper's president. The *Los Angeles Times'* second-quarter earnings would reflect the first year-to-year growth in five quarters, Willes announced, and it was time for him to return his undivided attention to the whole company. Both moves had their critics, but one of Willes's remarks deserves to be carved in stone: "Good leaders know when to get in, and they know when to get out." Amen.

We don't murder our top executives, we give them early retirement or a golden handshake, or they leave "to pursue other opportunities." (If that fails, you can punch up the press release on the computer that reads, "wants to spend more time with his family.") Be smart and avoid the humiliation of permitting someone else to set your date of departure. The end comes to even the most brilliant business careers. Take a page from the books of such immortal athletes as Joe DiMaggio and Ted Williams or more recently the basketball divinity Michael Jordan or hockey great Wayne Gretzky and step down before you're pushed.

And if you still find it hard to give up the power and glory, consider all the stress, anxiety, and grief you will also be putting behind you. After all, you're just quitting, not dying. And as Henry IV points out, at least you'll finally be getting a good night's sleep:

> How many thousand of my poorest subjects
> Are at this hour asleep! O sleep, O gentle sleep,
> Nature's soft nurse, how have I frighted thee,
> That thou no more wilt weigh my eyelids down,
> And steep my senses in forgetfulness?
> Why rather, sleep, liest thou in smoky cribs . . .
> Than in the perfum'd chambers of the great,
> Under the canopies of costly state . . .
> O thou dull god, why li'st thou with the vile
> In loathsome beds, and leav'st the kingly couch
> A watch-case or a common 'larum-bell? . . .
> And in the calmest and most stillest night,
> With all appliances and means to boot,
> Deny it to a King? Then happy low, lie down!
> Uneasy lies the head that wears a crown.
>
> KING HENRY IV, PART 2 (3.1, 4–31)

3

The Trusted Lieutenant

A Delicate Balance

. . . I have trusted thee, Camillo,
With all the nearest things to my heart, as well
My chamber-counsels, wherein, priest-like, thou
Hast cleans'd my bosom . . .

Leontes in The Winter's Tale (1.2, 235–38)

. . . Give me that man
That is not passion's slave, and I will wear him
In my heart's core, ay, in my heart of heart,
As I do thee . . .

Hamlet to Horatio in Hamlet (3.2, 72–75)

Aᴄ FTER the miraculous victory of Henry V's troops against the
French at Agincourt, the King of France asks Henry "to appoint
some of your council presently to sit with us once more" to negotiate the peace treaty. Henry agrees and quickly turns to his assembled nobles and gives this order:

> . . . Go, uncle Exeter,
> And brother Clarence, and you, brother Gloucester,
> Warwick and Huntingdon, go with the King,
> And take with you free power to ratify,
> Augment or alter, as your wisdoms best
> Shall see advantageable for our dignity,
> Anything in or out of our demands,
> And we'll consign thereto . . .
>
> KING HENRY V (5.2, 83–90)

Notice he doesn't say, "Meet with the French and report back to
me so that I can make the final decision." Henry gives his nobles
"free power to ratify, augment or alter" the French proposals according to their "wisdoms." Whatever deal the nobles reach with
the French, Henry promises to sign on to. Evidently, he has faith in
the ability of Clarence, Gloucester, and the others to represent his
interests. They are his "trusted lieutenants."

Such close aides to the king are common in Shakespeare's histories and tragedies. Kings, no matter how powerful or arrogant,
do not operate alone. It is easier for the head to wear a crown when
a trusted lieutenant is on hand to answer any call. And so we find
King Lear's loyal Earl of Kent, Timon of Athens's faithful Flavius,
King John's devoted Bastard, Henry VIII's manipulating Cardinal
Wolsey, Othello's ensign Iago, Mark Antony's aide-de-camp Enobarbus. Cleopatra has her Charmian, a close female confidante
who runs the Egyptian court and serves her mistress to the end. Of
course, a few of these trusted lieutenants should never have been
trusted (Iago and Cardinal Wolsey, for example). The dynamic between president and assistant to the president, chancellor and vice
chancellor, movie star and handler, entrepreneur and office man-

ager is the key to powerful leadership. A leader cannot do it alone. Who will be your personal backup? And if the leader commands or guides hundreds of people, does the personal assistant need to keep a finger on the pulse of the organization? Be your eyes and ears?

On every level of a business, success hinges in no small part on relationships between managers and the people reporting directly to them. The tension between those who lead and those who are being led can be constructive or destructive. But even constructive tension needs to be managed. A good personal assistant can keep the relationship between leader and followers healthy, harmonious, and efficient. Shakespeare raises questions helpful to modern management: How do you create an environment of trust so that the alliance between leader and personal assistant can flourish and everyone can benefit? When should you file for divorce? How do you find an Earl of Kent? How do you avoid creating an Iago?

The trusted lieutenant can be a powerful force for good in a company: filling in the gaps; explaining motives; creating laughter; making sure it all moves forward smoothly. However, because the trusted lieutenant knows the inside dope, has the ear of the leader, he or she has enormous influence and can create havoc if the relationship goes awry. The alliance between a leader and a top aide changes with time and circumstance. Not always do the leader and the lieutenant share the same needs, real or imaginary, and often their personalities are very different. Theirs is a very special relationship that will splinter unless it has a solid and consistent base. Bigger than both must be the goals of the enterprise, the company's mission. When both sides are aligned toward a common goal, then great things happen.

THE BENEFITS OF AN ALTER EGO

"I could not do the job without my right hand," says Tina Packer, who has had secretaries and assistants before, some very capable, but never anyone who could do most of the things she does and still do the detail work; she had never had an "aide-de-camp" until she hired Michael Hammond to be assistant to the artistic director of Shakespeare & Company. Hammond, still a working actor, director, and teacher with the company, took care of all the details of her job—scheduling appointments, arranging trips, making sure airplane tickets have been purchased, as well as bigger tasks such as negotiating contracts, doing the first leg of press interviews, even taking rehearsals and classes. Hammond soon emerged as Tina's alter ego:

> He told me what he thought, and where he thought I was lacking in my perception, if the decision I was making erred too much on the political side instead of on the artistic or vice versa. I conferred with him about all the decisions I had to make. He understood my mind very well. I trusted him to make decisions on my behalf because he knew how I thought.

Like Henry V to his trusted nobles, Tina gave Michael Hammond "free power to ratify" on her behalf. Hammond became the classic trusted lieutenant who does his boss's bidding, without bridling, but without being a doormat either. "I know he really did have to step on his ego sometimes," says Tina. "I saw him doing it." But he could gauge his response according to his knowledge of his boss, plus their shared commitment of getting Shakespeare & Company to be a top-notch theater company. "He was so good, I had to promote him. He now runs our Boston operations; he runs them the way he wants to run them, but I know he understands what I want, too. I am now looking for my new Michael Hammond!"

THE TRUSTED LIEUTENANT IS *YOUR* LIEUTENANT — SO TRUST HIM

At the supermarket chain John Marcuse was my first assistant to the president. (Because the job was a training position, I appointed a new "trusted lieutenant" every year.) His task was to find out what was going on in the company. He was my operative, my agent, my eyes and ears when he went into the field. All he had to say after a visit to one outpost or another was "I think you should take a look at that operation," and I was on my way. In the severing of the relationship between King Lear and the loyal Earl of Kent, Shakespeare offers a powerful example of the risk a leader takes when he ignores the wisdom of a trusted lieutenant. At the beginning of the play, the king appears to be a most successful monarch. In his eighties, Lear is still in command, surrounded by loyal family members and courtiers. However, by the end of the first scene, the king has made several alarming mistakes and is heading toward disaster.

Lear convenes his court to announce that he is "crawling toward death" and therefore is going to divide his kingdom into three parts, one for each of his three daughters—Goneril, Regan, and Cordelia. He seems to have decided already who is going to get what, because the map of the country has been previously divided. So it must be a whim of the moment that makes him declare that whichever daughter says she loves him the most will get the largest part of the kingdom. And he obviously expects his favorite, the youngest, Cordelia, to win because he's already rigged the map that way. Perhaps he sets up this silly test because her two potential husbands are in the court and he's proving that she loves Daddy best. In any case, it backfires. First Goneril effusively declares a love that "makes breath poor and speech unable." Her sister Regan essentially seconds her sister's pledge. And Cordelia? She's appalled by her sisters' hypocrisy. To her father's demand, "What can you say . . . ?" her answer is "Nothing." Lear presses her, and Cordelia, Shakespeare's staunchest heroine (so virtuous she seems almost angelic), informs her father,

> . . . I love your majesty
> According to my bond, no more nor less.
>
> KING LEAR (1.1, 92–93)

Lear begs her to reconsider. But Cordelia argues that any woman who pledges to "love her father all" is dishonest. In a rage

Lear disinherits her and divides her portion of the kingdom between her sisters.

Kent, the king's loyal adviser, steps in to try to stop this nonsense. Lear warns him not to come "between the dragon and his wrath!" Kent reminds Lear that he has earned the right to intervene:

> . . . Royal Lear,
> Whom I have ever honoured as my king,
> Loved as my father, as my master followed,
> As my great patron thought on in my prayers—
>
> KING LEAR (1.1, 140–43)

Kent points out that he has always performed his duties for the king and opposed his enemies; he argues that he must continue to do so even "when majesty falls to folly." He begs Lear to

> . . . Reserve thy state,
> And in thy best consideration check
> This hideous rashness.
>
> KING LEAR (1.1, 150–52)

Kent's courage is the courage that a trusted lieutenant must have when he is witness to catastrophic decisions. He boldly stares Lear straight in the eye and says, "thou dost evil."

How does Lear treat this most loyal of trusted lieutenants? He gives him five days to clean out his office—

> And on the sixth to turn thy hated back
> Upon our kingdom. If on the next day following
> Thy banished trunk be found in our dominions,
> The moment is thy death. Away! By Jupiter,
> This shall not be revoked.
>
> KING LEAR (1.1, 176–80)

It has to be one of the most brutal sackings in the history of personnel management. The first time one of my students asked me what I would have done if a subordinate had confronted me in Kent's manner, I replied, I'm afraid, "Like Lear, I would probably have fired him too." Lear was in such a highly charged state, I know that if I had felt like that, I too would have acted just as emotionally, just as stupidly. Kent was right to try to stop the folly. Could he have done it differently and been more effective? It's a very good question. Was Kent right to confront Lear in public? Maybe he should have waited and talked to him in private. Did Lear have the right to banish his loyal servant under pain of death? After all, Kent was doing the job Lear had chosen him for. As the king's adviser, he was meant to give the king advice.

And he gave him the right advice. By disinheriting Cordelia, Lear sets his tragedy in motion: the daughters who pledged their undying love turn on him, take away his authority, and drive his entourage from the palace, and he goes mad. By the end of the play all Lear has left is Cordelia's love. And Kent's love. The faithful Kent. Kent disguises himself and continues to serve the king: such is his tenacity as trusted lieutenant.

The tragedy of Lear's inability to listen to Kent brings up all the debating points about how leaders and their top subordinates must work together. What is the duty of the subordinate to the leader? Ought he to criticize his boss in public? I think so. Of course, a lot depends on the relationship that already exists between the two. Yet if decisions are to be made immediately as a result of a debate or a public forum, I believe that the trusted lieutenant has an obligation to speak up. Otherwise, why is he there? And while a top aide can always wait to collar his boss in private, sometimes waiting makes it too late.

It is the trusted lieutenant's job to challenge the leader. If the leader is smart, he will find an aide who complements his skills or compensates for his weaknesses. If you're not a master of high finance, find a loyal CFO; if you'd prefer to concentrate on operations and not press the flesh, find a face man.

I've had my Kents and, fortunately, I didn't fire them. On the contrary, I listened to them. And I had the good sense not to keep their wisdom for myself but to share the wealth by promoting them. At my advertising agency in Tulsa, Cecille Bales and Bill

Hussey spoke their minds, I listened, and we all prospered. When I arrived at Pathmark I found the usual turnaround situation: competitive attacks, internal dissension, system failures everywhere. My job was to fix these problems calmly and professionally, not to become part of the problem. However, without realizing how it sounded to others, I would say things like "You guys did that!" or "You guys should've done this!" Finally, my vice president of marketing, Ken Peskin, a former marine captain, tapped me on the shoulder and said, "John, now you are one of us." Ken's honesty and guts stopped me in my tracks—and perhaps even saved my job, for a few years, anyway. (Ken Peskin later went on to be president of Pathmark.)

LOYALTY IS A TWO-WAY STREET

Kent's loyalty is extraordinary. After the king banishes him, Kent risks his life to return to Lear's side—disguised as a servant—protecting him from murder and reuniting him with Cordelia at the end of the play. But no lieutenant should be required to go so far. In fact, once your boss stops trusting your advice, it is time to move on. Camillo in *The Winter's Tale* makes just such a decision. Leontes of Sicilia is sure that his best friend, Polixenes of Bohemia, is having an affair with his wife.

He asks his trusted lieutenant, Camillo, to poison Polixenes. Camillo strongly challenges his boss's perception. "You never spoke what did become you less / Than this," Camillo says to the king. However, Leontes will not be dissuaded. Camillo pretends to agree. Like any top executive, Camillo knows that following orders is to his advantage: "To do this deed promotion follows." But Camillo cannot murder a man who is innocent. As soon as Leontes leaves, Camillo informs Polixenes of the assassination plot, and they both leave for Bohemia. The king rages over Camillo's "treachery." One man's treason becomes another's good turn. Camillo becomes King Polixenes' number two for the next fifteen years.

However, unlike Camillo and Kent, some aides are close to the power in order to get promotions or line their own purse or promote their own agendas. Such a one is Iago.

CREATING IAGO

Iago, Othello's infamous aide, is a finely drawn, authentic, chilling villain. A debate centers around this question: Why is Iago, who schemes to turn the noble Othello into a crazed, jealous murderer, so evil? What are his motives? Some people are mystified by his obsession with revenge. The nineteenth-century poet Samuel Taylor Coleridge was puzzled by what he called Iago's "motiveless malignity."

But no business executive could read Shakespeare's great tragedy *Othello* and not understand perfectly well why Iago turned on his boss: the man had been passed over for promotion! Iago had served dutifully and bravely in the armed forces of Venice as General Othello's "ancient," or third in command; he had even been recommended by "three great ones" of the city of Venice as the clear choice for Othello's second in command. And what does the great Othello do? He gives the job to Michael Cassio, a man whose main attribute for the job is that he's a "great arithmetician." Iago is incredulous. Cassio has "never set a squadron in the field," while Iago has won battles for Othello. So while Coleridge might see no motive for Iago's guiltless glee in destroying Othello, anyone who has spent a few months inside a major American corporation (or university) knows exactly why Iago turns vicious. Being passed over can do terrible things to a person.

Shakespeare wastes no time in letting the audience know that Othello has created a dangerous enemy in Iago, who confides his outrage to his friend Roderigo in the first scene of the play. He will not be one of those timeservers, Iago points out, "a duteous and knee-crooking knave" who serves his master until he is retired "like his master's ass." Iago plans a craftier future: he will be one of those men who

Keep yet their hearts attending on themselves
And, throwing but shows of service on their lords,
Do well thrive by them, and, when have lined their coats,
Do themselves homage . . .

OTHELLO (1.1, 50–53)

Iago, passed over for promotion, has no intention of quitting. He prefers to get even. "In following him [Othello] I follow but myself." Iago intends to play the perfect employee; he will seem to care about "love and duty." But in reality, "I am not what I am" (*Othello* [1.1, 64]).

It is a chilling statement. In my classes and executive seminars, I have my students read Iago's speech. Every manager should; in fact, study the entire play with close attention to Iago's scheme to destroy Othello. He suggests that the love of Othello's life, his young wife, Desdemona, is cheating on him with—you guessed it, Cassio—the man who got Iago's job. It is a textbook case in psychological manipulation and the big payback.

Every manager, sad to say, should be prepared to discover that he will have to promote some people over others—and fire some people. Any leader who thinks that he will be loved and honored by all is a fool.

There are three ways to protect yourself from potential Iagos. First, stay involved with your work. As we have said earlier and will say later, leading is a demanding job and must be given close attention. The leader who daydreams or focuses too much on activities external to his job is vulnerable. The second thing you can do to protect yourself from Iagos is to create an open, trusting environment in your organization. When everyone else in the organization is working in relative harmony for a common goal with shared values, the Iagos of this world don't have such an easy time stabbing you in the back. Fair warning, though: some Iagos are so patient and crafty that they can work their mischief for years without being exposed. Your third alternative is to meet face-to-face with those who have been passed over and are potential Iagos. Let them make their protestations and then counter with your reasons. Have a plan ready to propose that shows them how they can have a chance at the next promotion. Or, if you have made up your mind that they won't have a chance, tell them so. Then you can assess whether they will continue to give their best efforts. If you believe they will not, then help them find a job somewhere else. You can't afford to have them around, grieving, festering, and, possibly, plotting.

Othello might have avoided creating his Iago. As Tina Packer points out:

> Othello clearly did not tell Iago why he passed him over for promotion. Iago has reason to believe he should be promoted. He and Othello have been to war together. Three important leaders of Venice support his promotion. But Othello appoints Cassio because he is a mathematician. That's the only reason we hear in the play. We suspect Cassio's role as a go-between during the period when Othello was wooing Desdemona may also have influenced the decision, but that's not mentioned in the text. Othello should have sat Iago down and said, "Good friend Iago, the only reason you were passed over is that we needed someone good at mathematics. Modern warfare means cannon, and placing the cannon at the exact angle, so the ball will do maximum damage to castle walls. Well, it's a science and you just don't have the science. If you want to get on, perhaps you should get some extra training. Also, you know as well as I do, ol' Iago, you are not the best politician in the army; you have a tendency to be rough with language." He might also have added, "I've heard you make racist and sexist remarks when you've had one too many. If it's true, you'll get fired."

Tina also points to a weakness in Othello's leadership that opens him up too easily to Iago's vicious manipulations (she has learned this from her friend, the actor Johnny Lee Davenport, who played Othello for Shakespeare & Company):

> For Johnny Lee, the most resonant aspect about the relationship between Othello and Iago is that Iago becomes, in effect, Othello's guide to the world of Venice. Othello is a professional soldier, a general, and the commander of the army. He's also a foreigner, a black

man from North Africa, who has never wooed a Venetian woman before, certainly not one twenty years his junior. Iago's closeness to Othello allows him to feed him false information. Johnny Lee considers Iago's misinformation similar to that of some history textbooks in school: "I never saw a mention of the contribution made by African Americans in building America. And I believed them. It created a kind of cultural schizophrenia in me. Where do I fit in here? Clearly, a man secure about his wife's love would ignore Iago's suggestion that she's having an affair with Cassio. But Othello, unsure about Venetian women, becomes crazed with jealousy; he trusts Iago instead of Desdemona, and therein lies his tragedy."

And thus Shakespeare offers the modern manager another useful lesson: The insecure executive is bound to be more vulnerable to the Iagos in his midst. So be strong; make your promotions as you see fit, but let those who get passed over know why and encourage them to throw their hats in the ring for the next promotion.

If that doesn't work, if you sense that, in spite of your encouragement, those you've passed over are simmering with outrage, fire them.

How Do You Spot an Iago (or a Cardinal Wolsey)?

If I learn that a lieutenant is willing to "cut corners" or "turn a blind eye"—even if it seems to be for the good of the enterprise—my guard goes up. Someone who uses duplicitous means tends to use them regardless of time, place, or situation. "Lions make leopards tame," says King Richard II. To which Mowbray replies wisely, "Yea, but not to change his spots." If someone uses deceit to help you, he can hurt you the same way.

In *King Henry VIII,* Cardinal Wolsey strengthens his place as the king's right-hand man by framing his popular rival, the Duke of Buckingham, and maneuvering his execution. The cardinal, whom one enemy claims has "witchcraft over the king's tongue," encourages Henry to divorce his wife, Katherine; however, behind the scenes he acts as if he opposes the divorce. Similarly, although Wolsey introduces Henry to Anne Bullen (Boleyn), he opposes the marriage. All under the pretense of protecting the king's interests.

Wolsey's real goal, of course, is to increase his own power. In Act 2, the cardinal shows his hand clearly to the audience when the king orders him to invalidate the taxes that Wolsey has imposed and the people are now rebelling against. Wolsey instructs one of his aides to make it look as if the change in policy came from his and not the king's office. Gradually, Henry VIII realizes that this cardinal, whom he had kept "next to my heart" and made "the prime man of the state," has been manipulating him to increase his personal power and amass "piles of wealth." Henry presses formal charges against Wolsey and orders the cardinal's wealth confiscated.

But Henry should have recognized that Wolsey's craftiness, so useful for the crown, could just as easily be turned against the crown. Another warning sign the chief executive should note: any top aide who is constantly affirming his loyalty and praising his boss is likely to have an ulterior motive. Wolsey and his sidekick Cardinal Campeius flatter the king unconscionably: "Your Grace has given a precedent of wisdom / Above all princes," says Wolsey (*King Henry VIII* [2.2, 84–85]). "Your Grace must needs deserve strangers' loves, / You are so noble," echoes Campeius (2.2, 100–101).

Other symptoms of a would-be conniver are changes in his or her usual habits. If your number two was always around and then starts disappearing, be careful. Similarly, if he has always given you some space and now won't let you out of his sight, watch out. Or maybe your aide seems reluctant to speak up at meetings, or she can't seem to shut up. Suddenly, a blizzard of memos comes from her office—or, even worse, memos to file. When a leader is in trouble, a disloyal number two is more likely to go on the record with information that will bolster his position after his boss is toppled.

And without succumbing to paranoia (although a little is a useful thing in spotting an Iago), the leader should assess whether her own demise or the demise of a colleague might advance the cause of a lieutenant. Julius Caesar sensed this when he pointed at Cassius and noted his "lean and hungry look." Caesar didn't act upon his suspicion of Cassius, and that contributed to his death. Earlier, I suggested that you create an open, trusting environment. Because that is not as easy as it sounds, it deserves special mention.

CREATING TRUST

I learned the most about trust in the scariest arena in business—the turnaround. The company in crisis has usually lost market share; cash is scarce, costs are typically too high, and in most instances jobs must be cut. The survivors are exhausted and dispirited. Morale plummets. The most important goal in a turnaround—next to conserving cash, that is—is to turn the people around. Achieving improved market position and lower costs is hopeless unless those who've escaped the ax are committed to creating a phoenix out of the ashes. And without creative and enthusiastic effort from the people on the front lines, I don't care how brilliant a turnaround strategist you are, you will never dig the company out of its hole.

To prove that you're creating a trusting environment in a damaged company, you have to do something dramatic and authentic. One small, symbolic act that I like is to remove time clocks. Workers are then told that they will be paid their normal wages, which will be adjusted up or down, but only if they report they have worked more—or fewer—hours than expected. Jobs have to get done, and getting them done is how we turn around. I instruct supervisors to deal humanely with issues such as time off for family problems. I think it's nuts for a company to try to gauge bereavement hours according to the family relationship: a week for a spouse, half a day for grandmothers and uncles, and so on. Union leaders hate this move; the employees recognize the humanity of it. Bean counting has its place in business, but not at a time when an employee is grieving for a loved one or needs to get a job done.

One of the most effective decisions I've made in a turnaround is to take away control of expense accounts from the financial office and turn it over to the employees. The first thing I do is call a meeting with all managers whose job includes traveling and entertaining customers. I remind them of the company's fragile financial health, laying out the details. Just when they're saying good-bye, in their own minds, to expense account dinners and nice hotels, I hit them with another command: "We need to travel more!" No company wants to signal to the business community that you're in more trouble than it thinks you are. Eager to cut costs, companies are inclined to rein in things like travel and entertainment. But if your managers aren't in the field, your competitors will clobber you. Managers will ask me, "Should I buy the customer a big steak?" My answer is simple: "If he's a big customer." And I definitely don't want managers in my company traveling at night or staying in fleabag hotels. When they meet customers, I want them to look fresh and feel good.

Less money, more travel? Right. Then I spring surprise number two: "Okay, we understand that we need to save money whenever we can. But you're a better judge of that than I am. So from this day forward, you don't need permission from me—or anyone else in the company—to travel. Then, when you turn in your expense accounts, they will be approved, automatically, no questions asked. I won't review them, and the controller will not question them." Radical? You bet. So radical that the three times I have tried this ploy in my turnarounds, *per diem expenses for travel have fallen by as much as 40 percent!* That means we were getting 40 percent more travel days for the same money. With these kinds of assurances from the company's leadership, the game of Beat the Controller on expense accounts ends. The message that I want to send is that we're all in the same boat and working for the same goal: the survival of the enterprise.

Will some people continue to cheat? Of course. But I'm not trying to change human nature, just save my company. Besides, you won't need a private police force to catch the cheaters. In my experience, they are usually exposed by their peers. The fact is that the money you save on expense account controls is more than you lose to the cheaters. If, however, you happen to catch someone stealing, cheating, or lying, you terminate them swiftly and dishonorably.

Two precepts have served me well in my management career: (1) Man can defeat any system man devises; and (2) The more controls you have, the less control you have.[6] The trick is to build a system that people understand, believe in, and willingly support. Trust will lubricate that system.[7]

***

Trust Must Be Earned

Trust is built daily, block by block, as leaders and lieutenants confront the world inside and outside the office. How does each person act under fire? And do they know one another so well that when the bombs are falling, a mere look gives the message? Do they admire one another's strengths? Are they willing to shore up one another's weaknesses? Or do they expect perfection? Do they feel compelled to check up on one another's performance? Does their relationship exclude others whose contributions are important to the enterprise?

The leader-lieutenant duo aware of such pitfalls and opportunities is more apt to build an enduring, rewarding relationship. If you are either a lieutenant or a leader trying to figure out how to operate with each other, or are already in a rocky relationship, you might wish to consider the following attributes as necessities for working together.

Competence

People are surprised that I identify this as the first and most important requirement. But if someone is not competent to do the job, then trust takes a holiday. The leader who is saddled with an incompetent lieutenant can end up doing both jobs. If you have an "assistant to the president," you ought to get your money's worth.

Alternatively, the lieutenant who works under an incompetent leader must constantly be on guard, covering up his boss's mistakes or helping him overcome his weaknesses. The big danger is that after working so hard to keep things afloat, the lieutenant is bound to start to wonder, "If I'm doing all the work, why is the boss getting all the glory?" In *King John,* the Bastard is unflinchingly loyal to King John, even though John is incompetent and cowardly. When the nobles say they've had enough and go over to the other side, the Bastard stays loyal. His steadfastness saves England from being handed over to France.

Competence, however, is relative. While some people may be born leaders, no one springs from the womb a chief executive of General Electric. We all have to do a lot of learning on the job. I like to think I did a pretty good job of rebuilding Pathmark. But, by definition, my first day as COO I was all incompetence. Sure, I knew something about crisis management and marketing. But my grasp of supermarket operation was nil, and I certainly did not know the capabilities of the people working for me. I was also ignorant of the logistics of the business as well as the operating systems that made it happen.

During my first few months as president, my incompetence, I'm sure, exhausted my stalwart lieutenants. And the journey was rough going. My mandate was to turn around a damaged company. To do so, I had to build on my previous skills in marketing and as a cash-savvy entrepreneur who also knew how to get people to focus on their opportunities rather than their problems. At the same time, I had to do my homework and learn supermarket operations, fast. When people saw what I did bring to the job and realized my commitment to learn, they began to relax a bit and help me get up to speed.

Every leader has what I call a "flat side," an area of competence where she or he is weak. In today's fast-paced world most executives are bound not only to change jobs often, but to change businesses, too. The most talented executives will be those who can quickly master any business they sign on for. To do that often requires the talented help of a trusted lieutenant.

But to keep from stepping on each other's toes, you both will need the following characteristic:

Commitment

First, commitment to the enterprise, then to yourself, and finally to the leader-lieutenant relationship. Friendships can flourish without a commitment to a cause, but the enduring boss-subordinate relationship flourishes *only* where there is a cause that transcends that relationship. Mark Antony's lieutenant, Enobarbus, is committed to Antony—until he decides that Antony's obsession with Cleopatra has destroyed his ability to act like the great warrior he is. "A diminution in our captain's brain / Restores his heart," notes Enobarus, who then announces to the audience that "I will seek / Some way to leave him" (*Antony and Cleopatra* [3.13, 203–206]). Enobarbus switches to Octavius Caesar's side.

However, Antony, when he hears that his aide has abandoned him, concedes that Enobarbus had good reason to do so. "O, my fortunes have / Corrupted honest men!" says Antony (4.5, 16–17), and he orders Enobarbus's belongings to be sent to him in the enemy camp. Enobarbus is stunned. Antony's gesture, says Enobarbus, "blows my heart," reviving all his love for Antony. In grief he dies of a broken heart. When Antony and Enobarbus lost their commitment to a common cause, they lost each other—and, ultimately, their lives.

Every leader (and every business) needs a "cause," a goal, an objective. In the turnarounds I lead, I never begin by making the traditional visits to outposts to gather intelligence. I believe you learn by doing rather than talking. So I begin by creating what I call a "marching song"—an important project that must be undertaken, a target that must be hit, like the twenty-four-hour store openings at Pathmark. With our marching song in place, my trusted lieutenants and I plot our strategy to reach our objective. As we work together, I learn far more about the strengths and weaknesses of my lieutenants—and they learn more about mine—than we ever would in days of office meetings.

What happens when you and your lieutenants disagree? Maybe you have different styles of management. No problem—if you are both clear about your objectives. Kent disagreed with Lear because he felt that the king's decision to split the kingdom and then foolishly cut Cordelia out of her inheritance would be a catastrophic blow to the future of the country. Even after he was fired, Kent was so committed to Lear that he was willing to risk his life by returning to Lear's side disguised as a servant.

Kent was not just loyal; he was also a man of conviction. Commitment to self is an absolute requirement for any successful partnership. We are persons before we are partners. For us to earn the respect of partners, we must respect ourselves. Carol Nan Wheat, one of the most prolific and creative writers at my advertising agency, once said to me as I was blithely editing her copy, "Where were you when the paper was blank?" She wanted to remind me of her worth. Penny Gaither, one of my vice presidents at the company, had just finished a massive project. Preoccupied with my own duties and problems, I began reviewing the project, when suddenly I noticed the fire in her eyes. She was furious, and I knew why: I had never thanked her for her prodigious effort. I quickly begged her forgiveness and assured her how much I appreciated her work, which I never took for granted again. Carol and Penny had a sense of their worth, and they insisted that I recognize it. Their candor only strengthened our relationship.

Managing Your Boss

Bosses, too, have fears and concerns, and you have to allay them. Bosses also need recognition. Not empty flattery, mind you, of the sort that King Lear or Henry VIII required. I'm talking about an honest appreciation of their worth.

Although we all know that true self-respect comes from within, a few pats on the back are likely not only to keep the boss up to speed but encourage him to spread some appreciation down through the ranks.

Every time the boss says something, a skilled assistant to the president runs through a list of questions in his own head: "What did the boss say?" "Did he really mean what he said?" "Did he sell the idea?" "What should he have said?" Their relationship should be so close that the trusted lieutenant can finish his boss's sentences. As Tina Packer said about her number two, "I trusted him to make decisions on my behalf because he knew how I thought."

The best lieutenants become their boss's alter ego. Enobarbus could anticipate Antony's every thought and move. When Antony pledges to marry Octavius Caesar's sister to cement their alliance as leaders of the Roman world, Enobarbus confides to others that Antony will never really leave Cleopatra; later, Enobarbus anticipates war between Antony and Caesar. It is easier to finish the sentences of your boss when you are both clear about the company's mission. Henry V's legates to France could speak for the king. The danger can be that a top aide speaks so often in the king's voice that he begins to think he *is* the king. Again it's a delicate balance: between pushing your boss for more responsibility and taking on so much of his job that you become a threat.

In *King John*, the king, weak and too willing to yield England to France without a fight, is not threatened when his loyal aide Philip Faulconbridge, known throughout the play as the Bastard, strongly disagrees. And so it is the Bastard, and not the king, who leads the English army against France. It is the Bastard who tries to negotiate peace with the Dauphin of France, assuring him that King John's "royalty doth speak in me" (*King John* [5.2, 129]) and proceeds to give the kind of speech worthy of a king:

> . . . know the gallant monarch is in arms
> And like an eagle o'er his aery towers,
> To souse annoyance that comes near his nest.
>
> KING JOHN (5.2, 148–50)

It is the Bastard, the loyal, trusted lieutenant, who saves his country—without ever giving up his loyalty to his king. The Bastard embodies another principle of the best lieutenant:

Honesty and Candor—but Not Too Much

"Threaten the threatener," the Bastard advises his king. "Glister like the god of war." In this case, the trusted lieutenant tries to make the king more kingly. King John's incompetence is maddening, but to the king's credit, he recognizes what a brilliant, brave, and loyal second in command he has. John may be afraid of the French and be a pushover for the pope's emissary, but he is not afraid of the truth, at least as it comes to him from the Bastard.

But if truth, the whole truth, and nothing but the truth were required in business relationships, most wouldn't last one week. The whole truth on important issues at the right time is imperative. But sometimes a white lie might do wonders to bolster courage, give confidence, create a team.

The trusted lieutenant who thinks that candor means blurting out everything that crosses his or her mind will muddy the water—especially if the boss is still formulating a plan. The leader has a broad view of the objective and the terrain, which the lieutenant can't always see; the plan might be better than it appears.

So the trusted lieutenant needs to hold back a bit and not rush to judgment. Continually put the small things right, and wait for the moment when the large action needs support. In *Antony and Cleopatra,* the Egyptian queen's attendant Charmian is her trusted lieutenant. "You think of him too much," says Charmian when Cleopatra is listlessly lolling about the palace in Antony's absence. In Act 2, Charmian tries to calm the queen's notorious temper when she draws a knife on the messenger from Rome who informs her that Antony has married Octavia. "Good madam, keep yourself within yourself," instructs Charmian (2.5, 75). The last act Charmian does for Cleopatra in death is to close her eyes and straighten her crown—before she follows her into the other world.

> . . . So fare thee well.
> Now boast thee, Death, in thy possession lies
> A lass unparalleled. Downy windows, close,
> And golden Phoebus, never be beheld
> Of eyes again so royal! Your crown's awry;
> I'll mend it, and then play.
>
> ANTONY AND CLEOPATRA (5.2, 312–17)

Charmian is honest, candid, and committed. Honesty is critical when the stakes are high and the time is right. The leader who is reluctant to give honest feedback during review sessions is doing a disservice to the subordinate. And likewise, the subordinate who is reluctant to buck his boss is doing him a disservice. When such shortfalls in candor occur routinely on both sides, the relationship is really in trouble.

If the relationship becomes so strained that reconciliation is hopeless, it is time for the lieutenant to leave. Only rarely does the boss get fired, and so the trusted lieutenant must take a cue from Enobarbus and "seek some way to leave him."

Communication—but Not Too Much

When someone says, "It's a communications problem," it often means that they don't know what the problem is. And talking about it seems to make it worse. It is frivolous to think that all problems can be solved if we just talk about them. Often too much talk can stoke a fire or make a gap wider.

Some differences cannot be reconciled (as Enobarbus and Mark Antony recognized). Sometimes, they should be accommodated. In *Timon of Athens,* Flavius, the manager of Timon's household, watches helplessly as his master's extravagant hospitality toward his friends bankrupts him. He has tried to warn Timon, who simply won't listen. "There is no crossing him in's humour," notes Flavius to the audience (*Timon of Athens* [1.2, 161]). But he remains loyal and sympathetic. "I bleed inwardly for my lord," says Flavius as he sees Timon's fortune dwindling (1.2, 206). And then the money runs out. Even when Timon, broke and desperate, leaves the city, Flavius, his faithful steward, vows to find him.

> I'll ever serve his mind, with my best will;
> Whilst I have gold I'll be his steward still.
>
> TIMON OF ATHENS (4.2, 50–51)

Flavius recognized that he could do nothing for the extravagant and sociable Timon other than be his loyal steward. Theirs was not a communications problem. Timon was convinced his friends would help him no matter what Flavius might tell him. Flavius had to let Timon play out his hand.

IN CONCLUSION

Two different people with the same goals; good at what they do; complementing each other's personalities and skills; willing to tell each other the truth; not afraid to compromise; journeying along a two-way street; committed. In short, a relationship built on trust.

Sounds like a perfect marriage, doesn't it? Tina thinks the analogy is particularly apt for the strongest combinations of leader and second in command:

> It's exactly how a good marriage works. And this holds true whether the woman leads and the man supports or vice versa. Look: you're working with someone who really does have the potential to do the job on his or her own. But this is a partnership, and partnerships can go further than a person on his or her own. So you keep talking to each other, always including each other in every decision. That's how a good business partnership or a good marriage works. And these days, with so many women in the workplace who have children, a husband and wife have to coordinate and support each other just to keep such a complex, modern family life afloat. Even if the wife stays at home to be with the kids, her husband must acknowledge that her role is as important to the collective family enterprise (which includes home and work) as is his traveling all over the place for business. Similarly, the boss-lieutenant team is a *unit*. Each figures out how to serve the other's needs and the goals of the enterprise.

Finally, I would say that it is impossible for anyone to be in a leadership position without a good lieutenant. I would bet that any gifted leader—in business, politics, arts, education, or sports—has an ace second in command, guiding, filling in the gaps, giving feedback, making sure the detail work gets done, making the boss look like the most competent person on earth. A good boss knows that she's where she is because she has an excellent lieutenant.

4

The Skipping King

Uses and Abuses of Perks,
Pay, and Privilege

All that glisters is not gold.

THE MERCHANT OF VENICE (2.7, 65)

I WAS once asked to help turn around a small, struggling company. The chairman said he was willing to cut costs, but he insisted on keeping his corporate jet. Apprehensively, I took the assignment, but I shouldn't have. I wasn't the CEO, and he was the major shareholder. Most of the costs were driven by his pet projects, many of which were as foolish as his jet. Even though he agreed with the logic of discontinuing them, when the time came, he refused to give them up. The turnaround failed. He lost his company and his jet, and I tarnished my reputation.

The Manhattan headquarters of a major oil company had a private elevator for its senior executives. The company is now out of business. An insurance company reportedly spent $4 million on a high-tech table for their boardroom: it didn't stop them from getting into deep financial trouble. A partner in a New York investment bank insists lunch be served in his office—on a silver tray by a waiter wearing white gloves. I'm waiting for the slide to start.

If I were a stockholder in any of these companies, I would wonder what all of these perks have to do with the health of the bottom line. I love to read business books (and to write them), but, frankly, when I find out that a working CEO has written a book, I short the stock. (John Sculley wrote a fine book—about the same time he was driving Apple Computer into near extinction.) I've been an admirer of H. Wayne Huizinga, the innovative entrepreneur who made millions from hauling waste and made more millions creating the Blockbuster Video chain and selling it to Sumner Redstone. But I'm keeping an eye on Wayne's most recent effort, Republic Industries, the auto retailing chain. Why? I read recently that Huizinga built his own private golf course with a clubhouse that cost $6 million.

Shakespeare had an apt and acerbic phrase for the leader who focuses more on the trappings of power than his job. He called him a "skipping king":

> The skipping King, he ambled up and down,
> With shallow jesters, and rash bavin wits,
> Soon kindled and soon burnt, carded [debased] his state,
> Mingled his royalty with cap'ring fools,
> Had his great name profaned with their scorns . . .
>
> KING HENRY IV, PART 1 (3.2, 60–64)

Power comes with trappings, whether you are an archbishop, a general, a movie mogul, a king, or a CEO. If you are a modern-day monarch, you've been in training for the job from the day you were born—whether you're suited for it or not. But if you are a CEO, the chance is you've made your own way through brains, courage, and talent. So why shouldn't you enjoy the rewards? And those rising to the top of the biggest companies can have access to jets and choppers, chauffeur-driven cars, star-studded parties, a picture on the cover of *Business Week,* and visits to the White House. The trappings of power are seductive; they can even be a motivating force to make us do some great work. But take care. Show some of that common sense that hoisted you up the ladder. Because if you let the big salaries and the symbols of your significance become the main goal of your career, if you don't manage your perks and position them for what they're worth, you're heading for trouble. You will be the hot manager "soon kindled and soon burnt." You will have attended too many galas only to mingle your royalty with "cap'ring fools." And your colleagues will be standing around the coffeemaker whispering about your foolishness, your "great name profaned with their scorns."

These are some useful perspectives on the pros and cons of the trappings of power offered by our man Shakespeare.

"All Hoods Make Not Monks"

Historically, the trappings of royalty had symbolic meaning. The crown, for example, was a derivation of the halo, proof that the king or queen was God's representative on earth and occupied the throne by "divine right." Shakespeare's own era, with one of history's most brilliant power players (and thus one of England's greatest monarchs) at the center, is worth studying. Have you ever looked at the paintings of Queen Elizabeth I? The famous "Armada" portrait, painted after England's defeat of the Spanish Armada in 1588, shows the queen on her throne with a lavish necklace of pearls as big as marbles. Her right hand rests easily on a globe, symbolizing that the entire world is in her control. In another portrait, Elizabeth's gown is covered with white flowers symbolizing the "Virgin Queen"'s chastity. In an early portrait, she is depicted outshining the goddesses Juno, Athena, and Venus, while carrying a ball-like object crowned with a cross. This is the traditional "sovereign's orb" that signaled that a monarch was the embodiment of God's power on earth.

Tina Packer points out that Elizabeth, who came to power in a dangerous period of English history, was thoroughly pragmatic and clever about how she used the trappings of power to solidify her reign (perhaps because her mother, Anne Boleyn, had been executed when Elizabeth was three and her stepmother, Catherine Howard, when she was nine and she had watched the mistakes made by her brother Edward, cousin Jane Grey, and sister Mary). The queen used the glitter of her crown and jewels to remind her courtiers who was in charge. She outshone everyone else in her court. She dressed to inspire awe—even though her personal taste was for simplicity. She also made elaborate "processions" through her kingdom accompanied by large numbers of her court to show all her people, no matter where they lived, their queen in person. Such personal appearances did much to unify a country that was still struggling with religious rifts. The monarchs of England have traditionally maintained palaces throughout the realm as symbols of their power in those areas (as the Bush family claims both Maine and Texas as home states); even to this day they stay at a certain castle at a certain period of the year. Elizabeth, however, was famous for her "economies" and often preferred to stay with local nobles and stick them with the bill for the parties and games that accompanied her processions. She was very keen on the bottom line—despite these seeming extravagances. She was the first monarch in decades to pay off the debts the crown owed to the city—and she earned the deep gratitude of her merchant class.

Symbols work the same way today. The modern corporate empire's limos and jets ought to signal, "This company is a great one." The district manager's salary should allow him to buy the appropriate wardrobe to alert customers that he is a successful agent of a strong company. If he drives hundreds of miles a week, he should have a comfortable car, which lets his colleagues know that the company cares about hard work and its employees. Other privileges such as access to the corporate aircraft, comfortable and well-equipped hotels, and an adequate budget for entertaining employees and customers are useful not only in order to do a good job, but also to recruit the best people and make sure effective executives stay at the firm. It can be delightful to enjoy these things. And do take joy in them. But don't be seduced by them. At the end of the day, Elizabeth had to run the country *well,* or the rebellions would start, and she could lose her life.

The trappings of power are a means, not the end. The corona of power can be blinding. Unfortunately, it blinds the leader as much as those around him. Too many of today's tycoons let their crowns tarnish their work efforts as well as their reputations. I would suggest that they melt some of that gold down and turn it into a small plaque for the office engraved with Shakespeare's words from *King Henry VIII:* "All hoods make not monks" (3.1, 23).

The fact that you have the same model of corporate jet as Jack Welch does not make you Jack Welch.

The Seduction of Power

Most of the imperial CEOs I know earned their power. Early in their careers they took on tough projects and succeeded. Their superiors singled them out for their "high potential." Next came promotion to division manager, where they proved they were no-nonsense, results-oriented performers. They worked behind steel-case desks, shared a secretary, ate in the company cafeteria, and flew coach.

Then they were appointed vice president. With the appointment come the first symbols of power and the first signs of potential danger: corner office, private secretary, lunch in the executive dining room. But they still have their eye on the ball, they're racking up great numbers, and so the perks get even better: access to the corporate jet, wining and dining customers at famous watering spots around the country, taking clients to the Kentucky Derby, the Super Bowl.

The trap is sprung. From their VP perches, they get a close look at power in all its glittering glory. They see the pay, the privileges, and the really serious perks of the skipping CEO, who's just announced he's traded in this year's Grumman corporate jet aircraft for next year's. Why? That's the kind of jet the CEO who runs the competition has! For years, they were sensible, hardworking executives working flat-out for the company. What happened?

They were seduced by the corona of power. Early in their careers, they probably laughed at a boss who bragged about his lunches at the Four Seasons or his access to the corporate jet. But now, after a few promotions and a taste of the good life, they begin to believe that the big job is their destiny, their divine right. Macbeth, too, might have resisted his own "vaulting ambition" if the witches' first few predictions hadn't come true. Even Julius Caesar refused the offer of the crown three times. But each time, his rejection got weaker. Like Macbeth, Caesar cannot resist the temptation of power. Shakespeare implies that a man who is ambitious for ambition's sake only (like Macbeth or Caesar) has trouble looking in the mirror without seeing a crown on his head. Even sober, solid Brutus, the noblest Roman of them all, could be tempted by power. Cassius stirs up Brutus's indignation toward Caesar by saying:

> Why, man, he doth bestride the narrow world
> Like a Colossus; and we petty men
> Walk under his huge legs, and peep about
> To find ourselves dishonourable graves.
>
> JULIUS CAESAR (1.2, 133–36)

Cassius continues to work on Brutus's ambition:

> Men at some time are masters of their fates:
> The fault, dear Brutus, is not in our stars,
> But in ourselves, that we are underlings.
> Brutus and Caesar: what should be in that 'Caesar'?
> Why should that name be sounded more than yours?
> Write them together, yours is as fair a name;
> Sound them, it doth become the mouth as well;
> Weigh them, it is as heavy; conjure with 'em,
> 'Brutus' will start a spirit as soon as 'Caesar.'
>
> JULIUS CAESAR (1.2, 137–45)

103

Shakespeare's insight into the dynamic of ambition is dazzling. Who among us has not looked at a superior and thought: "Why him and not me?" As Macbeth and Julius Caesar prove, such thoughts can have catastrophic ramifications.

"The Wasteful King"

As we argued in Chapter 1, there is nothing wrong with power in itself. Power is a freighted idea; it's what you do with it that counts. Becoming a "colossus" is one thing; believing it's your divine right and everyone else be damned is quite another. Devoting all your time to promoting your colossus-hood is even more dangerous. For too many chief executives, the trappings of power, instead of being the symbols of their success, become its reality. Tina again points to Richard II as the classic narcissistic leader; always talking about himself, always seeing himself as the star, whether as king or as deposed king:

> Down, down I come; like glist'ring Phaeton [son of the sun god],
> Wanting the manage of unruly jades [horses].
> In the base court? Base court, where kings grow base,
> To come at traitors' calls and do them grace!
> In the base court? Come down? Down, court! down, king!
> For night-owls shriek where mounting larks should sing.
>
> King Richard II (3.3, 178–83)

"Richard is obsessed with the style, the publicity of kingship," explains Tina. "He's interested not in his actions but their effects. And," she adds, "I can see this quality in myself. I've just been awarded my second honorary degree—and it's truly because of all the hard work and breakthroughs in education the whole company has made. It's not mine. But I find myself thinking, 'Oh, I wonder if I could get Yale to give me a doctorate next.' " Tina wants intellectual perks. Most CEOs want material perks. And the material perks start to affect the bottom line. Like so many high-flying chief execs, like my nemesis, the chairman who wouldn't give up his jet, Richard's "coffers, with too great a court / And liberal largess, are grown somewhat light" (*King Richard II* [1.4, 43–44]).

What does Richard do about his foundering finances? He orders his deputies to "farm our royal realm" for tax money and then force his richest subjects to bankroll what the taxes don't cover. This strategy raises money, but the king's popularity plummets. As one of his disgruntled nobles points out:

> The commons hath he pill'd with grievous taxes
> And quite lost their hearts. The nobles hath he fin'd
> For ancient quarrels, and quite lost their hearts.
> KING RICHARD II (2.1, 246–48)

Another concerned deputy notes that, unlike Richard's ancestors, "More hath he spent in peace than they in wars."

It is a conversation that could occur around the water cooler in any major American corporation where the CEO seems to be paying more attention to corporate frills than on the kind of deals that originally enriched the company. Richard rushes off to Ireland to put down a skirmish, apparently unaware that confiscating the lands of a subject will foment a rebellion at home that will threaten his reign. With his characterization of Richard, Shakespeare gives us a classic example of a chief executive who has forgotten what his real job is.

If James Robinson and Robert Buckley had paid attention to Richard's fate, they might have salvaged two of the more impressive business careers in America.

James D. Robinson III is a personable, politically savvy southern gentleman who seemed equally at home on New York's social circuit, on the Washington scene, and in the corporate world. After joining American Express as executive vice president in 1970, he took over as chairman and CEO in 1977. During his reign as American Express's chief executive, the company flourished and grew under Robinson's plan to create the largest "financial supermarket" in the world. In 1981, American Express acquired the brokerage house of Shearson. Then it added an institutional asset manager, a trust company, a Swiss bank, another brokerage, E. F. Hutton, and Lehman

Brothers, the oldest investment banking partnership on Wall Street. Robinson focused on the big deals, not the details. According to the gossip columns in the *New York Post, New York* magazine, and *W,* James Robinson and his chic wife seemed to be everywhere.

In January 1993, the company's board of directors, goaded by angry stockholders, asked Robinson to step down. What happened? In the more than fifteen years that Robinson ran American Express, the way business got done had changed. Robinson appeared not to notice. He seemed to be out on the town too much or playing the statesman from Wall Street in Washington. Suddenly, there was rough-and-tumble competition in almost every quarter. Shearson Lehman was on the ropes; the famed American Express cards, which required holders to pay up every month, were losing out to the more democratically minded and aggressive Visa, MasterCard, and other bank cards that let their cardholders maintain a balance, albeit at whopping interest rates.

Having proven himself a brilliant deal maker and strategist for fifteen years, Robinson seemed to lose interest in the day-to-day operations of his company, preferring to be a highly visible business statesman and a mover in New York society. More dangerous still, his internal decision model of the clubby, corporate world where charm and connections created business success fit a financial world that was slipping into history.

Robert J. Buckley seemed to have it all. He had worked his way up through the ranks at General Electric. He left GE to become, in 1977, the chief executive of Allegheny Ludlum Industries, then an industrial products firm and the ninth-largest steel company in America. Buckley decided to leverage Allegheny into international diversified consumer products. In 1981, he bought Sunbeam and changed the name of the company. Soon Allegheny International had acquired fifty companies. But not all of them were related to either the steel or consumer products businesses. Buckley seemed to be buying companies for the sake of buying companies. High interest and high SG&A (selling, general, and administrative) expenses left little room for error. Sunbeam's sales fell short of expectations in 1985, and a write-off in two unconsolidated divisions caused Allegheny's earnings to plummet. Buckley built a new

$100 million company headquarters in Pittsburgh that wags dubbed the Taj Mahal. He also bought palaces in the sky—six corporate jets. Just before the end, *Industry Week* honored Buckley with its Excellence in Management award. He was making more than a thousand speeches a year, addressing the problems of the American economy and how to fix them.

Too bad Buckley wasn't as eloquent with his bankers and his stockholders. He lost his job, his company, his Taj Mahal, and all six corporate jets. Buckley's situation is not unlike that described by Shakespeare's humble gardeners who tend the land and talk about their boss:

> . . . and Bolingbroke
> Hath seiz'd the wasteful king. O, what pity is it
> That he had not so trimm'd and dress'd his land
> As we this garden!
>
> KING RICHARD II (3.4, 54–57)

Instead of tending to their own gardens, the "wasteful kings" of the corporate world are off giving speeches or posing for the covers of magazines. And when they do return to their own gardens, chances are they're eager to make theirs bigger and more lavish than the garden across town, force-feeding the plants instead of watering, pruning, and fertilizing!

KEEPING UP WITH THE JACK WELCHES

Every year, CEOs from around the country turn up for the Business Round Table at the Greenbrier Resort, a beautiful, charming, comfortable getaway in the Allegheny Mountains of West Virginia. Greenbrier has the best service I've ever experienced. But this seductive watering spot has been the genesis of many a corporate disaster. Here CEOs meet annually to compare notes, exchange ideas, and listen to various gurus of management and economics. One year, the seminar themes might be "diversification" and "conglomeration"; the next year, "divestiture" and "focus"—whatever is the business fashion of the moment. In past years, management tools such as MBO (Management by Objective), TQM (Total Quality Management), and Six Sigma Quality have been extolled. At Greenbrier, economists have alternatively preached doom and gloom or unbridled growth and prosperity. On the surface, these intellectual exchanges seem benign. Some are in fact quite useful. However, too often they engender a game of Follow the Leader—a dangerous game if the leader likes to jump over the gorge but you fall in.

I've been to Greenbrier several times, as either a practicing CEO or a visiting guru. I have seen CEOs excited by Jack Welch's strategy at General Electric who go back to corporate headquarters and try to replicate that beautifully functioning behemoth. But they never seem to ask: "Can I become GE without GE's resources, human and financial?" Only rarely does the template for one company's strategy fit the needs of another company, even if they're serving the same market. Jack Welch makes a big conglomerate work; Robert Buckley, a GE alumnus, was unable to pull it off at Allegheny International.

Instead, these CEOs, entranced by every nostrum that business consultants can concoct, end up prancing around, plucking a garland of companies, hoping that one of their acquisitions will burst into a beautiful blossom.

In my experience, wanna-be emperors end up as nothing but skipping kings. Shakespeare's message is clear to every manager, especially those just starting up the ladder: the size of your expense account, like the size of your office and the quality of its decor, is not what your career is all about. In fact, some of the most successful and brilliant leaders in American business dispense with the trappings of power altogether. It's a sure way to win the respect of the most important people in your company: the rank-and-file employees who do most of the work.

Flying High with No Frills

Whenever I see a skipping CEO, a counter-image always comes to mind. His name is Sheldon Miller, the president of a small manufacturing company, whom I knew back in Tulsa. Sheldon had done quite well for himself. His company was located in an unattractive but functional building. Sheldon's office was neat but small. Frankly, the furniture looked as if he had bought it from the local junkyard: a battered gray steel desk, a small chair that looked uncomfortable, and a bolted steel-frame bookshelf for his *Thomas Register* and supplier catalogs. Sheldon must've noticed my gaze the first time I walked into his office because he immediately explained, "It would be foolish for me to spend money on a fancy office. Customers don't visit me here, and, if they did, I think they would see that I'm more interested in business than frills. But most of all, it would give the wrong signal to my employees."

And you don't have to be a small businessman to forgo the frills. When Franco Bernabè was head of Eni, Italy's large, energy-focused industrial group, which underwent one of the most dramatic turnarounds in recent history, he lived in the same house he had when he was assistant to the president. Warren Buffett has lived in his Omaha home for over forty years. He does his own taxes and also drives his own car. Such spartan habits have not kept Buffett's company, Berkshire Hathaway, from being one of the business and investment world's greatest success stories. A few years ago, I called Don Keough, who was then president of Coca-Cola. I asked the switchboard for the president's office, and the next voice I heard was Keough's.

My kind of CEOs. Throughout my own career, I've placed my own calls and answered my own phone, unless I was in a meeting. In the turnarounds I have led, I have specialized in banishing all ostentation. I have four things I do immediately, *the first day on the job:*

1. I personally paint out all the names on the parking places.
2. I take down the time clock. (In one turnaround, I had to use a crowbar.) I think punching a time clock is the most humiliating thing in the world.
3. I put locks on private executive bathrooms. (Later, I have the plumbing removed and turn them into storage closets.) Frankly, I've learned more about the companies I've run standing shoulder to shoulder than in any formal meeting.

4. At 4 P.M., I make sure everyone has a memo on his or her desk that says, "This is the last memo that will be written in this company for the next 30 days. If you want to communicate with someone, get up and talk to them. If they're too far away, telephone them. If they don't return your call, call me. [Signed] John Whitney."

That's just the first day. As soon as possible, I also go through a longer list: Corporate airplanes are sold (with the exception of the one that was owned by my bankrupt chairman friend). Everyone flies coach. (I don't even pay for upgrades out of my own pocket because I don't want my lieutenants to see me up front.) Any trips taken must be for serious business only, with immediate payoff potential. Country club memberships are canceled. Executive dining rooms—closed. I never have a desk, which I believe is only a stark symbol of separation of powers. I prefer a circular table, which signals that we're all listening to one another. I also like to redistribute the perks. In one turnaround, the owners had Mercedeses and Cadillacs. I informed them that the company car was a Chevy, but I was willing to sell them the luxury cars they were using. The biggest cars we had went to the district managers, who had to travel far and wide all day long to service their accounts.

The executives in the company are never crazy about these changes. But the rank and file love them. The best managers are good listeners, and that means paying attention to the concerns of all of your employees, not just the best paid among them.

STEP DOWN FROM YOUR THRONE— AND INTO THE WAREHOUSE

I remember taking my top executives to a luncheon meeting at General Foods where the executive dining room featured fine china and waiters wearing white gloves. I reciprocated by inviting the General Foods CEO and his top aides to join us for lunch, and they accepted. We took them into our executive dining room—the company cafeteria. As we stood in line, the General Foods CEO kept shooting glances around, looking for a private room, at least. Meantime, I sat down at a table with a few beefy guys from the warehouse, and so did my esteemed guest, though I got the sense he would've preferred to have been elsewhere. But for me and my staff, it was crucial to eat with our employees. We had Teamsters working in those warehouses, and we wanted them on our side, not on the picket lines.

Before his accession as Henry V, the young prince hung out at the Boar's Head Tavern in London's tenderloin district of Eastcheap, where he knew he was getting an education in dealing with his future subjects. "When I am King of England," Prince Hal says, "I shall command all the good lads in Eastcheap" (*King Henry IV, Part 1* [2.4, 13–14]). He knew his people. Shakespeare makes much of Henry V's skill at handling his men. He can be strong when necessary. (Stopping an assassination plot against him, he orders the conspirators to be executed.) But he also can show mercy. (Henry refers to freeing a man "that railed against our person," after he learns that his attacker was drunk.) At Pathmark, I held meetings with my employees so that I could speak to all 23,000 of them every year. I took questions from the floor, straight and unsanitized; they didn't have to state their names. They'd hammer me with their complaints, and I would stand there and take it and learn from it. Tina points out that such company meetings are comparable to Queen Elizabeth's processions through her realm. These royal appearances were not only to give her subjects a chance to see their queen, they also served the purpose of allowing the queen to hear what her people cared most about. Adds Tina: "In *Julius Caesar*, when the supreme commander Caesar moves through the city of Rome, the people throw notes at him, which Caesar's aides pick up. This was a way of informing their leader what they thought needed fixing in their republic."

Henry V, disguised as Harry Le Roy, moves among his troops before the Battle of Agincourt. Shakespeare makes sure the men he talks to are candid in their assessment of their chances. One says he wished the king were fighting alone. "So should he be sure to be ransomed, and a many poor men's lives saved" (*King Henry V* [4.1, 119–21]). Another hopes the king's "cause be good." Otherwise, he says, "the King himself hath a heavy reckoning to make when all those legs and arms and heads chopped off in a battle shall join together at the latter day and cry all 'We died at such a place' " and curse Henry for their deaths (*King Henry V* [4.1, 132–136]).

Even though Henry V had many flaws, including his cruel banishment of his friend Falstaff and his cynical invasion of France, Shakespeare portrays Henry as a heroic leader, and a large part of his skill in using his power is how he deals with subordinates and ordinary people. This skill should be learned by every executive.

Don't Play Favorites

I didn't paint out the private parking spots solely to make the point that the companies I run aren't about perks. I also wanted to change people's habits. If you don't have a special spot, maybe one morning you end up parking at the other end of the lot and have to walk a little farther than usual. During that walk, you bump into a colleague from another department or a worker from the warehouse. You say hello, you talk, and maybe you learn something about the business that you didn't know.

Tina Packer points out that Shakespeare shows repeatedly that the most dangerous force in any organization is a coterie. Richard III feared the growing power of the Woodville faction. Once Bolingbroke took power from Richard II, his next move was to cancel out the influence of Richard's "caterpillars," the coterie of Bushy, Bagot, and Green. Let me anticipate the reader's objection: yes, in the previous chapter, I advised that any new manager ought to have a loyal inner circle of top managers. That's definitely a good thing. But that coterie will have the overall objectives of the company in mind, not their own self-interest. As Tina points out with regard to Bushy, Bagot, and Green:

> They are the people Richard turns to, his companions. But they don't do anything other than swear at Bolingbroke and give the king bad advice, encouraging him to take the dying Gaunt's land

and money. They are men who follow their own interests. Richard spends his time with them—while ignoring others who are trying to get the business of the kingdom done.

They are Richard's flunkies, and once Richard is out of the way, Bolingbroke, now Henry IV, knows that their goals are not his, and he decides to get them out of his way. He's right. No enterprise should tolerate such selfishness (though my version of "termination" is not quite as final as Henry IV's).

DEMOCRACY, NO; MERITOCRACY, YES

The thing that has always impressed me the most about Shakespeare's varied portraits of royalty is the bravery of the kings who go to war, the men who put themselves in the trenches. Richard II went to Ireland to fight. He might have been a political incompetent, but he was not afraid of war. His successor, Bolingbroke, returns at the head of an army to retrieve his inheritance and then take the crown. For the next fourteen years as Henry IV, he puts down rebellions in his kingdom. His son, Prince Hal, trains among the common people. As King Henry V, he disguises himself as Harry Le Roy, moving among his troops to get a reading on their morale. And he leads his troops into battle at Agincourt. At the front. In the most danger. The people under your command appreciate that. Morale is bound to be higher when they know that their leader is with them on the battlefront and in the trenches. No one is likely to begrudge a warrior king his trappings of power.

The perks of power work best in the corporate world when they're rewards for a job well done. They are not displays of power but symbols of authority. Everyone wants something to aspire to, something to shoot for. Military leaders know the value of decorative ribbons. They also know the value of promotion. Privates would like to be sergeants; lieutenant colonels have a general's stars in their eyes. As soldiers move up the ranks, the symbols of authority change—more stripes on their arms, more brass and braid on their shoulders. As they move up the chain of command, officers are rewarded with more spacious quarters; they socialize only with their peers. Generals acquire a retinue of staff officers, drivers, and, until recently, orderlies.

While some of these symbols may be ostentatious, such trappings of power speak to a deeply held human belief that responsibility, authority, and privilege are intertwined. To be sure, this trio spawns envy. But to the extent that envy can generate accomplishment, such envy is useful. More important, some of these perks of power, such as assistants and drivers, are necessary for the speedy execution of a leader's duties. Although it might be good for a general's psyche to clean the stable, making him do it every day might keep him from the more important task of planning a battle.

Pay is one of the most visible and controversial trappings of power. Some sheltered academics and populist politicians want to replace the market system of compensation with a legal system. They want to put a cap on executive pay. A few egregious excesses might seem to confirm the wisdom of their proposals. (For example, the number one on the *Forbes* magazine's most highly paid executive list for fiscal 1998, Disney's Michael Eisner [$589 million], beat out the runner-up, CBS president and CEO Mel Karmazin, by almost $400 million.)

You can repress the market, but you cannot repeal it. The market may be imperfect, but I think it is still the best mechanism for determining executive compensation currently known to man. The measure of an executive's worth is what he can command on the street. If another company would pay Michael Eisner half a billion dollars in annual salary, then Disney is right to give him the compensation he receives. (However, I doubt whether the market would match Eisner's salary; Disney's profits during the last five years have woefully underperformed expectations.) The underlying assumption of the market system of compensation is that an executive's service creates value in excess of what he or she is paid in salary and perks. When a leader no longer creates that value, he or she should be demoted or deposed. But so long as they deliver, leaders should be well paid, and they should have their trappings of power. And if salary and trappings are the modern equivalent of honor, I agree with Henry V:

> But if it be a sin to covet honour,
> I am the most offending soul alive.
>
> KING HENRY V (4.3, 28–29)

But well-compensated executives should heed the Shakespeare who tells us in his plays, again and again, that the leader who treats the trappings of power as the end, not the means—that leader's ability to serve his company, his employees, and his customers is doomed.

Every executive who is riding high should read the speech of Shakespeare's Richard II the day he was deposed. After turning over his crown to Bolingbroke, the king asks for a mirror, and this is what he says:

> . . . O flatt'ring glass,
> Like to my followers in prosperity,
> Thou dost beguile me. Was this face the face
> That every day under his household roof
> Did keep ten thousand men? Was this the face
> That like the sun did make beholders wink?
> Is this the face which fac'd so many follies,
> That was at last out-fac'd by Bolingbroke?
> A brittle glory shineth in this face;
> As brittle as the glory is the face . . .
>
> KING RICHARD II (4.1, 279–88)

That said, Richard smashes the mirror on the ground. His reign is over. The only thing left for him to do in the play is lament the fact that the trappings of his kingship have gone on without him. At the end of the play, Richard sits a prisoner in Pomfret Castle and is visited by the man who tended Richard's favorite horse, Barbary. The groom informs Richard that the usurper, Bolingbroke, now rides Barbary. Their exchange continues:

RICHARD   Rode he on Barbary? Tell me, gentle friend,
How went he under him?

GROOM   So proudly as if he disdain'd the ground.

RICHARD   So proud that Bolingbroke was on his back!
That jade [horse] hath eat bread from my royal hand;
This hand hath made him proud with clapping him.
Would he not stumble? would he not fall down,
Since pride must have a fall, and break the neck
Of that proud man that did usurp his back?

KING RICHARD II (5.5, 81–89)

Then Richard realizes he is not his horse; the king is not the measure of his trappings. Barbary was the medieval equivalent of the latest-model Grumman corporate jet. And such trappings of power are not what life (or a career) is about. Shakespeare leaves us with this pathetic leader who failed to lead. Within half a page, "murderers" rush in and kill Richard.

Ironically (and Shakespeare can be very ironic), Richard predicted it all two acts before:

> . . . for within the hollow crown
> That rounds the mortal temples of a king
> Keeps Death his court, and there the antic sits,
> Scoffing his state and grinning at his pomp,
> Allowing him a breath, a little scene,
> To monarchize, be fear'd, and kill with looks;
> Infusing him with self and vain conceit,
> As if this flesh which walls about our life
> Were brass impregnable; and humour'd thus,
> Comes at the last, and with a little pin
> Bores thorough his castle wall, and farewell king!

KING RICHARD II (3.2, 160–70)

5

Women and Power

Shakespeare's Education and Transformation

Haply a woman's voice may do some good.

Queen Isabel in KING HENRY V (5.2, 93)

TINA Packer does not think the issue of women's equality with men in business is resolved yet. In this chapter—in Tina's own words—she gives us her views on this subject:

Carleton (Carly) Fiorina's accomplishments are staggering. Not only was she president of Lucent's largest division, leading Lucent's record-setting IPO, winning customers in forty-three countries, but now she's CEO of Hewlett-Packard, one of America's twenty largest corporations. Her "welcome" pay package approached $100 million. And she stated, "I truly hope that we are at the point where everyone has figured that the accomplishments of women across industry demonstrate that there is not a glass ceiling." Lest we believe her too quickly, *The New York Times* pointed out: "Ms. Fiorina's appointment reduces to 497 the number of companies in the *Fortune* 500 whose chief executives are men."

Oprah Winfrey, who is chairman and CEO of Harpo Entertainment Group, and who reaches some 33 million people weekly on TV, knows that for women there are ceilings after ceilings to be broken through, some as much internal as external. According to *People* magazine, Oprah had a 1-in-46 chance of attending college in 1972, a 1-in-13,342,000 chance of becoming one of the first black anchorwomen in history, and a 1-in-265,453,000 chance of becoming the most powerful person on TV.[8]

It's not that it can't be done. It's just that it's difficult to do.

In spite of talent and desire (which I—Tina—take as a given: no one is blind enough to think that women do not have either the talent or the desire to reach the top in the corporate world, or if there are such people, I don't want to talk to them), there are several important factors that still get in the way:

1. It takes about twenty years of experience to create a CEO. It wasn't until the 1970s that women began to attend MBA programs in any significant numbers so that there were enough starters to get some finalists.

2. Women still have to outperform men to get promotions— which means not only being good, but having general management and line experience with high visibility on the ladder upward in order to be noticed.[9]

3. Most women executives or would-be executives are married with kids—so home life and work life have to be integrated in ways that make sense.[10] (And, as women become equal in the workplace, this holds true for men as well as women.)

4. Some women still have to shift their own internalized picture of themselves—that there's something shameful about being ambitious, smart, aggressive when necessary, and actively interested in participating in making the world of commerce work.

5. And last but not least, there are some corporations and businesses that are still so stuck in their traditional ways that they just don't get it; one can only hope that their stodgy ways will get them into trouble as we move more and more to organizations that are fast-moving and lateral-thinking, and have more horizontal chains of command.

So, in acknowledgment of all those women working brilliantly in the workplace, knowing that churning up this information gets many people riled up (including me), I want to take a look at Shakespeare's experience of women and power and see whether it has useful information for us today. Certainly he has helped me find my way through the complicated business of becoming a leader.

In the Shakespeare plays there are around 170 roles for women, compared to about 700 for men. In *Fortune* 500 companies women constitute 11 percent of officers and 11 percent of corporate directors. So in the plays, as in life, the women have a different status from the men. Yet we are entering a period of history that has no precedent: men and women on equal footing. How we develop together is going to be different from how business was conducted in the past. While the marketplace helps define human consciousness, human consciousness helps define the marketplace. Men and women working together are going to alter the marketplace, we hope for the better, allowing it to have even more color, range, rhythm, and resonance! Will Shakespeare, being an enlightened fellow, had some feeling for the role(s) of women. And how he wrote about women when he was a young artist is very different from his writing as a mature man.

SHAKESPEARE AS A MAN WHO DOESN'T GET IT

In Shakespeare's early plays many of the women have a directness and vigor that change everyone's way of looking at the world. I'm thinking especially of Joan of Arc, who appears in *King Henry VI, Part 1;* Kate in *The Taming of the Shrew;* Tamora, Queen of the Goths, in *Titus Andronicus;* and Margaret of Anjou, Henry VI's queen and widow, who appears in the *Henry VI* plays and in *King Richard III*. These women have certain things in common: they fight their way to power, are very sexual, very sure of themselves. Joan of Arc, the teenage French heroine of the Hundred Years' War, was the embodiment of a woman who broke every barrier. In spite of the anti-French, anti-Catholic sentiments of Shakespeare's day, the playwright portrays Joan as a charismatic leader. Joan overcomes the obstacle of her sex to lead the French army; she transcends the barrier of class by getting the nobles to follow the ideals of a country girl. She is a leader who understands her constituencies. She challenges the abilities of her followers. And Joan dresses like a man. Then comes the caveat in this story: when she refuses to acquiesce to the powers that be, Joan of Arc is prosecuted (by men, of course, historically by the French, in Shakespeare by the English) for "heresy" and burned at the stake.

And it's not just in the story that Joan's role changes. It's in Shakespeare's attitude toward her. In the first scenes, Joan is charming and lovely, a woman who has God on her side. Then his language changes: it's as if he feels she's bewitched him; he has her sleeping with the dauphin, killing heroic Englishmen; he calls her a witch, the devil's handmaiden, a whore.

The pattern repeats itself with the second Frenchwoman, Margaret of Anjou. Margaret, like Joan, begins as a free-spirited young woman who leaps onto the stage of history (literally in the middle of a battle), where, through intelligence and courage, she emerges as a woman who leads armies and becomes a central figure in the Wars of the Roses. Then Shakespeare's attitude toward her changes. After her lover Suffolk is killed, she kills too—just as the men do. But Shakespeare pours invective on her head—unlike the male killers he treats as heroes. "A tiger's heart wrapp'd in a woman's hide," Shakespeare's Margaret becomes the embodiment of Vengeance (so does Tamora in *Titus Andronicus;* she even dresses as Revenge at one point). And the playwright loathes their foreign birth.

Clearly Shakespeare is fascinated by firebrand women and is also repelled by them. These early plays also depict another kind of woman—the idealized virgin, standing in counterpoint to the fire-brand and called Bianca or Lavinia or Luciana.

So it's obvious that the young Shakespeare didn't exactly trust women. He projects his hopes, fears, desires onto them. They are either terrifying or idealized: the whore or the virgin. And I hear the women reading this book sigh and say, "So what else is new?" (Just as Elizabeth I must have sighed 450 years ago, when she realized that in order to get her subjects to honor and obey her willingly she had to play Astraea or the Virgin Queen and be an icon worthy of worship.) And just as the men who run those firms that don't get it about women being smart, capable, and equal must be educated, coerced, and pressured into maturity, so Shakespeare had to grow up—which of course he did, being a great artist. And we are moving into a time when our culture encourages men and women to see each other as human beings, not as stereotypes. For this stereotyping is not, of course, how women see women. We see a complex picture, which has a multiplicity of levels. And in maturity, that is how most men understand women: as human beings of infinite complexity. Bill Hewlett and David Packard built a workplace that emphasized teamwork and respect for co-workers. When Sam Ginn, Richard Hackborn, and CEO Lewis Platt started to look for Platt's successor, they had the same openness. In fact, two of the four HP finalists for CEO were women. Equality had been built over many years at Hewlett-Packard. These men acknowledged women as equals.

That is true of Shakespeare, too. As he matured, Shakespeare's women characters in the plays gained a power and relevance equal to that of the men. And that, of course, is the goal of both our civilization and our workplace.

INTERNALIZING THE INFERIORITY

What happens when a woman has internalized a sense of herself as "lesser" than men (which of course may originate in background, culture, upbringing, attitudes of parents, or a hundred other places)?

In our business world, Katharine Graham must be an icon for all women who want to rise to the top. However, look at the way she saw herself at the beginning of her career. She gave an interview to *Women's Wear Daily* after she'd inherited the presidency of the Washington Post Company in late 1969. The magazine wrote:

> Kay Graham joins in the by-play, but does not dominate it, preferring to let the men, an assertive group, play the starring roles. It is a small slice of her life, one in which assertive strong-willed men have played a major part. . . . She says: "I rely on Fritz's—and other men's—judgment in every decision. . . ."
>
> "I think being a woman may have been a drawback for the job. . . ."
>
> "I can't see a woman as managing editor of a newspaper. . . ."
>
> "I guess it's a man's world. . . . In the world today, men are more able than women at executive work and in certain situations. I think a man would be better at this job I'm in than a woman."

Fortunately for us all, a friend of Katharine Graham's, *Post* reporter Elsie Carper, marched into her office, magazine in hand, and demanded, "Do you really believe that? Because if you do, I quit."[11] It shook her up—and Katharine Graham began the long journey of shifting her internalized assessment of herself (and all women). Over the next fifteen years she gradually changed from "little woman" to powerful executive. (There's nothing like a sister to get you on the road by telling you how it is!)

In December 1988 *Business Month* ran a cover story on the "Five Best Managed Companies," which included the Washington Post Company. And a few years later Graham received the Business Hall of Fame award from *Fortune*. In 1991 she stepped down, probably one of the most famous and powerful CEOs in the world, and a symbol for others to follow.

Katharine Graham's journey, of shifting her internalized idea of herself from incompetent and unworthy to competent, insightful, and capable, is a journey many of us are still on. It can be done only by noticing every time you accept someone else's assumption instead of knowing your own. It is a course of a thousand moments of retraining yourself.

Let's look at five plays—*As You Like It, Hamlet, Macbeth, Antony and Cleopatra,* and *Othello*. The women in these plays are in the center of power, wealth, and government. Each woman has a sense of her worth, and each woman changes throughout the course of the play. Yet only Rosalind in *As You Like It* ends up alive and well. The rest end up dead. Two go mad. Three kill themselves.

When I first started in business, I often thought I was going to die—metaphorically if not literally. It felt as if the job were too big for me. But I survived because I did something like Rosalind. Rosalind in *As You Like It* ends up living happily ever after—as do most of the women in the comedies. But how do they do it? Rosalind's life is every bit as disastrous as Ophelia's in *Hamlet* at the start of the play: she's banished from her uncle's court on pain of death, she has nowhere to go, no family (her father was already banished and her mother seems to be dead). What is she to do? Well, she does four things that seem to me to make a substantial difference: she gets some money (in the form of jewels), she joins with another woman (her cousin Celia) so that there are two of them on the journey; she takes along the Fool, so they laugh a lot; and she disguises herself as a man, so she no longer has to deal with other people's reactions to her as a woman. (Her status and the sexual harassment issue, for starters, are out of the way.) And she begins to see herself differently.

When I started Shakespeare & Company, I had a fellow traveler, our first director of training, Kristin Linklater (now head of the Theater Department at Columbia), with whom I discussed everything. I had two outrageous jesters, in the form of two ex-Jesuits, Kevin Coleman (now director of education) and Dennis Krausnick (now director of training and my husband). And I never got out of trousers. No little-girl dresses for me. Then I totally reassessed my way of looking at life. Just as Rosalind does.

Measure Rosalind against Ophelia, Hamlet's girlfriend. Ophelia is a "good" girl. She obeys her father, Polonius, when he makes her give back Hamlet's gifts. She loves Hamlet, but she doesn't make a stand for her own feelings and thoughts in the matter. She's untrue to herself and Hamlet when she pretends she doesn't love him. She doesn't object when he abuses her. And her needs and wants are completely ignored by the court as it goes about its business of treaties, deals, armies, and invasions. If she can serve the purpose of the court, then she'll be co-opted; if she can't, she's of no use and should stay out of the way.

Rosalind, meanwhile, with jewels, best friend, and the Fool, and dressed as a man, leaves the court and goes into the forest, able to do exactly as she pleases. She travels to the Forest of Arden, ostensibly to find her father, but once she's there, she chooses not to abandon her disguise and go to him, but rather to buy a cottage and some sheep (something only a man can do) and look after her "sister," Celia (dressed as a country girl: a disguise not quite as liberating as Rosalind's boy). Then she sets about teaching the young man she's in love with how he should court her and what he should understand about how women really think and feel. And because ostensibly he doesn't know that he is a she, Rosalind is perfectly free to do and say what she likes; the exploration is clearly more important to her than revealing herself and having a romantic relationship, at least for now. Trousers give her a freedom she has never had before.

To parallel Rosalind and Ophelia to Katharine Graham for a moment: if Katharine Graham hadn't had an Elsie Carper, and then her other strong women friends, she would never have ended up like Rosalind—she would have bought the picture of herself as unworthy and drowned herself (either metaphorically or symbolically) like Ophelia. Ophelia takes the only way she knows to get people to understand what's happening to her—she goes mad, singing songs and giving away flowers that have messages encoded in them.

> There's rosemary, that's for remembrance—pray you, love, remember. And there is pansies, that's for thoughts.
>
> HAMLET (4.5, 173–75)

Then she takes herself and her flowers down to the river (that symbol of the unconscious mind) and, singing old tunes, "as one

incapable of her own distress," floats downstream until her garments "heavy with their drink / Pull'd the poor wretch from her
melodious lay / To muddy death" (*Hamlet* [4.7, 178–83]).

Rosalind, on the other hand, flourishes. She organizes the
country folk, arranges four marriages, makes everyone think the
way she thinks, is witty, intelligent, and forceful. Could Rosalind
become a CEO? I think so.

It's as if the journey to the Forest of Arden and letting go of the
restraints of her life give Rosalind the power she never knew she
had. Anita Roddick, when she started the Body Shop, had no business training. She was passionate about traveling to distant places
and watching the local people use natural cosmetics on their skins
as they had used them for centuries. When she came back to England, she used what she had learned to create makeup for her
friends, then found a tiny corner shop from which to sell her po-
tions commercially. Even as the shop grew and the lines of cosmetics grew, she still traveled. And she still looked unmade-up and
slightly scruffy herself—creating a whole new attitude to makeup: it
could be fun, casual, funky. Then, as the business leaped forward
again, she instituted rules in the workplace she felt strongly about
—like leaving the customers alone if they wanted to browse, making sure all the salespeople took one day a week to do community or
volunteer service. Her spirit infused the workplace. Doing work in
the community built a strong sense of camaraderie among her employees and created the identity for her shops and advertising.
What she created came out of the very center of her interest.

Anita Roddick and her partner, who is also her husband, live a
high-profile and seemingly very equal life. It will be interesting to
see how they deal with the upheavals the Body Shop is currently
undergoing.

There is another point about women in power that comes out of
Hamlet. Hamlet's mother, Gertrude, watches Ophelia drown without sending for help or trying to help her herself.

Why would one woman watch a younger woman drown? Before
the drowning, Gertrude seems to like Ophelia, even says she
hoped she'd marry Hamlet. Shakespeare only hints at the reason
for her callousness: Gertrude serves the crown. Her power is de-

rived from being married to a king (first Hamlet Senior and then Claudius). Like Nancy Reagan or Princess Diana or Clare Boothe Luce, she must always acknowledge the primacy of this married relationship as the source of her power (whether she's happy or not!). Otherwise it's trouble. And Ophelia, in her madness, once she breaks from the constraints of her father, is trouble. Ophelia is dangerous. She's telling the truth and rocking the boat. And it's the boat Gertrude is sailing in that she is rocking. When women (or anyone else for that matter) derive their power in the first instance not through their own merits but through a personal relationship with the person at the top, difficulties can arise. Not all the truth gets told. It's difficult to challenge the individual because it feels like it's challenging the boss. And it's always difficult to know exactly how the relationship works. As we mentioned in the first chapter, there were many reasons for Jamie Dimon's leaving Citicorp. One we didn't mention was that Dimon was Jessica Bibliowicz's boss—Bibliowicz is Sandy Weill's daughter. Sandy Weill swore she should have no special treatment. It's interesting to note, however, that when Jamie Dimon took him at his word and didn't give Bibliowicz the job she wanted, he was forced to resign shortly thereafter.

Women have used this kind of substitute power for ages. Or, like Katherine in *King Henry V,* or countless CEOs' second wives, they are trophy wives. In the past, there was often no other way for them to get power. Gertrude is an obvious example of a woman who has power by proxy.

———

WOMEN CHANGING THE WORKPLACE

The journey of women changing their internal picture of themselves parallels the journey happening in the outside world. Pundits say the world has changed as much in the last forty years as in the preceding two thousand. One of the biggest changes in the marketplace is simply that women have entered it, are gaining ground, and soon will be equal with men. After thousands of years of being confined to the house and family, women can finally ask themselves: What do I want to be? Doctor? Politician? News reporter? Long-distance runner? Fighter pilot? Shop steward? CEO?

Women in the workplace are steadily altering the workplace. How? Is it for the better? And are women different from men? (To answer that last question: Yes. No. It depends on the woman. It depends on the man. And all of the above.) The fact that women are in the workplace as equal partners changes not just the chemistry but the structure, outlook, focus, and culture of our working lives. Women and men working side by side bring enormous benefit to both sexes. We now find those countries where women are hidden away, or where women are forced to do all the menial work, unenlightened, repressive societies. Yet in one way or another we were like that once. Because change is now so rapid, many young women in the United States have no sense of the past. But in Europe and Asia, the glass ceiling is still more like a concrete ceiling. Japan has no senior female executives; Britain only 5 percent; Germany 1–3 percent.

Women in the workplace are changing the relationship between business and the dynamic of the family. And that concerns both men and women. If our children are to be brought up with security, generosity, and focus, the interaction between home and work has to be carefully balanced. Can the place of business conduct its business without reference to the family? I think not, if women are to be an equal part of the equation. (Of course, start-ups are different, especially when the people—male and female—from Harvard, MIT, and Columbia hit the ground running. Then having children is the last thing in their minds. But within ten years they, too, will be dealing with families.) At my own company, Shakespeare & Company, authority, power, and influence are shared fairly and equally between men and women. There are as many women directors as men, as well as fund-raisers, marketing and press people, and so on. Perhaps the only place where there are more men is in the acting pool—because Shakespeare wrote more men's parts. (However, we sometimes cast a role with an actor of the opposite sex if we think it will add a new dimension to the play.) But in order to keep an equality of the sexes, we really had to think about how we would conduct the business of the company and bring up the children.

During the summer months, at the height of our season, school is out and we have no alternative but to find a place for our young children. Nurseries and camps don't go into the evening as well as all day. If we can't put the kids onstage, they organize themselves into acting classes, with one parent at a time looking after them. It works. And the kids grow up very bright. But it is an additional organizational issue we must think about, and often it feels like a pain in the butt. However, the alternative—women not being able to compete equally with men—is not acceptable to us.

Shakespeare & Company is small and in advance of its time for a theater company. But many, many organizations are thinking about the problems of families and children. For instance, at John Hancock Financial Services in Boston, they work hard to create an equal workplace. They have a family care mission statement that includes sensitivity training for managers on work and family issues, use of three days' paid sick leave to care for an ill family member, a flextime program, reimbursement of up to $2,000 for adoption expenses, a trade fair of summer camp information for working parents, an on-site child care center, and a Kids-to-Go program (for trips to museums, circuses, state fairs for employees' school-age children) on certain holidays at $25 per day, as well as generous maternity leave. SC Johnson Wax in Racine, Wisconsin, has similar programs, as well as a full-time day camp for school-age children.

This kind of societal transition has a precedent in the Renaissance. Then, women were breaking out of the rules that had governed them for centuries: there was a woman on the throne of England, something permissible for only some twenty years before Shakespeare's birth. (In the twelfth century, Empress Matilda fought her cousin King Stephen for the crown. Her brief reign was so bloody, the English decided "no more women" until Henry VIII declared his son, two daughters, and a grandniece his heirs.) Middle-class women were demanding their own rights under the expanded religious freedom; in the spiritual domain both men and women were arguing that perhaps women might have souls of their own and were not the appendages of their husbands or fathers; women poets were beginning to be published (though actors were not yet women, no matter what the film *Shakespeare in*

Love depicts); widows automatically received a third of their husbands' worldly goods. However, women weren't allowed to own
property in their own right if they had a husband, but some were
very good businesswomen, nonetheless.

One of the wealthiest people in the country, besides the queen,
was Elizabeth Hardwick, who started life as the daughter of a member of the minor gentry. She married four times and invested her
widow money in land, holding mortages for impecunious noble-
men, lending money—and also giving it away generously. Bess of
Hardwick built several magnificent houses, including Hardwick
Hall and Chatsworth. She is a brilliant example of what brains and
hard work can do, even when the cards are stacked against you.
And the big women in Shakespeare's mature plays have far more
in common with Bess and Elizabeth I, Carly Fiorina, Anita Roddick, and Andrea Jung than they do with the Virgin or the Whore.
But their lives still have major problems.

When women work alongside men in the marketplace, the
chemistry changes. It's healthier, it's more alive, it makes more
demands upon us, and, in the end, the balance and emphasis of
the workplace will be more harmonious with the quality of our
lives. For those men (fortunately, getting fewer and fewer) who are
not used to women being part of their work life, having a female
boss can be a scary proposition—not least because they think of
women only as mothers, lovers, wives, and secretaries, or just plain
"different," but not as everyday equals—and they don't know what
to do with the awkwardness or resentment they feel when asked
to work alongside, or be in a department of, a female boss! (It's
not the purpose of this chapter to look at sexual harassment,
though we'll touch on it—and Shakespeare of course had a play
or two with that as one of its themes, most notably *Measure for Measure* and *Cymbeline*. However, laws against harassment are among
the marks of women entering the workforce and are steps forward in our culture, though awkward and dangerous in many
ways to both men and women.) Women have been dealing with
these kinds of men for centuries—but the relief is enormous when
a company decides to confront the problem openly. And a man
who learns to change his attitude toward women becomes a bigger

person—and a better, more insightful team player for the company.

Not only are women conscious of others' reactions to them, but the choices they make about families and children affect their work and pose a question that is at the forefront of everyone's mind when looking for a new job. Statistically, 90 percent of women executives will marry, 20 percent will not have children, 26 percent will postpone having children,[12] and quite a few will have very supportive husbands who are willing to relocate to support their wives' careers. Occasionally they will have husbands who will abandon their own careers to support their wives (Carly Fiorina, for example). But men overcoming their fear of women, and women working to accommodate home and career, alter the dynamic of the marketplace.

Gender and sexual energy, of course, aren't taken into account when looking at Wall Street projections; it's what the figures show, how the business is being run, and what next quarter's projections will be that count. Yet sexual identity, sexual drive, sexual imagination are an integral part of the fuel that creates the energy to build the business world—whether it's the drive to make beautiful things, to be the best CEO, to win the blue jeans war, or simply to spend your money on high living after you have sold your toothpaste on the grounds that it improves your sex life. And the men and women working alongside each other are propelling a new openness.

You only have to look at the old photographs of the J. P. Morgans, Carnegies, Vanderbilts, and Westinghouses looking into the camera with somber airs, drooping mustaches, and ponderous expressions to see the difference. Donald Trump is out there with his towers and his wives, glint in his eye. King Donald is founding his empire, and his amorous adventures are reported as much as his business. And our Freds, Jacks, Garys, and Johns beam at us from the pages of *Fortune,* full of energy and life. Having women in the workforce makes a difference in the way business gets done; the power struggles are more complicated; dress codes loosen up; conversations have more variety; feelings have been known to be discussed; the vision of the organization includes more things women want, such as nurseries and flexible hours; the retreats and conferences have a wider range of topics and are more fun; sexual harassment has been slapped on the hand; and maternity leave (for both men and women) has advanced enormously.

GETTING THE PROMOTION

Let's look at Lady Macbeth. Lady Macbeth has become the archetype of the scheming monster woman. I say her story is that of a powerful woman who knew nothing about power. Lady Macbeth has courage and decisiveness, can organize others, and certainly knows how to put her fingers in the dike when the flood is about to swamp everything. But she is ignorant about the freight of power. And every action she takes is ostensibly for her husband; never does she look within to find her own true desires.

The moment Macbeth hears the prophecy from the witches that he will be king, he communicates that news to his "dearest partner of greatness." It's as if he knows he won't be able to achieve the high position by himself. She immediately defines what she thinks is the problem for both of them: neither has the killer instinct. But to her the witches' prophecy is an opportunity not to be missed—and she certainly isn't going to wait around to see if it happens by itself. She's going to make sure it happens. So before Macbeth even gets home, she asks the "murth'ring ministers [evil spirits], Wherever in your sightless substances / You wait on Nature's mischief" to unsex her and fill her from "the crown to the toe, top-full / Of direst cruelty" (*Macbeth*, 1.5). She also asks them to turn the milk in her breast to gall (so we know she's had a baby who must have died not long ago) and that the "access and passage to remorse" be stopped up in her. That done, she knows she's now tough enough to back her husband all the way to the crown. And she does. Inciting him with shame when he wavers, insulting him when he shows remorse, plotting with him moment by moment on how to do it—worse, invoking their dead child, saying she would dash his brains out if she had sworn to be king as he has. This is strange, because nowhere do we see Macbeth actually swearing that he will kill Duncan, only admitting to the feeling that he'd like him "removed," so she actually puts words in his mouth, which he accepts.

When Macbeth finally acquiesces to her passionate prompting, he tells her to

> Bring forth men-children only!
> For thy undaunted mettle should compose
> Nothing but males.
>
> MACBETH (1.7, 73–75)

Obviously sex and bed and male children and succession are major factors in the Macbeths' life: urges that all get diverted in this drive to gain the throne.

As John has pointed out earlier, the murder of Duncan has no other purpose than to give the Macbeths the top job in the country. The price of getting the top job—wanted for selfish ends and no other—brings not a single desired result. The Macbeths' relationship falls apart, though she's able to prop him up for a while at the coronation feast. When Macbeth sees Banquo's ghost, she convinces their guests there's nothing amiss and breaks up the party. But psychologically, he leaves her once he is king. He becomes addicted to his relationship with the witches, seems to sleep no more (which the voice as he murdered Duncan told him would happen), and ceases to confide in her.

> Be innocent of the knowledge, dearest chuck,
> Till thou applaud the deed.
>
> MACBETH (3.2, 45–46)

The purpose of Lady Macbeth's actions is to gain power for her husband and take their collaboration to the highest pinnacle. But the price she pays is too high—for her, for her marriage, and for the country.

Power is a freighted idea. At what or whom is it aimed? While she attains what she set out to do, Lady Macbeth's life ends miserably. She sets her incredible skills to work for something that has no benefit for anyone other than her own desire for top status. She never knows why she wanted it or what it will cost. She has no idea what happens to people who murder, and she uses powers that are beyond her comprehension. She finds out about evil in herself and her husband on a level she never imagined. She goes mad and kills herself. So Lady Macbeth is not as smart as Eva Perón or Jiang Qing, Chairman Mao's wife, though they have many qualities in common.

Many women find it difficult to assume authority—it's easier to remain lower on the totem pole. And look, not everyone has to aspire to the top. If you are happy where you are, stay there. But if you are determined to go for it, do as Rosalind does, get a buddy. It's a very good idea to have a woman friend (or any friend, man or woman) to keep checking in with, not one who will watch you drown. Get a cushion of cash if you can. And keep your sense of humor. After performing beyond all expectations, top women say that finding a working style men are comfortable with is the most important asset.[13] So if it means wearing trousers, wear trousers. As women acquire equal power, we will shift the ethos.

So what can you do if you are performing extremely well, you've got your buddy and sense of humor, you've found a style that all the men around you are comfortable with, you are philosophical about the fact that you have to make the adjustments and they don't—and you still don't get the promotion? What do you do? Again, do as Rosalind does: change your place of operations.

It's the moment for THE BIG MOVE. If you look for another job, let your bosses know you are looking; it may be the wake-up call they need. If you tell them where you think you should be going next, they might wake up to the idea, might even like it. And if they don't, you don't want to be working for them anyway. There's nothing worse than working for years below your potential. You and your family will end up unfulfilled. Know that time is on your side—the wave of the future is equality between men and women in the workplace. Just make sure the business you go to has a far more enlightened outlook than the one you've left!

We've discussed the corporations that don't like women in power, women's internalized picture of themselves, and what a good workplace for women with children might be like. Now let's go to the woman who can outperform any man, Cleopatra.

OUTPERFORMING THE MEN

In those businesses where traditionally women are not discriminated against—cosmetics, furnishing, fashions, and media—the Anitas, Tinas, Lauras, Marthas, and Donnas have been competing very favorably with the Tommys, Calvins, Ralphs, and Freds. And Oprah is in a class all by herself.

But it is in the new fields of the information superhighway, the Internet, that women are making dramatic gains. The online auction house eBay's Margaret Whitman; Mary Meeker, Morgan Stanley Dean Witter's top Internet analyst; Dawn Lepone of Charles Schwab; Joy Covey of Amazon.com; Jan Brandt of America Online—these are the women now at the top of their field.

And so we come to Cleopatra, the most fascinating of all Shakespeare's women, and certainly at the top of her field.

There are many women at the height of their careers who have the Cleopatra syndrome thrust upon them. Cleopatra in life was a different person from the one who has passed into our imaginations. Historically Cleopatra was extremely good at her job, rather a plain woman, and a very able administrator. It was Octavius's historians who wrote about her as a temptress who seduced Antony and took him away from his Roman duties. (Because, of course, the winners write history.) This fiction was passed on to Plutarch, who passed it on to Shakespeare, and Shakespeare turned it into his vibrant version. Then Hollywood turned it into a vehicle for Elizabeth Taylor and Richard Burton and exploited the story some more. The longevity of the fascination with the tale obviously has to do with the inherent sexual energy between a couple with power—especially if she might have even more power than he! I think this has some parallels with the enormous amount of press coverage, and the quality of coverage, female CEOs receive. And some, like Jill Barad, play into it. When Jill Barad became CEO of the top toy maker, Mattel, she had some 717 articles written about her and glamorous pictures taken, as opposed to 263 and very few pictures for Alan Hassenfeld, her more successful opposite at Hasbro. As the sales of Barbie fell, the tone of glee in the press could hardly be contained. And as Mattel's market share plummeted, the critical articles commented on Barad's feminine style, as if that were to blame rather than bad judgments made about her purchase of The Learning Company. When Jill Barad finally resigned in February 2000, *The New York Times* ran a glamorous picture of Ms. Barad with Barbie in the background. While the analysis of her departure was serious (apart from mentioning "The Jill Factor"), Ms. Barad's physical attractiveness assured an extra sizzle to the story. Martha Stewart thrusts herself in front of the television cameras at every turn, selling everything she can think of in every way. She sells homemaking, and style, and celebration. She's associated with what she sells—but she doesn't live like that. She's a businesswoman. And when she went public last year, it paid off in the billions! Similarly, a leader like Tina Brown, who ostensibly is promoting other people's careers, has her own rise to fame reported on at every turn. Her rise from ordinary journalist in Britain to editor of *Vanity Fair* magazine, to *The New Yorker* to Miramax is mapped in minute detail. People who never met her have ideas about her—somehow they know she's sexy and bossy and unpredictable. Stories about her abound. Some very powerful men have backed her, and a lot of other powerful men would like to get rid of her. A lot of people say she has no substance—it's all hype and parties and style (Did *The New Yorker* EVER get into the black?)—and a lot of others think she's the wave of the future: this is what the newspaper/magazine/film industry is going to look like, now and in time to come.

If men were leading these initiatives, they would not get the coverage these women get. I'm not complaining. I'm glad they get the coverage—mostly it helps them do a better job. I'm just pointing out that it's the unusualness of women in power coupled with their sexual attractiveness that makes them the focus of so much attention. Most actors (men or women) would rather play Cleopatra than Antony. Jill, Martha, and Tina all play the part, either consciously or unconsciously, exuding sexual energy, just as Cleopatra does. But, come to think of it, Jack Welch makes not a bad Antony; and Bill Gates has a lot of Octavius Caesar in him (eventually becoming Emperor Augustus) and ruling the known world.

Before *Antony and Cleopatra* opens, Cleopatra has already had two major Roman leaders as her lovers, Julius Caesar and Pompey. She seems to like to sleep with the powers—and they certainly seem to like to sleep with her. She makes power very personal. Her court is filled with life and laughter; she and Antony like to dress as ordinary people (often changing sexes) and wander through the crowds incognito. And yet her country is rich (historically Egypt was the wheat basket of the Roman Empire), with a large navy and a huge treasury. We don't see Cleopatra working much, but her household and country function well. And she is *exciting*. So much so that Antony wants to stay in her arms forever. "Let Rome in Tiber melt . . . Here is my space! . . . The nobleness of life / Is to do thus [kissing her]" (*Antony and Cleopatra* [1.1, 34–38]).

Antony has forsaken the traditional Roman marriage and is living in sin and equality with Cleopatra. They are still mad about each other after some twelve years of cohabitation. Cleopatra's problems start when Egypt and Rome go to war. Egypt is a sovereign country but pledges allegiance to Rome. It's a delicate balance and one Cleopatra has maneuvered with great skill in the past (having the leader[s] of the Roman world as her lover[s] is only a part of her negotiating ability). Cleopatra's mistakes start when she acts like a man—when she assumes Egypt should fight Rome (which is under the leadership of Octavius Caesar) instead of negotiating as she always has done in the past. Worse, she decides to go into battle herself, but knows nothing about it. She gets scared and runs away.

Now, I'm not saying women should not go into battle if they want to: there have always been heroic warrior women, from Boadicea and her daughters, who led the English rebellion against the Romans around A.D. 60, Jinga in West Africa, Joan of Arc in France, and Rani of Jhansi, who led the rebellion against the British in India in the mid-1850s, to Deborah Sampson, who fought as a common soldier in the War of Independence (along with hundreds of other disguised women) and now is the official "heroine" of the state of Massachusetts.

No, Cleopatra's problem is that she takes on a role she is unfit for and knows nothing about, that someone else could do better. Yet what is marvelous about Cleopatra is that she manages to keep a sense of herself no matter what other people think of her. And once she gives up the idea of going directly into battle and goes back to her old way of mixing sex and politics, she gets onto sure footing again.

Cleopatra does overtly what many women over the centuries have done covertly. Being curtailed in having direct power, women learned to take their power underground, either as Rosalind does, by disguising themselves as men (or as nuns or as foreign princesses as women do in other plays), or by using their sexual attractiveness to get what they want from men. Lady Elizabeth Grey (née Woodville) in *King Henry VI, Part 3,* is probably the best example of this: the moment she knows he's attracted to her, she gets the womanizer Edward IV to marry her by subtly leading him on and then cutting him off. It drives him crazy, and so, as it's the only way he can have her, he marries her. She becomes Queen of England, bears him at least seven children, builds up a huge power faction, mostly with her brothers and the sons from her first marriage, turns a blind eye to Edward's mistresses, and outlives her husband by a decade.

Cleopatra, however, enjoys exerting her sexual powers, and she enjoys having others watch her showing her stuff. Maybe her high status keeps her protected from others' thoughts, or maybe she doesn't care: she's queen anyway.

The way Cleopatra exerts her sexuality in negotiations is subtle. ("She's cunning beyond thought," says Antony in despair.) For example, if she and Antony are fighting Octavius Caesar as a couple, she has limited power—because of course Antony is acknowledged as her man, and therefore, she's not really available to other men. When that's the case, all that other men want to do is to kill her. But if Antony is *not* her man (she lets Octavius think she may betray Antony), then she has more room to maneuver—there is then the possibility that someone else can be her man. She turns her charms on Thidias first, then on Proculeius and Dolabella, and finally Octavius Caesar himself.

You can see her toying with the idea: Shall I seduce Octavius Caesar? (Her fourth Roman!) Certainly it would be a way of retaining her power—and Cleopatra loves the game of power. Like Elizabeth on the throne of England, she entertains proposals of love in order to manipulate. Even in the last years of her reign, when she had no teeth and very little hair, Elizabeth was putting herself forward in the marriage market. And England had forty years of peace, in part through this political maneuvering.

Ultimately Cleopatra finds that there is something more important than power: love. She agrees with Antony that the nobleness of life is to love. And she loves Antony. Moreover, the time for her to step down has come; she hasn't the taste for playing cat-and-mouse games with Caesar. (If I can get him to fall in love with me, will he still force me to be paraded through the streets of Rome in the victory march? How much autonomy will he allow me in Egypt? And so on.) She'd prefer to be dead and united with Antony than living and dealing with Caesar. And anyway she knows she will have finally beaten Octavius Caesar if she kills herself—then he cannot take her captive back to Rome; she will not be a trophy for him to parade.

So she stages her death beautifully, sensually, and dies in orgasmic bliss, calling to Antony.

Are women still being indirect about their use of power? Are Shakespeare's women still among us: the woman who reacts only to what other people say and has no purpose of her own? Or the older woman who won't help the younger when she's in trouble? The woman who takes on power beyond her expertise and knowledge? The woman who uses her sexuality to get what she wants? The woman who can travel far if she is disguised, has a best friend to help her, and then withdraws into marriage?

And of course, these attributes—lack of clarity, deception, acting without knowledge—apply to men, too. So it is as relevant for men to ask these questions about their power plays as it is for women.

Finally, we all need to hear the story of yet another woman: Desdemona in *Othello*. Desdemona has all the attributes of a good CEO—just like Rosalind. And she doesn't have to put on trousers in order to plead her case, marry whom she pleases, go to war, be the advocate for her friend. She can do all these things with ease. No, her problem is that she will operate only as if the world is good, sticking to her ideals of Christian marriage and love even while Othello is strangling her and she's in her death throes. She cannot bear the fact that she loves someone who is mad, that he's killing her and it's best to get out of the way. (Even if he's your partner. Especially if he's your partner.)

All these women, fictional and real, have cleared the way so that we can see ourselves, use their stories, and live full and productive lives. The computer age will put the final nail in the coffin of inequality. Just as the printing press and the translation of the Bible into native tongues broke the tight bondage of women in the Renaissance, so the Internet will level the playing field now. As access to information becomes easier, there will be less and less need for creaking, overdefined hierarchical management structures. Fewer ways of keeping women out. More ways of working at home. Many people can have the knowledge and many can act on it, which gives rise to collegial relationships, something women understand well.

I do not think women are like men, except 80 percent of the time. It's in the remaining 20 percent that the differences range. And it is exciting that there is that difference. And that difference will enhance the workplace.

If the tales about ambassadors and cabinet members finding Margaret Thatcher attractive are true; if Martha Stewart's share of the action is even a tenth of what the rumors say (all in the name of building the happy home, of course); and if Bill Maher is not boasting, then sexual attraction in the marketplace is here to stay. But there is no reason for inequality in this phenomenon, providing women stay true to themselves. Sexual energy has always been there hidden away, but now, like many other things, we get to look at it.

Charged energy can inspire workers, lighten their load, make work fun, make it more interactive, less competitive, but still alive with vitality. As women's brains and talent win them ever larger sections of the workplace, we'll have more humane work hours, more project-based tasks to be coordinated with school schedules, more jobs that can be done jointly by husband-wife teams, more concern about how the kids are being brought up without mandating that it's always the woman who has to give up her career. We will support men who share equally in parenting duties and pay more attention to creating a challenging, but not overburdened, work schedule that allows both men and women to know themselves, each other, and their children. We will be able to run highly innovative and exciting places of business.

The demands that businesses put on families will be coordinated with bringing up those families. If we do not have healthy families, we will not have a healthy society. A healthy society—one with a low crime rate, a good education system, no homeless on the streets, and men and women knowing that they have equal opportunity—is something that should concern us all. It is our legacy to our children. How to get there? . . . Ah, there's the rub.

But as Hamlet says in an enlightened moment:

> Sure he that made us with such large discourse,
> Looking before and after, gave us not
> That capability and godlike reason
> To fust in us unus'd.
>
> HAMLET (4.4, 36–39)

With luck, having women in the workplace and using our godlike reason, we will devise workloads that will truly allow us to have it all: beauty, love, the enjoyment of raising our children, and deep satisfaction in doing a good job!

Part II

ALL THE WORLD'S A STAGE

Business as Theater

—

6

All the World's a Stage

Playing the Part

> . . . All the world's a stage,
> And all the men and women merely players.
> They have their exits and their entrances,
> And one man in his time plays many parts . . .
>
> As You Like It (2.7, 139–42)

LEADERSHIP is theater. The way a manager walks into a room, the clothes he or she wears, the way his office is designed, the props he uses when addressing his aides, employees, or stockholders—these are key components of his effectiveness.

My Tulsa business associate Sheldon Miller did not operate out of that spartan office just because he was naturally a no-frills kind of guy. Sheldon's office also made a statement to his employees: "The priority of the man in these sparse surroundings is work." It was theater. So were the sports shirts and khakis he wore to work to signal to his employees that though he owned the store, he was one of them. The scene changed when Sheldon visited customers at their offices. He wore a suit and tie, thus playing a different, more public role, the CEO. At Pathmark, I made sure none of the store managers parked close to the front door. I felt it was important for employees to see their boss walking through the parking lot, gathering errant shopping carts and pushing them toward their corral.

More theater. Elizabethans were acutely conscious of rank, privilege, and the ceremonies that accompanied them. The clothes they wore, for instance, signaled immediately their place in the Great Chain of Being (the name given to the preordained hierarchical ordering of the Universe). Those few who were able to boost themselves up through the social ranks had to learn to play a new role in society. (The financial and social success of Shakespeare allowed him to acquire a coat of arms for his father, John, which gave John the title of "gentleman," something he had aspired to in his merchant days at Stratford but had not been able to pull off on his own.) As a professional actor, Shakespeare was acutely sensitive to the performances going on around him in Elizabethan society. At the Globe, the audience sat according to rank. As a playwright, he clearly enjoyed making the connections between great leaders and great actors, and his insights are sprinkled throughout his histories and tragedies. Says Macbeth: "Life's but a walking shadow; a poor player, / That struts and frets his hour upon the stage" (*Macbeth* [5.5, 24–25]).

Shakespeare's leaders have much to teach modern business executives about how the form and substance of wielding power can complement each other. In Shakespeare, the canny leader knows how to perform in public, how to tailor his presence and remarks to the audience of the moment. Such acting skills are crucial to any business leader who must impress customers, win the confidence of bankers, or inspire employees when his company is up against the wall. Above all, Shakespeare forces us in business to think hard about the parts we play as leaders and followers, not men and women merely "making believe" that we're in business but people with a real job to do, plumbing the depths of our personalities and talents to learn how who we are can contribute to our *roles* in the marketplace and in society.

All the world really is a stage, and businesspeople eager to succeed must be willing to play a number of parts in their working lives; they must also be prepared to put in award-winning performances.

The Leader as Actor

Richard III was one of Shakespeare's first great roles, and fine actors have always been eager to play him, from Richard Burbage, the leading actor of Shakespeare's day, to such modern-day stars of stage and screen as Laurence Olivier, Ian McKellen, and Al Pacino. One of the obvious attractions of Richard III is that Shakespeare's king is himself a brilliant actor.

He is worth studying. In his very first speech of the play, a soliloquy, Richard makes it clear that as he is deformed, a hunchback, in a time of peace with a "true and just" king on the throne, his possibilities are limited:

> And therefore, since I cannot prove a lover
> To entertain these fair well-spoken days,
> I am determined to prove a villain,
> And hate the idle pleasures of these days.
>
> KING RICHARD III (1.1, 28–31)

Richard decides to create his own destiny. He announces to the audience, "Plots have I laid . . . To set my brother Clarence and the King / In deadly hate, the one against the other" (1.1, 32–34). How does a misshapen madman, whose own mother has reservations about him, emerge as the most popular choice to assume the crown? Richard is a master of deceit, the consummate actor. And he proceeds to prove it throughout the play. Richard plays a loyal follower of his brother King Edward IV, though he is merely waiting for him to die. He plays the friend and confidant to his other brother, Clarence, whom the king (having been duped by a wizard in Richard's pay) has just ordered to be imprisoned. Richard claims to be appalled and promises to do everything to get Clarence released. Three scenes later, Richard's henchmen enter Clarence's cell and murder him.

In the scene immediately after he deceives Clarence, Richard accosts the Lady Anne (as she follows the late king's body to be re-buried) and explains with tears in his eyes the reason he killed her father-in-law, King Henry VI, and her husband:

> Your beauty was the cause of that effect;
> Your beauty, that did haunt me in my sleep
> To undertake the death of all the world,
> So I might live one hour in your sweet bosom.
>
> KING RICHARD III (1.2, 125–28)

Anne spits in Richard's face. But Richard turns her spittle into erotic foreplay: "Never came poison from so sweet a place." He persists in a performance of sexual harassment so brazenly brilliant that he turns a woman who asked God to strike him dead and the earth to swallow him up into his lover and eventually his wife. When Anne leaves, Richard turns to the audience and asks:

> Was ever woman in this humour woo'd?
> Was ever woman in this humour won?
>
> KING RICHARD III (1.2, 232–33)

And we, the audience, laugh with him, instead of being appalled. And thus he's seduced us too! There is no end to his chutzpah. We may disapprove of Richard's Machiavellian deceptions, but we have to be impressed by his brilliantly malevolent performance. After King Edward dies and Richard keeps the king's young heirs in the Tower, he and his trusted lieutenant the Duke of Buckingham conspire to persuade the people to offer Richard the crown. Richard questions whether Buckingham is up to the serious acting that will be required of them both:

RICHARD   Come, cousin, canst thou quake and change thy color,
Murder thy breath in middle of a word,
And then again begin, and stop again,
As if thou wert distraught and mad with terror?

BUCKINGHAM   Tut! I can counterfeit the deep tragedian,
Speak and look back, and pry on every side,
Tremble and start at wagging of a straw,
Intending deep suspicion. Ghastly looks
Are at my service like enforced smiles,
And both are ready in their offices
At any time to grace my stratagems.

KING RICHARD III (3.5, 1–11)

Not only is Buckingham prepared to act his part by spreading the rumor that the young princes are illegitimate (because the late king was betrothed to someone else and therefore his subsequent marriage to Elizabeth was bigamous and thus not legal: a bit far-fetched, but what the hell—play it for all it's worth!), he also advises Richard to confect the following ruse to convince the lord mayor that the people should offer the crown to Richard:

And look you get a prayer-book in your hand,
And stand between two churchmen, good my lord:
For on that ground I'll build a holy descant.
And be not easily won to our requests:
Play the maid's part: still answer nay, and take it.

KING RICHARD III (3.7, 46–50)

When Richard appears, between two bishops, no less, and with a prayer book in his hand, the mayor is impressed. Richard continues to "play the maid's part" beautifully, refusing the very crown he is conniving and murdering for. "I am unfit for state and majesty," he says. He explains why he is not their man: "Yet so much is my poverty of spirit, / So mighty and so many my defects, / That I would rather hide me from my greatness" (*King Richard III* [3.7, 158–60]). No would-be president has ever demurred so well. Fi-

147

nally, the mayor's delegation heads for the door; Richard swiftly calls them back:

> Since you will buckle fortune on my back
> To bear her burden, whe'er I will or no,
> I must have patience to endure the load.
>
> KING RICHARD III (3.7, 227–29)

As a would-be king, Richard shows how a leader must gauge his audience and play his part accordingly. As a character onstage, he has a great actor's ability to charm theatergoers despite the fact that they see before them a serial murderer. If his ability to do good had matched his ability to act, England would have had a formidable king! (Do not think for a moment that I am recommending Richard's actions to those who aspire to power. On the contrary, as we see in Shakespeare's plays and in our daily lives, those actions destroy the kingdom. I am using Richard only to show Shakespeare's knowledge of acting as an attribute of leading.)

Henry V is a less Machiavellian example of how the Shakespearean leader must play the right roles. As we saw in Chapter 4, Henry moves through the campfires of his troops disguised as Harry Le Roy. Confronting the frank doubts among the foot soldiers about the pending Battle of Agincourt, Henry argues that the king's cause is just and honorable. "That's more than we know," says Williams. And then, speaking for common soldiers past and present,

> But if the cause be not good, the King himself hath a heavy reckoning to make, when all those legs and arms and heads chopped off in a battle shall join together at the latter day and cry all "We died at such a place," some swearing, some crying for a surgeon, some upon their wives left poor behind them, some upon the debts they owe, some upon their children rawly left. . . . Now if these men do not die well it will be a black matter for the King, that led them to it . . .
>
> KING HENRY V (4.1, 132–43)

Williams delivers a strong antiwar statement, which Harry Le Roy counters. (Whenever Shakespeare gives a character his own

name, whether in tragedy or comedy, Tina Packer thinks the scene
has an extra bite.) The undercover king remains cool, calm, and
collected, staying in character, not betraying his mission, learning
the thoughts and feelings of his men. Harry Le Roy goes so far as to
confide that the king is likely to be as scared as the common soldiers but can never show his fear:

> Yet, in reason, no man should possess him with any appearance of
> fear, lest he, by showing it, should dishearten his army.
>
> KING HENRY V (4.1, 109–11)

In the turnarounds I have led, I have had my Agincourts. My
troops, too, have been afraid. All leaders have to know that doubts
and fears like these reside in their followers. In a turnaround, I'm
just as afraid, scared to death, in fact. When you go into a crisis
turnaround, you don't know if you're going to make it or not. I
have won some and lost some. But, as Shakespeare has Henry
point out, the great leader cannot show his fear. What troops
would follow into battle a leader who has lost his courage? My advice to managers under the gun—whether facing a hostile banker
threatening to pull the plug or an important employee or customer who is threatening to defect—is similar to Shakespeare's,
though a lot less eloquent: *Don't let them see you sweat.* You've got to
act the role of fearless leader. It's a performance. But you also have
to be honest and explain the situation to your employees and how
you think you can all come out the other end in one piece.

Larry Bossidy, the CEO of Allied Signal, the New Jersey–based
diversified manufacturer, is probably the last person his friends
would describe as a man of the theater. But whether or not he
would appreciate being identified as such, he is a fine actor. Let me
set the scene. In 1991, when Bossidy took over Allied, the company
was not growing, not making money, and the price of its stock was
languishing. Allied was caught in the post–Cold War defense
spending cutbacks and was getting hammered by an economic
downturn. Bossidy lined up financing, revitalized some divisions,
divested others. Above all, he devised a customer-friendly strategy
using "Six Sigma" as Allied's marching song. He quickly placated

Allied's shareholders, and over the next few years he turned the company into a major supplier of materials to chemical companies as well as a leading seller of safety instruments to airlines.

Wall Street was impressed. Bossidy was clearly a talented chief executive. As I said before, he was also a consummate actor. When I first met him in the late '80s, Larry was a member of the four-person executive office at General Electric and Jack Welch's most trusted lieutenant. I was one of twenty-four academics and consultants hired to advise on GE's famed "Work-Out" project aimed at understanding business processes in order to remove unnecessary work and bureaucracy from the system. The objective was to work with speed, simplicity, and self-confidence. Bossidy was the point man for "Work-Out," and I got to watch him close up. He is a big man, with big shoulders and big hands and a rough-hewn face. He can be warm and friendly or gruff and grim; he can be relaxed or determined—whatever the moment requires. Bossidy also moves like the natural athlete he is (as a college pitcher, he once had offers from major-league teams). His is a commanding presence, and Bossidy uses his emotional flexibility to great advantage, presenting to his public a big man with big ideas. In 1998, Allied's revenues were more than $15 billion.

Bossidy announced that he will retire in April 2000, and there was much concern about his successor. Using his talent for the dramatic, with less than a year to go before his retirement, Bossidy had secret talks with Michael Bonsignore, the chief executive of Honeywell, the Minneapolis-based maker of electronic controls, and hammered out a merger between the two companies. Honeywell International, as the new company will be called, will have $25 billion in sales and a market capitalization of more than $45 billion. Bossidy is chairman, but when he retires, Bonsignore, fifty-eight, will add the chairman's title to his job of chief executive.

FOLLOWERS ARE ACTORS, TOO

Shakespeare has Jaques say in *As You Like It,* "All the world's a stage / And all the men and women merely players."

All the men and women? That raises an important question: How can you know what's really going on in a company if everyone—leaders and followers alike—is an actor? You can't. And that's what makes corporate life so interesting. Perfect understanding is impossible. The best any of us can do is to approximate. But one thing I do know for sure (and for once I have to disagree with Shakespeare): the follower will have a more difficult and more stressful job as an actor than the leader.

I've been both, boss and employee, and playing the role of loyal subordinate was always a challenge. Trying to figure out what a leader really wants, reconciling that with what you really want, then performing that task in a manner that will enhance your self-esteem is not easy. It is even harder when you have to factor in the interests of the others who are simultaneously tugging at you—your colleagues and your family.

I worked for several years in my first advertising job wondering why the company was not getting bigger. We were doing fine, but I reckoned we could have been doing a lot better. We were an eight-person firm. To go after bigger and more profitable accounts, we needed to hire more talent. The owner of the agency resisted our pleas to increase the staff. My confusion turned to disgust. I was still pretty green in the ways of business, but I knew that you couldn't increase your profits without increasing your business, and in advertising that added up to more brains in the room. Finally, I discovered my boss's reason for sticking to the status quo: according to state law, any firm with more than eight employees had to pay state unemployment insurance. The owner of the agency, I learned, had been so scarred by the Great Depression that he could not bring himself to reinvest any profits into the business. He was a fine, honorable man, but his excessive thrift made it impossible for his people to serve him and the enterprise as well as we could.

This experience dramatized to me that followers have their special problems. Of course, ambitious young managers tend to see themselves as only temporary followers. Nevertheless, I encourage the members of my executive seminars and my students to recognize that it will take them at least a few years to become CEOs, and, in the meantime, they should learn from their roles as followers. Followers serve at least five different constituencies: the needs of the enterprise, their boss's needs, and their own, not to mention the needs of their colleagues and their families. It's a tall order. The secret of success, I've observed, is not to get hung up serving the needs of any one constituency—especially yourself. Sometimes, for example, even though you don't agree with your boss, he might actually be right. Equally problematic is the person who is preoccupied with pleasing the boss. But can you know, without a doubt, what your boss might or might not want? Better to tell it as you see it, but be careful how you tell it. This is where your acting skills come in: you have to tailor what you tell your boss to the kind of person he is, to the situation at the moment, and to any other variable that you can factor in.

I have learned that the best guide to serving the five constituencies (self, boss, enterprise, family, and colleagues) is to weigh your decisions and actions in favor of the primary variable in that mix: the enterprise. Let the company's objectives and goals, its mission in the marketplace, be your guide. After all, that is the reason why you're all there, boss and employees, leaders and followers. If, in trying to serve these different constituencies, you find yourself miserable, or if someone asks you (or, worse, orders you) to break the law or violate your own moral principles, then you always have one other solution available: Quit!

WHAT IF YOU'RE A BAD ACTOR?

Larry Bossidy happens to be a good actor. Like Henry V, he's a natural. Most of the really talented leaders I know are comfortable in front of a crowd (or have learned how to appear to be). A good leader, however, must also know his limitations on the stage. There are some roles certain leaders should avoid. Even staunch haters of President Richard Nixon could admit that he was a brilliant performer in the arena of foreign affairs. But remember those famous photographs of Nixon walking on the beach? The Kennedys were great at that casual, sporty, wind-in-their-thick-hair look, walking barefoot in the sand, their khakis rolled up. When Nixon tried it, the beach part was all right, but the tie? The tightly zipped jacket with the presidential seal? The black cordovans? Nixon undermined himself by trying to act the role of a Kennedy. The president to study is Ronald Reagan. Ronald Reagan took the leader-actor to new heights. Reagan was a real actor who became a real leader, who also knew when, as a leader, he had to put on a show. The best role he ever played was president.

Instead of imitating the competition, sometimes it's better for a leader to establish how different he is. Tina Packer recalls catching a television profile of Scott McNealy, the CEO of Sun Microsystems, during the government's antitrust trial against Microsoft:

> It was a genuine performance. McNealy literally roller-bladed onto the stage. He displayed several placards with remarks denoting the differences between his company and Microsoft. He's a very witty speaker, who earned a lot of laughs by deriding his main competitor, Bill Gates. He even mimicked Gates. It was a very persuasive performance. And what struck me about it most was that he was playing the fool to Bill Gates's king. How else can you make an impact on something as big as Microsoft? You do something outrageous, play the little guy (though Sun Microsystems is hardly little), throwing spears and lances at the giant. However, if he had looked like Bill Gates or used the same language as Gates, or if he had come off as self-righteous or looking for pity, he wouldn't have gotten the same kind of attention or applause. But his attack on Microsoft, charging that it's become a monster and the world needs to go in another direction, was very canny and very entertaining.

Not every manager can be a witty speaker or display a commanding presence to an audience. But that doesn't mean you cannot be a performer, using your own skills and appearance to your advantage. Remember Frank Perdue, the chicken king? A funny-looking guy, he was hardly anyone's first choice for TV pitchman. But he used his down-home appearance and accent to play the man of the people. He even began to look like a chicken, and he sure sold an awful lot of chickens to the people.

PLAY THE PART AND KNOW YOURSELF

Good acting, like a good golf swing, is not a natural phenomenon. A golf swing uses muscles in a way that they're not accustomed to being used. Good actors use their bodies and voice along with their emotions and their intellect in ways that they might not use them in their offstage lives. An actor speaks so that her voice will project to the back row under the balcony; physical movements and emotions are defined and heightened so that the back row can see and feel them. An actor's intellect is bent to the understanding and projection of words that began as someone else's but now are aligned with her own emotions in order to evoke the response from the audience that the playwright intended. (Tina particularly enjoys playing characters prone to violence, a psychological trait she does her best to repress in real life.)

Here are some pointers from Tina Packer about qualities and attributes that are important to business leaders as well as actors:

- *Physical stamina.* Just think about it: An actor playing Henry V will be onstage for three hours, talking or exhorting his troops, fighting two major battles, and leaping through the breach in the wall at Harfleur. Many of Shakespeare's other plays feature wild dances, complicated deaths, and acts of physical daring such as swordfights, swaying atop a ship's mast, and leaping over walls.
- *Mental stamina.* Learning the hundreds of lines an actor must speak when she plays in a repertory of plays is only a small part of the job. A Shakespearean actor is constantly arguing and debating, actively thinking about complex issues, not to mention putting ex-friends to death or being assaulted, sexually or physically. Characters in Shakespeare ricochet from anger to love to derision to fear to loneliness and back again to love. Once a play has started, the Shakespearean actor is off and running and, like an airline pilot (or CEO in motion), can't pull over and think about the next move. In Shakespeare's day, actors got only one or two rehearsals of the play before they went in front of a paying audience. Often

they didn't know the whole story line until rehearsal. Actors received "sides," which included only their speeches with the two lines preceding theirs. Onstage, actors had to be listening like mad for their cues.[14]

• *Energy.* If an actor's energy does not infect the audience, there is no play. Like a preacher or pop singer, an actor has to have motors that are turning over deep and fast to grab the attention of the whole room with her performance. The audience is the other half of the creative act, and the actor must be open to the energy of the audience. As we all have noticed, some audiences are better than others, more inclined to laugh or cry or get scared. A skilled actor knows how to take advantage of a lively audience and reignite a dud. (Great comedians, for instance, are brilliant at turning a joke that has fallen flat into a laugh, typically by making fun of themselves, or the joke, or maybe even the audience.) The audience's attention can inspire an actor to be more focused than before and then proceed to use the energy of the audience to transcend the boundaries of what is possible, thus becoming an even greater actor.

These three ingredients, energy, mental focus, and physical stamina, are the attributes needed by a great leader as well as a great actor. Infecting the troops with your energy, listening hard, speaking with conviction, being emotionally available, empathic without sentiment, and able to keep going for long periods of time, sorting, distilling, disseminating—if you can do these things, you will be a great CEO.

CREATING A NEW REALITY: THE ACTOR'S ART

Let me anticipate an objection: "Aren't you advising me to make believe I'm someone I'm not?" Absolutely not. Tina and I want to stress that we're talking about the need for executives to be able to perform in all kinds of situations. But we are not suggesting that the route to success is simply to imitate your idea of what a good business leader is. There has to be some there there. (I can't resist quoting Goethe, who said, "If you would create something, you must be something.")

This brings us to what actors actually do onstage. Curiously, while all our lives most of us have been watching actors perform in the theater, in films, and on television, we don't really know what it is they actually do. This is partly because many actors (like magicians) are reluctant to discuss their craft and its secrets lest their audience become interested in watching the mechanics instead of being caught up by the whole story. But we can't very well encourage executives to act without coming clean on exactly what actors do. And since I have a genuine professional at my side, I'll defer to Tina here:

> Great acting is not about putting on disguises and being something you're not. Great acting is about taking off, stripping off the masks we all wear, to reveal the human being inside. Acting well is not about "faking it" at all. (Though, when all else fails, then fake it. Sometimes the action of faking it creates a reality, and you can pass from pretending into being.) Good acting is about becoming more yourself. It's true that this self on the stage might move or speak differently from the "you" of everyday life; but the character you're playing is an expanded version of yourself, no longer confined by the habitual patterning of your upbringing. If an actor is not "being," then the audience is aware that the person they're watching is just an actor. When it's just the mechanics of "acting" that the audience is watching instead of a human being "being," it's awkward: there is no art, no creativity, no vulnerability revealed. Good actors make us forget that we're in the theater; they persuade us that we're watching something truthful, something real. But they have to create that reality by letting it inhabit their minds and bodies; that's the art of it.

That's precisely what Tina and I believe great business leaders must do—create the reality of what they are proposing in the present moment. With body and mind. And the audience believes them. Paradoxically, by learning to act, you are more likely to discover who you really are (or at least allow that person to appear in public).

How many people do you know who are charming and entertaining in private, but who freeze when they get up in front of a group? Many of us are inclined to think that the difference between us and actors is that they're comfortable performing in public or don't mind making fools of themselves in front of hundreds of strangers (or have some kind of psychological need to "show off"). The fact is that most actors are no less terrified up there onstage than you would be. Again, listen to Tina:

The reason people stiffen up in public is because suddenly they experience a whole new level of self-consciousness. One on one, they're relaxed enough to be themselves. The trick about being able to act onstage is to be relaxed enough to pull it off. Actors have to learn all kinds of exercises that will help them relax, no matter how many people are watching. Self-consciousness sets off a number of physical reactions: your throat constricts, your breathing gets very shallow so that you no longer pick up what others are thinking, your jaw clenches because you're going to say something that you fear will not be the right thing, something that will let you down.

Anyone speaking in public, whether an actor or business executive, is bound to have a high energy level because all the primitive "fight or flight" buttons are being pushed. What you have to do is learn to relax so that your breathing can drop deep into your body, to allow you to get back in touch with what you are feeling. If you are afraid, you have to stay with your fear instead of letting it dominate you. Allow it to be there and breathe deeply. Don't cut yourself off from yourself. It's not that you stop being frightened, because the fear does not stop; you just learn how to use it better. In fact, if you suppress fear, all your energy will go toward that, and what we will watch is someone who is very frightened and can't bear it.

As an actor you have to be what you are and be able to expand into a bigger sense of who you are. You can't think, "I'm scared, so I'll try to think about something completely different." No, you have to walk into your fear and say, "Okay, I'm really scared. Where do I feel this fear?" Usually, the "fight or flight" response churns up your stomach. So you should try to relax your stomach. You can feel your intestines tightening up. "I'm really holding on for dear life,"

157

you tell yourself. At that moment, an experienced actor can begin to release. As you release, you start feeling strength and power. When you breathe more deeply, you bring in more oxygen to the body, which increases the energy flow and makes you feel invigorated. (The appeal of yoga to many people these days is that it is an ancient technique for breathing deeply, which is why so many people find that doing yoga exercises increases their energy level.)

A lot of the training actors undertake is to find ways to live truthfully in the situations their character inhabits—whether that be in fear, lust, excitement, anger, a state of anticipation. Take on your characters—imagine yourself going out to speak to four hundred people, imagine yourself speaking with passion; then rehearse it, let your body find out what it feels like. And then do it over and over again.

The good actor uses energy to create a reality onstage. Shakespeare is quite clear that the best leaders succeed in creating the reality around them that they need. In a way, such leaders are not just performing their roles, they are producing and directing them as well. Larry Bossidy at Allied Signal would be the last man in the world to characterize his activities as theatrical. But he plays all the roles we have just described—playwright, performer, producer, and director. And he plays them superbly. When he took over Allied, he devised and implemented a customer-friendly strategy based on quality. In this sense, he was a playwright and a performer. And like a producer, he lined up the finances and placated his patrons and shareholders. Finally, Bossidy played the part of director, assessing his cast, promoting some people into new roles, getting rid of others, and hiring new players who would pack the house.

Good leader-actors not only prepare themselves for their parts but also set the stage, make sure the lights are right, and then thoroughly enjoy the audience.

SETTING THE STAGE

At Pathmark, I not only collected supermarket carts on my way into the store, I advised all my people at headquarters that when they visited a store, they, too, should park on the far edge of the lot and collect carts on their way in. I wanted to set the stage. Inside the store, if I noticed a gum wrapper on the floor, I hurried to pick it up. Before long, it became a race between me and the employees accompanying me to see who could get to the gum wrapper first. More stage setting.

That lunch I told you about in Chapter 4, when the CEO of General Foods invited us to the executive dining room, to a sumptuous feast served by waiters with white gloves on fine china with sterling silver settings and crystal water- and wineglasses—well, that was his stage set! And when I reciprocated and brought him and his people to my "dining room"—the company cafeteria—that was my (mischievous) effort at theater.

The skilled leader is not only a canny performer, he also has to be able to take advantage of the trappings of power and ceremony. As we saw in the previous chapter, Richard II thought that acting like a king was being a king. Shakespeare points out that the great leader uses the trappings of power to blind others, never himself. Queen Elizabeth I used her "processions" through the English countryside to show her people the glory of their monarch and find out what their concerns were. Henry V points out that it is not "the sceptre and the ball. / The sword, the mace, the crown imperial" nor the "thrice gorgeous ceremony" that makes the king. Ceremony—the symbolic actions and words that great leaders use—is merely a tool of the trade, and not the trade itself. As Henry V says: "I am a king . . . and I know."

The leader who knows what Henry knows (namely, the difference between power and its symbols) will be able to use ceremony to his advantage. When Shakespeare has Richard III "play the maid's part" to perfection, he is once again showing how important it is for leaders to set the stage. Richard and Buckingham are, in effect, putting on a little play for the lord mayor. When Richard appears before the lord mayor bookended by two bishops, Buckingham, already part producer and part director, now plays drama critic, pointing out to the mayor:

> Two props of virtue for a Christian Prince,
> To stay him from the fall of vanity;
> And see, a book of prayer in his hand—
> True ornaments to know a holy man.
>
> KING RICHARD III (3.7, 95–98)

Buckingham and Richard have set a perfect stage for the appearance of a devout, modest prince. Richard, of course, is a faithless, arrogant monster. But his performance wins over the mayor and the people.

THE BEST USES OF CEREMONY

As a professional actor and director, Tina Packer has thought a lot about how cultures and other smaller groups use ceremony to their advantage. Ceremony, she points out, is the rites and rituals that allow us to belong to a group. In order to have harmony, in order to empathize with one another, in order to feel camaraderie, we need to believe that there is a collective good as well as an individual good. In order to say, "This is important," we create ceremonies.

To celebrate success, we create ceremonies. Sports teams and Japanese corporations have long recognized the benefits of ceremony. The dancing girls, the mascots, the chants—even the hot dogs and beer—are part of the ceremony in sporting events. New Zealand's All Blacks rugby team has a special ritual, a kind of Maori war dance, that they perform on the field, complete with grunts and growls, to put awe and fear into their opponents even before the match begins (and most of the time, it succeeds). Scottish fighting forces used to go into battle accompanied by the sound of special bagpipe cries, also designed to terrorize the enemy before the fight began. Japanese firms have "welcome to the workforce" ceremonies that help newcomers bond to a company that wants them to be employees for life. The Japanese also celebrate various rites and rituals and sing the corporate anthem when employees get promoted or finally retire.

At U.S. companies we might have a party for new retirees, present them with a gold watch for their good work and loyalty, but we are not very good at collective ceremonies. Perhaps it's because our Puritan ancestors frowned on parties and the ceremonies of the Roman church. However, any new king or queen knew it was best to get crowned as soon as possible. Coronations required every follower to swear allegiance to the crown, and the more elaborate the public ritual, the more difficult it would be for any subject later to break an oath made in the presence of so many people. In *King Richard II,* moments after Richard has agreed to abdicate, Bolingbroke's first words are "On Wednesday next we solemnly set down / Our coronation." As soon as Richard III accepts the lord mayor's offer of kingship, discussions begin about when to schedule his coronation. Even today, coronations and other royal ceremonies are done with as much pomp and circumstance as possible to create a reality that transcends the everyday and thus make it more significant and memorable. (Remember Charles and Diana's wedding? Diana's funeral?)

So why not invent a few rituals for your company appropriate to your team and the job they're doing? They need not be centered around rewarding the person who has made the most sales. Wednesday could be the day you all have lunch together, and each time a different person sets the agenda (for example, to eat a food you've never tasted, to hear a speaker from a different walk of life, to sing a song someone has written, or to acknowledge a team member). A company where middle management all go out for a drink after work on Friday nights or have a company softball or soccer team that competes with other organizations' is likely to be a healthy place to work. Managers should recognize that small rituals such as these can allow their employees to laugh together, get to know one another better as people, and care for one another. Such employees are likely to end up working together more coherently and creatively.

NEW ROLES, NEW CEREMONIES

In his speech about all the world being a stage, Jaques goes on to say: "And one man in his time plays many parts," from "first the infant / Mewling and puking in the nurse's arms," to schoolchild, to lover, to soldier, to judge, to old man, and finally to the second childhood of senility.

Notice that Shakespeare anticipated that a person might have two occupations as an adult—soldier and judge. He himself earned his living at perhaps more than ten jobs: he began as an apprentice to his father the glove maker, then himself became a glove maker (which would have required killing and skinning cattle and then stretching, cutting, and stitching leather). The young Shakespeare, according to one near-contemporary writer, worked as a tutor in the home of a noble family. The writer Anthony Burgess (among others) speculates that Shakespeare might have clerked for a lawyer.[15] An early source claims that Shakespeare's first jobs in the theater were tending horses outside and prompting the actors. Eventually, he became an actor, then a playwright, and finally a shareholder in the Globe Theatre. Success allowed him to become a landowner and householder. (Some scholars have also claimed that the young Shakespeare might have even gone to sea.)

Shakespeare's many careers make him something of a modern man. While our own fathers, mothers, grandfathers, and grandmothers typically had only one job all their lives, today's young workers can look forward to multiple careers over a long working life. I myself began in the advertising world, then ran a consulting company and a public relations firm. Then I went to teach at the Harvard Business School, where I also served as associate dean and did consulting work for various corporations. One of them, Supermarkets General Corporation, hired me to help turn around its floundering Pathmark Division. After Pathmark, I was president of a flowers-by-wire company and an oil exploration company, and CEO of a publishing company. In 1985, I returned to the academic world to teach at Columbia Business School and have continued to do consulting. I also sit on four boards. Tina began her working life as a journalist and then became an actor. She now works as a director, producer, and manager of her own theater company. She's learned marketing and fund-raising. In the meantime, she and her colleagues began working closely with public school systems to set up "arts-in-education" programs for kids. She trains actors and teachers. More recently, Tina has added another career as a university teacher.

Why not create new ceremonies to help us in the transition from one job to the next? If you're likely to have five or six different kinds of jobs over the next thirty years, how exciting! Why not embrace the unknown? Ceremony and ritual can prepare you for change and challenge. We have graduation ceremonies (also called, fittingly, "commencements"). Tina and I suggest "preparation ceremonies" to teach five steps: (1) you are going into unknown territory; (2) you will experience fear and excitement; (3) if you are really doing a good job, you will not know what will happen next; (4) you will be supported by an unknown force and your own brains; (5) and this, too, is only a stage toward your next journey, so enjoy it while you can.

In fact, this is what most actors feel when they step onto a stage. It's unknown; it's frightening; learning the lines was not the most important part, it's being able to create a reality out of those lines, to keep telling the story but in such a way you do not know what's going to happen next or how you are going to relate to the other actors on stage; it's creating a reality *together;* and it's over soon, so play each moment with every ounce of life you have!

As Puck, the mischievous goblin who initiates the plots, twists, and turns in Shakespeare's comedy *A Midsummer Night's Dream,* says:

> What, a play toward? I'll be an auditor;
> And actor too perhaps, if I see cause.
>
> A MIDSUMMER NIGHT'S DREAM (3.1, 74–75)

We all have cause. Don't be an auditor. Be an actor.

7

Lend Me Your Ears

The Art of Persuasion

> Is it not monstrous that this player here,
> But in a fiction, in a dream of passion,
> Could force his soul so to his own conceit . . .
> Tears in his eyes, distraction in his aspect,
> A broken voice, and his whole function suiting
> With forms of his conceit? And all for nothing!
> For Hecuba!
> What's Hecuba to him, or he to her,
> That he should weep for her?
>
> HAMLET (2.2, 550–60)

I N the turnarounds I have led, there have been hundreds of problems. No one man could have fixed them all. The secret is to find the keystone—the one problem whose solution will resolve the others. Solving that one problem will give the company the overall focus it needs to get healthy again. This special focus I call the company's marching song. At Allied Signal, Larry Bossidy made "Quality" his marching song. When I was at Pathmark, I took an idea that was already being kicked around the company before I arrived—keeping the supermarkets open twenty-four hours a day—and turned that into our marching song.

I called a meeting of all our store managers and assistant managers, five hundred strong. Frankly, like Henry V's troops before the Battle of Agincourt, they were scared and concerned about the future. They knew the company was in trouble; they had watched their stock options plummet by a multiple of 12. And here's this new COO standing before them, with no supermarket experience, whose most recent job was teaching at the Harvard Business School! But in a turnaround, the employees tend to be willing to give the new man some room to move, particularly if he proposes to do something fresh and exciting, something dramatic.

Mammoth supermarkets in a major metropolitan area staying open twenty-four hours a day was definitely a dramatic move! I trumpeted the fact that we would be making history in the supermarket business. As the idea caught hold, the store managers' thoughts turned from dismay to optimism, from optimism to enthusiasm. Once the meeting was over and we got back to work, "Open-Twenty-four-Hours-a-Day" became our new marching song and invigorated the whole company. An entirely new way of doing business forced us all to address dozens of operating problems both old and new. Old logistics problems were no longer relevant as we devised new systems to make sure the right products got to the right stores at the right time. In our marketing, we no longer had to react to local competition. Our own company's revolutionary twenty-four-hours-a-day campaign created so much excitement that we blew right by our competitors.

We had set our own stage, and we had certainly created a new reality in the supermarket business. But you will never be able to make new ideas happen unless you can communicate how exciting they really are to others. The power to persuade, through both the written and spoken word, is a requirement for effective leadership that is often overlooked. Indeed, Tina and I believe that being a persuasive communicator is the number one tool of leadership. No matter how good a leader's ideas are, they mean nothing if he cannot communicate them to his followers. As an actor-playwright-producer, Shakespeare recognized the importance of getting people into the theater and then making them glad they came.

In this chapter, we will look at three of Shakespeare's most famous speeches to show that persuasion is not just a matter of what you say or even how you say it, but of properly assessing your relationship with your audience—and then choosing an appropriate approach to accomplish your goals. In *King Henry V, Julius Caesar,* and *Troilus and Cressida,* Shakespeare points to two requirements for persuasive communication: what you say must be *simple* but *compelling.* Of course, some leaders can win over an audience on the strength of their credibility alone. The character of Ulysses in *Troilus and Cressida* is a good example of the force of content over form, and we'll discuss it in detail. But more often than not, you will need some rhetorical techniques on your side. Two of Shakespeare's most effective speakers, Mark Antony and Henry V, use *repetition, imagery,* and *emotion* to win over their audiences. Few modern business leaders will face tougher crowds than Henry or Antony did.

HENRY'S CALL TO ARMS

In *King Henry V,* the English army, with Henry at its head, sails across the Channel and invades France. Henry has been persuaded that his claim to the French throne is just. Any doubts that he might have had about going to war with France disappear when he receives the French ambassador, who conveys a message from the dauphin. The dauphin scorns the king he has heard is a ne'er-do-well from Eastcheap. To express his disdain, he sends him a box of tennis balls! The insult spurs Henry to revenge. Angry, but in full control of his emotions, Henry declares war on France:

> But I will rise there with so full a glory
> That I will dazzle all the eyes of France . . .
>
> KING HENRY V (1.2, 279–80)

"Now all the youth of England are on fire," Shakespeare's chorus announces at the beginning of Act 2. When the king and his troops break through the wall and take the coastal city of Harfleur, Henry quickly proves to the French that they are up against a stronger opponent than they had bargained for.

But the siege of Harfleur lasts a month, and the troops that Henry leads inland are bloody, exhausted, hungry, and dispirited. They are also outnumbered, and, as we saw in the previous chapter, on the eve of their next major fight—the Battle of Agincourt—the English forces are wondering whether their king's cause is just. Henry knows he will have to blot out the fear and uncertainty demoralizing his troops. But how? With a word picture so simple and compelling that Henry V, against all odds, spurs his troops to greatness and immortality.

The modern manager can learn a great deal about how to inspire employees from a detailed reading of Henry V's famous speech before the Battle of Agincourt. First, let's look at what the king doesn't say. He does not address the harsh reality that his troops faced: the hunger, the exhaustion, the fear. Who knows better than they? And one look across the field confirms that they are outnumbered, five to one. Henry's comments to the soldiers moving around the campfires in disguise reveals that he (dare I say it?) "feels their pain." But he refuses to pander to it. Nor does he try to debate their doubts that his cause is just. Over time, a leader ought to make a direct response to the fears of his followers. But if Henry had chosen that moment to do it, the French army would have finished his speech for him. Instead, what Henry does is to pick two themes that tap the emotions of his troops: *honor* and *brotherhood*. Throughout the speech, he repeats those themes, using imagery that inspires each soldier to visualize life at home after Agincourt.

Returning to his command post from the campfires, Henry overhears his cousin Westmoreland complaining:

167

> O that we now had here
> But one ten thousand of those men in England
> That do no work today!
>
> KING HENRY V (4.3, 16–18)

That remark inspires one of the most focused speeches in all of Shakespeare. Listen to his uses of honor and brotherhood:

> . . . No, my fair cousin:
> If we are marked to die, we are enough
> To do our country loss, and if to live,
> The fewer men, the greater share of honour.
>
> KING HENRY V (4.3, 19–22)

Henry points out that he himself covets neither gold nor fine clothes:

> But if it be a sin to covet honour
> I am the most offending soul alive.
> No, faith, my coz, wish not a man from England.
> God's peace, I would not lose so great an honour
> As one man more, methinks, would share from me
> For the best hope I have. O do not wish one more!
>
> KING HENRY V (4.3, 28–33)

He then begins to paint a picture that will distract his men from the muddy battlefields of France and turn their imaginations to what it will be like to return to England as the heroes of Agincourt. And because the battle will take place on the feast of St. Crispin, that holiday will be forever linked in the minds of the English people with their exploits at Agincourt:

> This day is called the feast of Crispian.
> He that outlives this day and comes safe home
> Will stand a-tiptoe when the day is named
> And rouse him at the name of Crispian.

He that shall see this day and live old age
Will yearly on the vigil feast his neighbors,
And say, 'Tomorrow is Saint Crispian.'
Then will he strip his sleeve and show his scars,
And say, 'These wounds I had on Crispin's day.'

KING HENRY V (4.3, 40–48)

Shakespeare completes the picture so that each soldier sees himself back at home, surrounded not just by family but by England's greatest names. The implication: for posterity, every foot soldier will be numbered among England's nobility, unforgettably:

Old men forget; yet all shall be forgot
But he'll remember, with advantages,
What feats he did that day. Then shall our names,
Familiar in his mouth as household words,
Harry the King, Bedford and Exeter,
Warwick and Talbot, Salisbury and Gloucester.
Be in their flowing cups freshly remembered.

KING HENRY V (4.3, 49–55)

They will become part of history. Imagine your names as "household words." Who can resist immortality?

This story shall the good man teach his son,
And Crispin Crispian shall ne'er go by
From this day to the ending of the world
But we in it shall be remembered . . .

KING HENRY V (4.3, 56–59)

And in case anyone still has a shred of doubt about charging into battle, Shakespeare describes how posterity will also remember the veterans of Agincourt, in three of the most famous lines ever written:

We few, we happy few, we band of brothers.
For he today that sheds his blood with me
Shall be my brother . . .

                                    KING HENRY V (4.3, 60–62)

Heady stuff for dirt-poor farmers, day laborers, all commoners, facing battle in France with their nation's greatest names and as soldiers of the king—their *brother.* Shakespeare's Henry V uses repetition (honor, St. Crispin's Day, never to be forgotten), imagery (standing proudly on tiptoe, showing battle scars, generations of Englishmen telling the story of Agincourt to their children), and emotion (the prospect of fame and immortality, until the end of the world, "we few, we happy few, we band of brothers").

No wonder Winston Churchill used Shakespeare's words to inspire the English people during World War II. (It was also no accident that Laurence Olivier's great film version of *Henry V,* which he produced, directed, and starred in, was made during the worst days of the war.) A great leader must persuade his followers that they are a part of a team with a joint mission. He must convince them that at the end of their labors, there will be large rewards. Henry's audience, of course, was looking for inspiration. Similarly, most employees want to be inspired; they would prefer their work to have meaning. I have found that the smallest compliments, the slightest pat on the back, will make employees want to vault through walls for you. But what does a leader do when he faces a hostile audience, employees looking for more than inspiration? A good place to find the answer is Mark Antony's funeral oration in Shakespeare's *Julius Caesar.*

MARK ANTONY'S BRILLIANT TURNAROUND

Here's the situation Antony was up against. A gang of conspirators, led by Brutus and Cassius, has just assassinated Julius Caesar. They ambushed Caesar in Rome's most political place, the Capitol, to prove that they were killing Caesar for the good of Rome. Their argument: that Caesar wanted to turn their republic into a monarchy, led, of course, by Julius Caesar. Brutus makes the assassins' case before the people, who seem to buy it. Then Mark Antony persuades Brutus, much to Cassius's distress, that he should be allowed to address the crowd with a simple funeral oration "to bury Caesar, not to praise him."

The speech that Shakespeare puts into Antony's mouth is a masterwork in the art of persuasion. Anyone who ever anticipates facing a hostile audience ought to study the rhetorical techniques Antony uses to turn an angry mob into *his* angry mob. In Elizabethan times, former schoolboys like Shakespeare and the London lawyers who were regulars at his plays were as well trained as their Roman counterparts in the principles of rhetoric. But part of the genius of Antony's speech is that he knows when to throw the rule book away. Those buttoned-down American companies that require every internal communication to begin with an "executive summary" would not be an easy place for a Mark Antony to rise in. Nor would he pass muster in the traditionalist approach, which mandates that every paragraph begin with a simple declarative sentence that states the main thought, followed by another that supports it, and end with a conclusion that wraps up that same thought. As the old bromide goes: "Tell them what you're going to tell them. Tell them. Then tell them what you've told them."

Such rigid formulae might serve for training manuals, but if you want to persuade people in the real world, you must quickly gauge your audience and build a case in such a way that your conclusion is inescapable. And if you're up against a hostile audience, as Antony was, you have to be careful what you reveal at the outset. If Antony had led his funeral oration with his conclusion—that Brutus and his fellow conspirators are traitors—the crowd would have murdered him on the spot. They have already heard Brutus make a strong case that Caesar's assassination was the right thing to do. Brutus explains his motive:

> Not that I loved Caesar less, but that I loved Rome more. Had you rather Caesar were living, and die all slaves, than that Caesar were dead, to live all free men? As Caesar loved me, I weep for him; as he

was fortunate, I rejoice at it; as he was valiant, I honour him; but, as he was ambitious, I slew him.

JULIUS CAESAR (3.2, 21–27)

When you look at Brutus's words on the page, one thing immediately becomes clear: he is speaking in *prose*. Shakespeare's great speeches are written as poetry, classic iambic pentameter. The form of Brutus's speech fits its argument, hardly subtle or complicated; what Brutus has to say is, in fact, quite prosaic: Caesar was too ambitious, he was going to destroy the Roman Republic, take away your freedom and mine, so we had no alternative but to destroy him first. It was the patriotic Roman thing to do:

Who is here so rude, that would not be a Roman? If any, speak; for him have I offended. Who is here so vile, that will not love his country? If any, speak; for him have I offended. I pause for a reply.

JULIUS CAESAR (3.2, 30–34)

If we had been in the audience, I doubt any of us would have raised a hand and said, "I am vile, Brutus. I hate my country, and you have offended me." Tina reminds me that Brutus was a philosopher, an intellectual; he had a reputation as a fair man, a measured man, an honest man, not a rabble-rouser. True to form, noble Brutus uses considered arguments, repeats his phrases, and wins the approval of the people. Shakespeare has members of the crowd give Brutus a thumbs-up rating. ("Give him a statue with his ancestors," says one Roman. "Let him be Caesar," suggests another.)

Antony has his work cut out for him. As he takes the podium, Shakespeare has the crowd murmuring with hostility. (" 'Twere best he speak no harm of Brutus here!" says one person. "This Caesar was a tyrant," warns another.) Every business executive is bound to find himself in Antony's shoes. And she who makes it through her business career without ever having to deal with a hostile audience is likely to have had a boring career. I myself have addressed a large audience of employees not even realizing they were hostile. A month after I created my first triumph with the Pathmark store managers by announcing our twenty-four-hours-a-day campaign, I went for a second win. I hired an auditorium at Rutgers University and assembled again the store managers and assistant managers. This time I wanted to thank them for their hard work and commitment. They all, I said over and over, had been essential to the company's newfound success.

What I didn't know was that most of the people in the room were seething with resentment. Yes, they had been working hard, literally twenty-four hours a day. I had appreciated that. But they wanted more than words of praise. Finally, one brave man rose and said, "That was a great speech, and we really appreciate you thanking us. But . . . we need more money. Our meat managers are taking home more money than we are, and we're responsible for running stores with three hundred employees!"

Having arrived only a few weeks earlier, and having spent every waking hour on the twenty-four-hour program, I had no idea they were so underpaid. But I quickly checked with my colleagues on the dais. "We haven't gotten around to that problem," I was informed. The people running the meat departments were members of the butchers' union and making more money per hour than the store managers. I quickly opened the meeting up to the floor, asking for suggestions for what else we might do. I made it clear that I viewed the store managers as our most important employees. As a result of that meeting, we reviewed our compensation policies and made some dramatic changes. In some instances, managers' salaries were doubled. We also made sure those running stores in tough neighborhoods got more time off.

A better-prepared leader would have known that the managers felt underappreciated before he rented the hall. (Faced with a company in meltdown from day one, I was working twenty hours a day on the logistical problem of keeping the stores open day and night and had neglected to look closely at the company's personnel problems. That's my excuse, and not a good one. But at least I was able to take a punch and recover. Being fast on your feet is a crucial talent for leadership.) Mark Antony had the advantage of knowing that his audience was against him at the outset. He had to create his own agenda and make it work with his own particular style. As we all know, he begins, "Friends, Romans, countrymen, lend me your ears" (3.2, 74). So he asks them to listen. Then he sets out to win their hearts. At first he moves carefully and gently, assuring the crowd, "I come to bury Caesar, not to praise him."

And then quickly, the first subtle shift:

> The evil that men do lives after them,
> The good is oft interred with their bones;
> So let it be with Caesar. The noble Brutus
> Hath told you Caesar was ambitious.
> If it were so, it was a grievous fault,
> And grievously hath Caesar answer'd it.
>
> JULIUS CAESAR (3.2, 76–81)

Here Antony repeats Brutus's argument—that Caesar had to be killed because he was too ambitious. He slips in an "if" to open up doubt but swiftly moves on, implying that he is willing to accept that argument. Why? "For Brutus is an honourable man . . ."

That is Brutus's reputation among his fellow Romans, and Antony is not about to begin by attacking Brutus. But notice how he positions himself. Antony says he has come to speak at Caesar's funeral only because "he was my friend, faithful and just to me." Notes Tina:

> While Brutus says he loved Caesar and weeps for him, we never see it. By pointing out that Caesar was his friend, "faithful and just to me," Antony puts his speech on a very personal footing. As angry as his audience might be over a man Brutus said wanted to turn them into slaves, they relate immediately to the death of a friend.

With that modicum of sympathy on his side, Antony now points to some of Caesar's undeniably finer actions, which brought blessings to everyone:

> He hath brought many captives home to Rome,
> Whose ransoms did the general coffers fill:
> Did this in Caesar seem ambitious?
>
> JULIUS CAESAR (3.2, 89–91)

Antony knows his audience. After all, he is a man who likes sports, competes in races, is the Michael Jordan of his day. Unlike Brutus, Antony is no intellectual, and he points out that Caesar's military exploits filled the "general coffers"; those ransoms did not go into Caesar's pocket but into the treasury. Antony then throws in a dash of hyperbole to stress that Caesar, too, had the common touch:

> When that the poor have cried, Caesar hath wept:
> Ambition should be made of sterner stuff . . .
>
> JULIUS CAESAR (3.2, 92–93)

Very effective. But he still concedes that Brutus has argued that Caesar was ambitious, and "Brutus," he repeats, "is an honourable man." This is one of Antony's most effective devices: to repeat again and again that "Brutus is an honourable man." It is true, but not in the context of Caesar's assassination, which Antony will soon prove. Tina points out that what that repetition does is provide an emotional trigger for Antony's argument. Every time he returns to it, the emotion builds. Listen to the speeches of our great civil rights leaders. They use the same devices. To make his case against Brutus, Antony mixes emotion with facts familiar to his audience. At this point, Antony throws in a fact known to everyone in his audience who had recently seen Antony himself offer a crown to Caesar at a public event, which Caesar, Antony reminds them, "did thrice refuse."

> . . . Was this ambition?
> Yet Brutus says he was ambitious,
> And sure he is an honourable man.
>
> JULIUS CAESAR (3.2, 98–100)

Antony assures his audience, "I speak not to disprove what Brutus spoke," which is exactly what he is doing. But before his fellow Romans can figure that out, Antony takes his speech to the next level by exploiting the emotion of the moment. A great actor,

Antony has worked himself into tears, but he must also allot time for his emotional state to infect his audience:

> . . . Bear with me.
> My heart is in the coffin there with Caesar,
> And I must pause till it come back to me.
>
> JULIUS CAESAR (3.2, 106–108)

It's a startling image, Antony's beating, grieving heart, lying there with the dead Caesar. And the ploy works. Antony doesn't have to dissemble: he really is in pain about Caesar's death. But he's using his emotion, not being dominated by it. As Antony pauses to regain his composure, Shakespeare allows members of the audience to report on how well Antony's doing. "Methinks there's much reason in his sayings," says one. "Poor soul! His eyes are red as fire with weeping," reports another. A third citizen adds, "There's not a nobler man in Rome than Antony."

How do we know he's not faking it? The audience member who notes that Antony's "eyes are red as fire with weeping." And in any case, the crowd can feel his deep anguish. When Tina directs an actor in the role of Mark Antony, she says the feeling of genuine emotion is the key to making the scene work, as well as Antony's knowledge that such emotion is exactly the right thing to express at this time to his audience and the audience in the theater. Tina explains how an actor can help an audience feel the same emotion the speaker is feeling onstage:

Every actor consciously opens himself up to a sense of the audience. If the audience is with you, you can feel it viscerally. See if your skin starts to tingle when you are onstage. It's almost as if something chemical happens in your body, and you can feel if things are going right or not. If they're not with you, it feels as if you're moving through sludge. But if you allow your emotions to be there, neither exaggerated or repressed, the audience gets it. Don't pretend to weep or laugh, just let go into the situation you are in. Caesar was Antony's best friend. When that Roman citizen says of Antony: "Poor soul, his eyes are red as fire," Antony's audience is commiserating with him. Antony weeps, and he is also aware of his audience's reaction to that weeping. And they begin to weep together. Tears beget tears. Laughter spreads laughter. And now Antony knows that the people are beginning to trust him. If you really want people to follow you, you have to make an emotional connection with them. Ronald Reagan did this. Like Antony, he personalized things, made his speech emotional. Martin Luther King, Jr., was brilliant at sparking emotion in his audience. And, like Antony, he used the device of repetition. So, God help us, did Hitler, using his eloquent power for evil. Emotion is a powerful tool of persuasion.

Thus Antony brings the crowd into his corner. Notice how Shakespeare, through Antony, shows us that though individual men and women might be rational, a crowd is not. The lesson for the leader is clear: If you do not manipulate the crowd, it will manipulate you. For those of you who recoil at the word *manipulate,* consider your own efforts to persuade someone to do your bidding. You can call it persuasion if you like, but your planning makes it manipulation, and honestly so. Manipulation is part of the art of persuasion.

In fact, it is downright dangerous for any leader to ignore the risks of "mob psychology." I learned that firsthand when I called that meeting of the store managers without knowing that they were underpaid and rightly resented it. I advise my MBA students and the members of my executive seminars to be careful about calling a meeting. Never do so without knowing what you intend to say. Be ready to answer every question. Let there be no surprises. I tell them to listen, not only with their ears but with their eyes and every fiber of their bodies. Pick up the cues and tailor your words and actions accordingly.

Antony certainly knew what he was up against. He can tell his audience:

> . . . if I were dispos'd to stir
> Your hearts and minds to mutiny and rage,
> I should do Brutus wrong, and Cassius wrong,
> Who, you all know, are honourable men.

> JULIUS CAESAR (3.2, 122–25)

Shameless! Inciting a riot was exactly what Antony had in mind from the beginning. Such skill proves that Antony is a brilliant orator. The irony is almost too much to bear. Brutus asked the crowd to "awake your senses, that you may the better judge" (for the Romans, like the Elizabethans, knew that all the senses needed to be alert to understand), but it is Antony who succeeds in capturing the emotions of the crowd. Knowing the audience is his, Antony administers the coup de grâce:

> But here's a parchment with the seal of Caesar;
> I found it in his closet; 'tis his will . . .
>
> JULIUS CAESAR (3.2, 129–30)

This is where Antony proves how devious he has been. Strange that someone in the crowd did not say, "Pardon me, Antony. But Caesar has been dead less than half an hour. How did you find time to go to his house, ransack his closet, and find his will?"

The crowd begs Antony to read the will. Antony demurs: "I fear I wrong the honourable men whose daggers have stabb'd Caesar." That's all the crowd needs. They are with Antony. They denounce the conspirators as "traitors," "villains, murderers." They want to hear the will, which Antony will read to them, of course, but not before he further increases their animosity toward Brutus and Cassius. Antony invites the crowd to move closer to Caesar's body, where he can really work on their emotions: "If you have tears," he says, "prepare to shed them now."

This is a great moment in the speech. The crowd is in high dudgeon, and Antony pumps them up even more. He points to Caesar's "mantle," the loose sleeveless coat the Romans wore over other garments, and recalls that Caesar had worn it first the day he beat the Nervii. He points to the stab wounds, including "the most unkindest cut of all"—from Caesar's friend Brutus. The irony would be clear to his audience remembering the triumph over the enemy Nervii, who failed to kill Caesar. It was left to his fellow Romans to do him in. Antony can now rage at the conspirators with impunity and denounce the murder of Caesar as a "bloody treason." The crowd is now ready to "burn the house of Brutus."

Now is the moment for Antony to refer to the contents of Caesar's will. Antony stirs the audience's imagination, getting the listeners to create their own mental images of what he is describing—in this case the delights that Caesar would have showered on the Roman people had his will been executed.

> . . . he hath left you all his walks,
> His private arbours, and new-planted orchards,
> On this side Tiber; he hath left them you,
> And to your heirs for ever: common pleasures,
> To walk abroad and recreate yourselves.
> Here was a Caesar! when comes such another?
>
> JULIUS CAESAR (3.2, 248–53)

That's all it took—about fifteen minutes, and Antony has turned around a crowd that would have lynched him had he admitted at the outset that he had come to praise Caesar and criticize Brutus. In the middle of the speech, he had assured them once again:

> I come not, friends, to steal away your hearts.
> I am no orator, as Brutus is,
> But (as you know me all) a plain blunt man . . .
> For I have neither wit, nor words, nor worth,
> Action, nor utterance, nor the power of speech
> To stir men's blood; I only speak right on.
>
> JULIUS CAESAR (3.2, 217–24)

Of course, he has proved himself brilliant at stirring up men's blood. (It is also, by the bye, the first time "right on" appears in the English language.) By the end of this scene, a servant sums up Antony's success to him:

> . . . Brutus and Cassius
> Are rid like madmen through the gates of Rome.
>
> JULIUS CAESAR (3.2, 269–70)

I am not suggesting that any executive set out to be as devious as Antony. But the techniques he uses to win over an audience are impressive and available to you: the repetition of words and phrases ("But Brutus is an honourable man . . ."); the self-deprecation ("I am no orator . . . a plain blunt man"); the imagery ("he hath left you his private arbours"); the skill at tapping into people's emotions ("My heart is in the coffin there with Caesar, / And I must pause till it come back to me"). Tina points out something else about Antony's speech that is essential for the business leader: Antony respects the intelligence of his audience. To turn them against Brutus finally he uses the facts: Caesar turned down the crown; he had the public's interests and pleasures in mind, according to his will. This is a reality that the audience can refer to.

Good speaking skills have always been important to great leaders. And in our media age, where CEOs give interviews to the press or appear on videotape or videoconferencing, learning how to speak in public is an even more crucial managerial skill. While some talented speakers can improvise before a crowd, most of us have to be well prepared. Learn Antony's lesson well. The secret is to be well prepared, to have rehearsed your speech long and carefully out loud, to have written it in such a conversational style that as you deliver it, your audience will think that you're making it up as you go along, that it's spontaneous, in the moment. And then allow yourself to respond to the audience as they respond to you!

That's the art of great communication. And yet . . . we are not all poet-kings like Henry V; nor are we likely to be brilliant orators like Mark Antony. And even if we have access to terrific speechwriters, they are not likely to be Shakespeares. Usually, the best and most effective speech need not be as emotional as Antony's. Reason and credibility can be as compelling as emotion. And a lot more simple.

So let's turn to a rather dull, rather plodding speech, which ends up being as compelling as Henry's and Antony's emotion-packed words, and just as persuasive.

ULYSSES, THE CREDIBLE, PEDANTIC PERSUADER

I have had the good fortune to work with the legendary business consultant Dr. W. Edwards Deming, the architect of the most astonishing economic turnaround in history, the rise of the Japanese economy after World War II. (Toyota has a large portrait of Dr. Deming, alongside those of its founder and current chairman, in the main lobby of its headquarters in Tokyo.) When he consulted for American auto manufacturers, Ed Deming would first spend hours with the workers, researching their take on the company's problems, and then hit the top executives with his opinions based on what he had learned. In the 1980s, I watched Dr. Deming face off with the CEOs of General Motors and Ford and tell them exactly what he thought was wrong with their companies. He did not mince words. When I asked him why he was so blunt, Dr. Deming, who was in his mid-eighties at the time, joked, "There's so little time." (He actually lived until age ninety-three.)

But Ed Deming had enjoyed being candid with the world's most powerful CEOs throughout his long career because he had something that you cannot fake: *credibility.* For decades he had taught and written about corporations; he had consulted for the biggest companies in the world; Dr. Deming was the man who in my opinion put "quality" back into the vocabulary of businesspeople everywhere. He could be blunt, but everyone in the room listened. Credibility, too, can be very persuasive, and Shakespeare gives us a very good example in his play *Troilus and Cressida.*

In spite of the play's title, I believe that the central character in the play is Ulysses, King of Ithaca, a leading figure in the Trojan War. He is also, of course, the central character of the great Greek Homeric epic the *Odyssey,* the story of Odysseus's return from Troy. (Ulysses was the Latin name for Odysseus.) To the ancients, Ulysses/Odysseus was known for his craftiness. ("Wily Odysseus" is Homer's usual description of him.) Shakespeare is kinder to Ulysses, portraying him as the voice of reason at Troy, where the

Greeks are fighting a bad war for a pointless cause. The Trojan prince, Paris, has run off with the King of Sparta's beautiful wife, Helen,

> . . . a pearl
> Whose price hath launch'd above a thousand ships,
> And turn'd crown'd kings to merchants.[16]
>
> TROILUS AND CRESSIDA (2.2, 82–84)

To defend King Menelaus's honor, the combined armies of the Greek kingdoms laid siege to Troy—for ten years. Shakespeare's play is set in year seven of the Trojan War. Generals on both sides are questioning whether this battle over Helen, whom Shakespeare portrays as a simpering, fashion-obsessed society wife, is worth the lives of so many men. Agamemnon, the Greek commander in chief, advises his fellow generals not to let their inability to conquer Troy discourage them, and invites Ulysses's opinion: "We shall hear music, wit, and oracle" (*Troilus and Cressida* [1.3, 74]).

What we actually hear from Ulysses is, I think, a plodding, pedantic declamation diagnosing the Greek failure at Troy as a lack of order and discipline. Scholars argue that Ulysses is speaking for Shakespeare, noting that the speech would not have seemed tedious to an Elizabethan audience: the idea of order and harmony in the heavens and universe spreading through nature and including humankind was a potent principle in the Middle Ages and Renaissance. And for topical reference was the fact that Shakespeare's story of lovers in the middle of the Trojan War was an enigmatic satire of an abortive rebellion against Elizabeth's rule that took place the same year Shakespeare began writing the play. In 1601, the Earl of Essex, a major political figure in the later Elizabethan court and possibly a lover of the queen, tried to raise the city of London against her. The rebellion failed, and Essex was executed. (The plot of the recent popular film *Elizabeth* was built around the queen's relationship with Robert Dudley, Earl of Leicester, who afterward became stepfather to the Earl of Essex.) Implicated in the plot was Essex's close friend the Earl of Southampton, Shakespeare's patron.

Shakespeare's personal connection to Essex and Southampton would have tugged at his commitment to law, order, and hierarchy.[17] But in Ulysses's speech he makes his preference clear:

> . . . But when the planets
> In evil mixture to disorder wander,
> What plagues and what portents, what mutiny,
> What raging of the sea, shaking of earth,
> Commotion in the winds . . .
>
> TROILUS AND CRESSIDA (1.3, 94–98)

Everything in the world has its place, its "degree." And "when degree is shak'd," Ulysses warns, "the enterprise is sick." Shakespeare makes this point repeatedly in the speech by varying the metaphors for order and discord, returning finally to the crucial role of the leader in any hierarchy:

> . . . The general's disdain'd
> By him one step below, he by the next,
> The next by him beneath: so every step,
> Exampled by the first pace that is sick
> Of his superior . . .
>
> TROILUS AND CRESSIDA (1.3, 129–33)

It is this kind of disorder in the ranks that is keeping the Greeks from winning, and not the strength of Troy:

> And 'tis this fever that keeps Troy on foot,
> Not her own sinews. To end a tale of length,
> Troy in our weakness stands, not in her strength.
>
> TROILUS AND CRESSIDA (1.3, 135–37)

Ulysses has made a straightforward argument, no tricks, no surprises, and just one point, stated in the first sentence of the speech: "the speciality of rule hath been neglected." Internal disputes and disrespect for rank have stymied the Greeks, not the Trojans.

The speaker backs up his straightforward argument with one

powerful asset: his credibility. Every business manager should work hard to build credibility. When you have it, credibility can be a powerful tool of persuasion. Never do anything to destroy your own credibility. As a turnaround specialist, take it from me: nothing is harder to restore than credibility ("Reputation, reputation, reputation! O, I have lost my reputation!" weeps Cassio in *Othello*. "I have lost the immortal part of myself, and what remains is bestial." I'm not sure I'd go this far, but he makes a good point.) The Greeks do overcome the Trojans in the end—but not by aligning themselves in perfect order, more by cunning, dishonorable actions and muddling through.

But to return to credibility. Every action you take will be more effective if you have credibility to back it up. Credibility helps you overcome limitations as an actor and speaker. It's more useful, of course, for a leader to have both the linguistic skills and the credibility gained from knowledge and performance. But if I have to choose between wit and wisdom, I'll take wisdom every time. Alan Greenspan is one of the most persuasive men in the world, not only because of his power as chairman of the Federal Reserve Board, but because he earned that power. He knows of what he speaks. When he talks, Wall Street listens, even though it might be difficult to stay awake. Similarly, when Jack Welch speaks, I take notes.

On this point, I leave you with one final, inspiring fact for those of you at every level of business suffering from stage fright: Jack Welch is a lifelong stutterer.

Part III

THE SEARCH WITHIN

Integrating Values, Vision, Mission, and Strategy

8

Polonius's Paradox

Choices and Consequences for Man Alone and Man in Society

> This above all: to thine ownself be true,
> And it must follow as the night the day
> Thou canst not then be false to any man.
>
> HAMLET (1.3, 78–80)

S HAKESPEARE gave the famous words in the above epigram to Polonius, a wily politician who was Lord Chamberlain to Claudius, recently crowned king of Denmark. As you may recall, Claudius had secretly murdered his brother, the former king (Hamlet's father), assumed the throne, then swiftly married Gertrude, Hamlet's mother and widow of the dead king. Claudius enlists Polonius's help in spying on the young prince, whom he doesn't trust. There is no evidence that Polonius knows of Claudius's murderous tendencies, but that's no matter. Polonius is reprehensible enough in his own right. He spies on his son, he spies on his daughter and Hamlet, then on Hamlet and his mother, who are having a heated argument about her hasty marriage in Gertrude's chamber. It is in this last invasion of privacy that Shakespeare indicates his own distaste for the old man. Polonius, hiding behind a curtain, cries out when he believes that Hamlet is going to harm Gertrude. Hamlet, responding to the noise, runs his rapier through the curtain, killing the meddling old man. Shakespeare's epitaph for Polonius is Hamlet's unrepentant lines:

> Thou wretched, rash, intruding fool, farewell! . . .
> I'll lug the guts into the neighbour room.
> Mother, good night indeed. This counsellor
> Is now most still, most secret, and most grave,
> Who was in life a foolish prating knave.
>
> HAMLET (3.4, 31, 214–17)

Shakespeare's genius for irony lives not only in these words, but in the fact that only a few scenes earlier he had Polonius saying, "To thine ownself be true." During the action of the play Polonius is never true to himself—or if he is, it is as a scheming, exploiting busybody; faithful to the crown but not to himself or his family. Hamlet delights in leading the old man around by the nose:

HAMLET   Do you see yonder cloud that's almost in shape of a camel?

LORD POLONIUS   By th'mass and 'tis—like a camel indeed.

HAMLET   Methinks it is like a weasel.

LORD POLONIUS   It is backed like a weasel.

HAMLET   Or like a whale.

LORD POLONIUS   Very like a whale.

> HAMLET (3.2, 378–84)

Polonius was consistently false to all those around him other than the king. Shakespeare knew what he was doing. Polonius's aphorism, so widely quoted, is nonsense, a true paradox. One can be true to oneself and one can also try hard to be false to no man, but, as we shall see, these two noble attributes do not follow each other "as the night the day." Indeed, they are often at odds; they dramatize a dilemma faced by mankind long before Shakespeare's time and with us to this day. But it takes a Shakespeare to frame the issue so cleverly that, in order not to be misled, we must think about it closely. And because the problem is universal, we will not, in this chapter, limit our discussion to Shakespeare's insights, but will look at how the great religions and legal systems have also tried to deal with the paradox. We will also review an essay of Ralph Waldo Emerson, whose words "Trust thyself: every heart vibrates to that iron string" are often associated with Shakespeare's "To thine ownself be true." Finally, we will touch on the social sciences, particularly through classical and Austrian economists, who at first might seem to be an unlikely source. But these social philosophers, by observing the actions of humans who are trying to reconcile the inherent conflicts of "Man Alone" versus "Man in Society," brought us not a solution, but a better understanding of the paradox. The paradox confronts us all but is particularly vexing to leaders, whether they be CEOs, middle managers, or first-line supervisors.

THE LEADERSHIP PARADOX

In an earlier chapter we said that leaders are not sponges to soak up and squeeze out the same muddy water. Good leaders, "true to themselves," stand for something. They are creative and innovative, and in many cases they march to a "different drummer." Leadership traits like these nearly always evoke criticism from some quarter, whether employees, investors, bankers, or the press, but effective leaders know that if they try to please everyone all the time, they are doomed to fail. Well and good! But here's the paradox: The essential requirement of leadership is followers. Although some people might be coerced to follow for a time, sooner or later the effective leader must strike a responsive chord in the hearts and minds of enough capable people to accomplish the tasks at hand. Otherwise, his steadfastness, his innovations, even his good intentions are to no avail. Like the leader who marches only to his own drummer, he too will be doomed to "suffer the slings and arrows of outrageous fortune."

The dilemma is illuminated in many of the plays. Julius Caesar paid the price for too much conviction just as Henry VI paid the price for his passiveness. But true to his fashion, the Bard makes us think about the leader's paradox more carefully than we would if he simply categorized Julius Caesar as arrogant and Henry VI as passive. And, also true to fashion, he did it with the well-crafted lines we saw at the beginning of the chapter:

> This above all: to thine ownself be true,
> And it must follow as the night the day
> Thou canst not then be false to any man.

At first reading, Polonius's advice seems sound. "To thine own-self be true" has a nice ring to it; and who would admit the desire to be "false" to any man? But as we noted earlier, when you connect those two thoughts with "it follows as the night the day," the aphorism becomes a bit troublesome. For example, just what does "false to no man" really mean? If it means that any deeply held conviction is okay just as long as you make it clear to others who you are and what you stand for, then Adolf Hitler, Slobodan Milošević, and Chairman Mao would meet Polonius's requirements. But so would Jesus, Moses, and Mohammed. So far, the advice is useless. Let's take another approach. If being "false to no man" means that your actions taken while being "true to yourself" will never do harm to others, the aphorism is patently absurd. Man does not live in this world alone, nor do all men and women have similar goals, values, and aspirations. Julius Caesar was being true to himself when he banished Publius Cimber. Brutus was being true to himself when he helped assassinate Caesar. Mark Antony was being true to himself when he went back on his word to Brutus and convinced the

Roman citizens that Brutus and Cassius were not "honorable men." Octavius Caesar was probably being true to himself when (in *Antony and Cleopatra*) he defeated his old ally Antony in battle, an action that contributed to Antony's suicide.

And so it goes. Shakespeare presented this paradox repeatedly in his history plays and tragedies, and indeed in many of his other plays. But he also presented a paradox for the ages, even for lovers of popular music.

CONSEQUENCES GOOD AND BAD, OLD AND NEW

What man or woman has not felt a lump in the throat when they heard Frank Sinatra sing:

> And now, the end is near;
> And so I face the final curtain.
> My friend, I'll say it clear,
> I'll state my case, of which I'm certain.
>
> I've lived a life that's full.
> I've traveled each and ev'ry highway;
> But more, much more than this,
> I did it my way.[18]

But even his most ardent fans, like me, remember when Sinatra, the Chairman of the Board, banished his old friend Sammy Davis, Jr., from the "Rat Pack." Then we think of other people in Sinatra's life, including his family. Could they do it their way while Frank was doing it his way?

In 1968, I did it my way. I sold my advertising agency and took a 92 percent cut in pay to become a lecturer in business administration, the paramecium of the faculty food chain at the Harvard Business School. It made sense to me, but what about my family? My wife had scrimped for years as I reinvested our profits in the business. Our sons were juniors and seniors in high school. It was tough for all of them while "I did it my way" and was "to mine own self being true"!

As we will see later in the chapter on Falstaff, Shakespeare pummels us almost into insensibility when he has Prince Hal, now King Henry V, cruelly banish his old buddy Falstaff. Hal was being true to himself—and the kingdom—and even though he had given signals that when he became king he would turn "away from my former self," he was terribly false to Falstaff.

Al Dunlap, deposed chairman of Sunbeam Corporation, has been true to himself. Like Iago, Othello's nemesis, he announces his intentions—slash and burn, cut costs with a chainsaw. And he announced his intentions in books, television and radio interviews, presentations to Wall Street. In this context, he was not false to those whose jobs he eliminated—he warned them. But in my view, he was false to many whose jobs were cut in order to prop up the company's short-term results; and those short-term profits were extremely detrimental to the company's growth and future prosperity. And I'm quite certain that the investors who, in March 1998, paid $53 for a share of Sunbeam's stock, which six months later traded at 4¾, feel that Dunlap was false to them.

Donald E. Petersen, CEO of Ford Motor Company from 1980 to 1990, had worked with my late colleague W. Edwards Deming, who persuaded him of the importance of consistently good quality. In late 1980, the entire Ford organization was eagerly awaiting the introduction of the new Ford Escort. "We desperately needed the Escort to prove that Ford could build fine automobiles, especially a fuel-efficient front-wheel-drive car." Red Poling, chief of North American operations, flew to the Escort plant for sign-off on the test run of the first one hundred cars. This was usually pro forma, but he saw that the quality measurements of the new cars "weren't up to par." It cost Ford millions of dollars, but Poling delayed the introduction until the bugs were worked out. "Let us know when you get this straightened out," he said. "We'll start production then, not before." And Petersen backed him up. The investment community was sore, Ford dealers were disappointed, but Petersen was being true to himself—not just because he had committed to

Dr. Deming, but because he had committed to himself that Ford would stand for quality. Was he false to Wall Street and his dealers? In the short term, perhaps, but in the long term, no. Ford was on the way to better market share, better profits, better employee relations because of better quality.[19] This example introduces another dimension in being true to oneself: time.

FALSE TODAY, TRUE TOMORROW

In the early stages of the supermarket chain turnaround that I led, Wall Street was furious at us; our stock price had plummeted in less than a year from the mid-twenties to less than three dollars a share. As I have mentioned before, the founders and I were often at odds with each other, but we stood firm on the premise that, even though we had made mistakes, we were in it for the long haul. We were determined to recapture the loyalty of our customer base, even if it meant that our financial performance would grow slowly for a year or two. And we had turned the corner—we had broken into the black and were naively happy when it was time for a regularly scheduled meeting with our Wall Street analysts. But we were in for a surprise. I remember one hotshot analyst, in his mid-twenties, telling us how to run our stores—raise prices, slash payroll, and cut back on store hours. If we did those things, he assured us, we could show quarter-by-quarter profit improvement, and it would be consistent. While I agreed with him that consistency in earnings stream was important, it wasn't nearly as important as rebuilding trust with our customers. And we were not going to do that by raising prices and slashing payroll. When he argued back, I suggested that he sell his stock. He did—and missed out on an increase from about $2 a share to well over $100 a share when the company was taken private some years later. Doing it "my way" seemed "false" to the analyst and maybe other stockholders at that time, but over the long term it worked out well.

The time dimension makes the paradox even more difficult to resolve. If I, in my infinite wisdom, say to others, "Trust me; everything will work out in the future," then, in theory, I can get away with anything. In practice, of course, it doesn't work that way. More about the time dimension later.

Throughout this book, Tina Packer and I have emphasized that the job of leaders is to stand for something, to make the tough decisions when necessary, and then take the consequences like mature men and women. Tina has taken her lumps and so have I—and have we, at times, become Caesars or any of the characters who are arrogant or false to others while being true to ourselves? Certainly we have, but we have been fortunate enough to have colleagues, friends, and family to pull us back to reality and help us find the balance we needed.

So far, however, we have provided only anecdotes and case histories. Are there any enduring principles—rules to live by, signposts that tell us when we're veering off the road? Like Shakespeare, we don't have any pat answers, nothing you can write on an index card to carry around in your pocket or purse. But we can provide a framework that has been useful to us. We will look first at the work of Ralph Waldo Emerson, the American transcendentalist, to see if he can provide a workable theory to help resolve the inherent conflict between Man Alone—"to thine ownself be true"—and Man in Society—"And it must follow as the night the day / Thou canst not then be false to any man."

EMERSON — THE HALF-RIGHT SOLUTION

In the second act of *Hamlet*, when Polonius says to the young prince, "My lord, I will take my leave of you," Hamlet replies:

> You cannot, sir, take from me anything that I will not more willingly
> part withal—except my life, except my life, except my life.
>
> HAMLET (2.2, 215–17)

Ralph Waldo Emerson would have wanted to get rid of Polonius, too. I can think of nothing that Emerson and Polonius have in common. Polonius is obsequious, dishonest, duplicitous, pandering, and intellectually challenged. Emerson was stalwart, honest to a fault, direct, sometimes rude, and always brilliant. Emerson and his friends in the Transcendentalist school certainly understood "To thine ownself be true." They wrote forcefully about the power and potential of Man Alone. Here is a passage from Emerson's famous and stirring essay "Self-Reliance":

> Where is the master who could have taught Shakespeare? Where is the master who could have instructed Franklin, or Washington, or Bacon, or Newton? Every great man is a unique. The Scipionism of Scipio is precisely that part he could not borrow. Shakespeare will never be made by the study of Shakespeare. Do that which is assigned you, and you cannot hope too much or dare too much.

He also said, in this same essay, "Trust thyself: every heart vibrates to that iron string." As I began this chapter, I thought: Who better than Emerson to solve Polonius's paradox, especially since Emerson also said, "In every work of genius we recognize our own rejected thoughts: they come back to us with a certain alienated majesty."

Then I read the essay more carefully. Emerson spoke beautifully to the first half of the paradox "To thine ownself be true," and I have no evidence at all that he was ever "false" to his friends or family—or any man, for that matter. But then I thought, "What if the world were populated only with Emerson and his friends?" It would be as if the world were populated only with Julius Caesars, all "constant as the northern star." What if the world were populated only by men like Henry VIII, who divorced his faithful wife, Katharine of Aragón, on dubious premises, then did away with two other wives, divorced another (and also had one wife who died in childbirth and only one, the final wife, who managed to outlive him), all while being true to himself? (And, ostensibly, to his kingdom.)

Emerson loved Shakespeare but, I believe, did not understand Polonius's paradox. One of his lines is particularly revealing:

The doctrine of hatred must be preached as the counteraction of the doctrine of love when that pules and whines. I shun father and mother and wife and brother, when my genius calls me.

In fairness to Emerson, that statement is not in context with another part of his essay:

I shall endeavour to nourish my parents, to support my family, to be the chaste husband of one wife.

But this protestation does not recant his central theme: that man should fiercely resist society's influence.

As I pondered Emerson's criticism of society, I recalled some of my most memorable encounters with the mind of this genius. When I was on the faculty of the Harvard Business School, I lived in Weston, Massachusetts, a ten-minute drive to Walden Pond, where Emerson's friend and colleague Henry David Thoreau lived in solitude for two years. On several Sunday mornings, I gathered up the book of Emerson's essays along with a couple of Thoreau's tomes, drove to Walden Pond, found the modest cairn that marked the site of Thoreau's hut, then read for a couple of hours.

While writing this chapter, I reflected on those peaceful Sunday mornings, and it finally dawned on me what was missing in Emerson's advice. It might have been great advice for hermits like Thoreau, a Man Alone, but incomplete for Man in Society, especially leaders and managers, who must influence and be influenced by others. A final glance at Emerson's essay confirmed my suspicion.

Society everywhere is in conspiracy against the manhood of every one of its members. Society is a joint-stock company, in which the members agree, for the better securing of his bread to each shareholder, to surrender the liberty and culture of the eater. The virtue in most request is conformity. Self-reliance is its aversion.

I still agree with many of Emerson's stirring aphorisms about self-reliance, but I don't agree that it is impossible to be self-reliant and a happy and productive member of society at the same time.

———

DOES RELIGION HAVE THE ANSWER?

At first, one would think so. Religion should give us a framework that helps us to know ourselves; it puts us in touch with the ordering force of the universe, whatever that might be. And the great religions also prescribe behavior toward one another. In theory, then, religion alone could give us the answer to Polonius's paradox. But in practice, it has been "weighed in the balance and found wanting."[20] The problem is circular. The problem is not with religion but with man practicing his religion. It was in the name of religion that Henry IV wanted to mount a crusade to the Holy Land to drive out the infidels, a pejorative term for people with a different religion than his. Indeed, Shakespeare gives mixed reviews to men in religion. Cardinal Wolsey, adviser to Henry VIII, is not only dishonest and politically ambitious, but also a procurer. He arranges the bacchanalian party in which Henry meets the beautiful Anne Boleyn (Elizabeth I's mother and a lady-in-waiting to the queen). Wolsey and Campeius, the church's emissary from Rome, play a disgusting role in the king's divorce from Queen Katharine.

Religious leaders in *King Henry V* seem similarly flawed. The Archbishop of Canterbury, hoping to avoid the crown's levy of taxes on the church, produces a tortured analysis of why Henry should conquer France. On the other hand, we see in *King Richard II* the courageous Bishop Carlisle, who is willing to speak his mind, condemning the usurpation of Richard's throne and correctly predicting civil strife if Richard were deposed. Bishop Carlisle is one of the few "good guys" from organized religion in Shakespeare's plays. And Shakespeare, if he had any, was careful to conceal his own religious persuasion. (Some say he died a papist, a dangerous belief in Elizabethan England. Tina thinks he was far beyond worshiping in any one denomination: that his awareness of God was deeply spiritual but not particularly attached to any sect.) However, before and after Shakespeare's time we see how religion has been corrupted by man. And we can confirm that, so far, religion has not given us the answer to Polonius's paradox. In the service of "being true to one's religion," we have seen holy wars, inquisitions, terrorism sanctioned by religious leaders on all sides of the conflict in the Middle East. Machiavelli chronicled the activities of the venal Pope Alexander VI and his son, Cardinal Cesare Borgia. We have also seen the violence with which the ascetic Girolamo Savonarola conducted his inquisitions, opposing venal practices in the church and Italian society. And in the United States, supposedly founded on the precepts of religious freedom, we killed the "witches" in Salem, Massachusetts.

Religious beliefs, like Emerson's advice, have seemed to be helpful in understanding part one of Polonius's advice—"To thine ownself be true" (Man Alone). In theory, they should have been helpful to us in understanding part two—"Thou canst not then be false to any man" (Man in Society). But human intervention is flawed in practice. As we will demonstrate in the following section, when man designs and administers a system, the power is often abrogated to the designer and administrator, who can be counted on to be true to himself, but cannot always be counted on to avoid being "false" to others. To extrapolate from Cassius (in *Julius Caesar*), "The fault, dear Brutus, is not in our *religion*, / But in ourselves, that we are underlings" (italics added).

Religion may play a part in our solution to the paradox, but religion alone has, so far, not been able to solve it.

LET'S *NOT* KILL ALL THE LAWYERS

Through the ages, legal systems have been created in the attempt to adjudicate the inherent conflicts between Man Alone and Man in Society. They have met roughly the same lack of success as religion. Because they have been designed by man (or, in the case of religion, explicated by man), and because they are interpreted and administered by man, the designer (or explicator) tends to be at the apex of the system; therefore, control of the system tends to move to the center. Even the United States Constitution with its Bill of Rights, which was designed to protect individual freedom in the context of society's rights, has failed to stem the flow of power to the center. Whether this is good or bad, just or unjust, is not the issue under discussion. All one need do is look at the tens of thousands of pages of regulations that have transmogrified the intentions of the Constitution's founding fathers. Emerson would be horrified.

Shakespeare had a keen interest in legal governance systems. Anthony Burgess, among others, speculates that the Bard might have spent some early years clerking for a lawyer. Portia's sly tactics in her defense of Antonio in *The Merchant of Venice,* Dick the Butcher's "First thing we do, let's kill all the lawyers" from Jack Cade's rebellion in *King Henry VI, Part 2,* the tortured anguish of the lawyer Angelo in *Measure for Measure,* all reflect Shakespeare's knowledge of the legal profession. In his Roman tragedies and English history plays, he regularly addresses the legal issues raised by Polonius's paradox. He makes certain that we understand that Bolingbroke (the future King Henry IV) has just cause to return from banishment to reclaim his inheritance after Richard II confiscates his dead father's estate. And Shakespeare leaves no doubt in his audience's mind that Richard had abused his power with confiscatory taxation and inequitable distribution of power among his nobles. Governance was a major theme in both *Coriolanus* and *Julius Caesar.* In *Coriolanus,* we see the struggle between the tribunes (representatives of the people) and the Roman Senate, which, the plebs believed, was hoarding corn, thus causing shortages and high prices. Indeed, Elizabethan England suffered from several short famines, so the plight of the Roman plebs had special meaning for the folks standing in the Globe's pit.

Abuse of power—or the threat of it—was the prime mover of action in *Julius Caesar.* But Shakespeare leaves us with no simple notion that only leaders corrupt governance systems: he shows the Roman citizens murdering a hapless poet (who happened to have the same name as one of the conspirators) when they go on the rampage after Mark Antony's speech. Polonius's paradox plagues all—the common folk as well as the high and the mighty—and history has taught us that governance systems alone will not solve it, whether in the Roman Republic, an English monarchy, or the Land of the Free.

What does all this have to do with business? Plenty: every corporate leader I know struggles with the paradox. On the one hand, innovation, today's driver of productivity and progress, is stifled when individual freedom is stifled. On the other hand, a successful business is not an anarchy. It is a society of individuals who should be working for common goals.

Business's religious system is its vision, mission, and values. Its legal system is the body of goals and objectives, policies, practices, and procedures. As in society at large, neither system alone is sufficient. I have seen both for-profit and not-for-profit enterprises with wonderful values but with no sense of direction, no creative energy to drive them forward. And I have also seen enterprises where both systems ("religious" and legal) were in reasonable shape but the motivation wasn't there. It is my opinion that in most underperforming societies, the missing ingredient is the market system, which measures (not in financial terms alone) and rewards (not in money alone) the humans in our society.

CHOICES AND CONSEQUENCES: THE MARKET SYSTEM

What in the world does the market system have to do with William Shakespeare? He died long before Adam Smith or David Ricardo or the Austrian economists, those people so closely associated with free and open markets. And, more to the point of this chapter, what does the market system have to do with Polonius's paradox?

Let's discuss the first question before we proceed further. Shakespeare could not escape the market system. It has existed in some form since man walked upright. Even in hunter-gatherer societies, people divided their labors, each doing what he or she could do best; in collaboration they shared, trading the products of one skill for the products of another. Adam Smith did not invent free enterprise or the unseen hand. He merely observed it, understood it, and then chronicled it beautifully. He demonstrated that although the market system can be tampered with, it cannot be repealed. For example, Elizabethan England was a closely controlled monarchy, with rules and regulations that were inimical to a market system as we know it. The prices farmers could get for agricultural goods were strictly controlled, as was the interest rate at which money could be lent. (Shakespeare's father, the "merchant" of Stratford, was twice fined for lending money at above 10 percent interest.)

Nonetheless, Shakespeare's London was a hotbed of free enterprise and international trade. The fall of Antwerp, across the English Channel, to Spanish armies in 1576 and again in1585, forced the merchants of that city to relocate to Amsterdam. They brought Europe's first stock exchange and Antwerp's set of global trade networks with them. (This critical density of economic activity generated "the embarrassment of riches" that gave birth to investment capitalism there.)[21] In 1600 the British founded the East India Company in response to increased Dutch competition. London tradesmen of all stripes, innkeepers, landlords, street vendors, global merchants (yes, the global economy existed before the twentieth century) flourished or failed depending on chance and fortune, but, what is more important, depending on their industriousness and ability. You may have had to get a license from the crown to import, say, Rhenish wine. But it could be applied for, fought for, held, and traded. Shakespeare's father in Stratford was a glove maker, and by virtue of his trade was probably a butcher and a tanner. His business flourished for a time but also suffered reverses. Shakespeare himself certainly understood the market system. To survive in his trade he had to sell his acting and playwriting ability. We know that he experienced the thrill of a full house, and he probably also experienced that empty feeling when the theater was empty. I'm certain also that, like producers and directors today, he kept tinkering with his productions, adding lines, cutting scenes, until he met the needs of his market. When the playhouses were closed (usually because of an outbreak of plague), the company broke into small groups of actors with reduced scripts, to play the provinces. They kept the cash coming in, one way or another.

So that leads to the second observation: Shakespeare not only wrote Polonius's paradox—Man Alone versus Man in Society—he understood it and he lived it. Moreover, his plays dramatized the paradox—the choices man must make in resolving the tensions between Man Alone and Man in Society. Choices, however, have consequences, and that's what gives life its savor and is certainly what makes Shakespeare's dramas so compelling.

Choices and Consequences

At the heart of the market system is the philosophy that man is free to do as he chooses (within legal and ethical bounds) as long as he is subject to the consequences, whether they be good or bad. Indeed, he or she can act outside legal and ethical boundaries but must expect to take the consequences. Thus, I can rob a bank if I am willing to risk a jail term. I can lie, cheat, and steal if I am willing to be excluded from decent society. Obviously, I am not recommending this course of action, but I am noting that despite legal, ethical, moral, and religious codes, no matter how rigorously they might be administered, some misanthropes still choose to violate them. As much as it would desire to do so, society cannot coerce all people into decent behavior; so, out of necessity, we have prescribed harsh consequences for untoward actions.

Throughout his plays, Shakespeare dramatized his understanding of choices and consequences. Henry IV, as we saw in Chapter 2, was willing to depose Richard II, and he paid the price—a turbulent and troubled fourteen-year reign. He died from exhaustion, worn out by the tensions of kingship. Antonio in *The Merchant of Venice* chose to forfeit a pound of his flesh if he could not repay Shylock's loan. That was the contract he signed. Shylock chose to exact the penalty, and the duke's court of Venice upheld that decision—until Portia (not the first to give lawyers a bad name), disguised as the brilliant Balthazar, shows the court how to avoid the legal murder. Shylock can have Antonio's flesh, but if he draws blood while extracting it, or deviates even by a hair's weight in the measure of it, he will lose both his goods and his life. And for good measure, she points out that any Jew seeking to take a Christian's life will be executed.

Hamlet complained to his college friends that he "lacked advancement," but he did nothing to win the support of those who could help him win the throne. (Denmark at that time had an elected monarchy—elected from within the royal family.) In Chapter 10 we will meet an outrageous but delightful character, Sir John Falstaff, who was bright enough to do anything he wished (he had a title so was not constrained by the class system) but chose to be a wastrel—and he paid the price: he was banished.

In economic terms, we can choose to offer any product or service that suits our fancy, but society can choose either to buy or not to buy it. In governance terms, when people no longer "buy" what the leader wants to "sell," they often choose to depose him—even a leader who might seem to be protected by a legal system, an army, a group of sycophantic nobles, or a friendly board of directors. It usually takes too long to oust an ineffective or despotic ruler, but sooner or later the market works, even, if necessary, in the form of rebellion or revolution. The Romans overthrew the Tarquin king in 510 B.C. and kept the republic together until Julius Caesar's time. When Mark Antony chose Cleopatra over his interest in governance (questionable at best), he was overthrown by Octavius Caesar, who, although he emasculated the Senate, was able to convince enough senators and Roman citizens (their choice) that he was worthy of becoming Caesar Augustus. Prince Hal turned away from his profligate ways and became medieval England's most successful king.

Shakespeare's queen, Elizabeth, was an absolute monarch. In theory, she could do anything she pleased. In practice, however, she knew that even though the "people" might pay a dear price, they could choose to depose her. Of the fourteen monarchs in the two hundred years previous to Elizabeth's reign, only eight died of natural causes,[22] and Charles I, the son of her successor, was beheaded. Elizabeth ruled for forty-five years (1558–1603), not because of a divine right, but because of a divine gift. She hung on because she knew how to satisfy her market. She chose to balance the imperial "we" with common sense. She curried people's favor when necessary, just as she knew how to persevere when tough decisions were required.

The market works for all of us, not just monarchs and CEOs. It certainly worked for Shakespeare. True to himself, he forsook his father's profession—tanner, glove maker, butcher—and hied himself to London to be an actor. Then, as a playwright, he was true to himself by writing about controversial subjects—Richard II's deposition, lunatic leaders, artistic parasites. Yet, as the song goes, he was true to himself "in his fashion" because most of his plays were written to please the commoners, the middle classes, the queen and her court.[23] Without audiences and patrons he might have needed to reconsider the glove-making trade back in Stratford.

Tina Packer, though in the not-for-profit world, knows the economics of choices and consequences. As she has told us, unhappy with the limitations imposed on her interpretation of Shakespeare, she chose to leave a promising career in England and came to the United States, broke but with a vision. Now she is not only interpreting but producing Shakespeare in a way that is authentic to her vision. Knowing her as I do, I am sure she thinks about her audience as she pushes the envelope in her productions. Like Shakespeare, she has to keep the theater full and the patrons interested. She doesn't want to put on productions that no one comes to, but she does want to introduce new perceptions. Where is the balance? It is not unusual for misguided, even well-meaning, people to tamper with the market. Let's look at what happens when they do.

Central Control: The Enemy of Choices and Consequences

Who knows best, the leader or the people? Leaders, of course, believe they know best, and quite often they do. They might have more experience, greater ability, and more information than their followers. So the natural tendency of leaders is to want either to limit or to influence the choices of their followers to those actions that serve the leaders' goals or enterprise. Leaders also want to consolidate their power, using rewards (either extrinsic or intrinsic) and punishment to focus attention on their goals. Often this system works well. Good leaders do make a difference. I have served on several boards of directors where leadership changes at the top transformed the organizations from tarnished losers to sleek and shining winners. *But I have noticed also that the most enduringly successful leaders acknowledge that the collective experience, ability, and information of their followers are orders of magnitude greater than their own.* My friend and colleague E. T. "Bud" Gravette, former chairman and CEO of the Turner Corporation, certainly understood this verity. He was no stranger to the construction industry, but he had never led a troubled $4 billion construction business. Bud drew on his considerable experience in banking and his sound understanding of good management practices. His genius, however, was his ability to unleash the considerable talents of Turner's senior and middle managers. As the turnaround progressed, we on the board of directors came to realize that the dozens of names we had known only as positions on the organization chart were indeed formidable leaders in their own right. Bud gave them responsibility, authority, and tools; he also distributed rich rewards when they were deserved. Like any wise leader, Bud modestly acknowledged that "they"—the managers—had accomplished the turnaround. We on the board knew, however, that just as Bud could not have accomplished the turnaround without them, they could not have accomplished it without him. Too few leaders understand this simple, but profound, notion. Like Al Dunlap and other infamous hatchet men, they are blinded by the corona of power. They begin to think that they alone are the saviors of the businesses they run. Like Julius Caesar, Richard II, and King Lear, they embrace the doctrine of their own infallibility. They shut out the collective wisdom of their followers.

Shakespeare had no blind admiration for mobs, but he put wise words in the mouths of commoners. In the opening scene of *Julius Caesar* he shows us that the commoners were not clay merely to be molded by the leader's wishes but, indeed, were capable of matching wits with their "betters." The tribunes Flavius and Marullus are trying to force the tradesmen to go back to their homes, rather than attend Caesar's victory parade. Here is an interchange that should sober any leader who believes that he or she, alone, has the wit, wisdom, and intellect to lead. Marullus and Flavius are questioning a cobbler:

MARULLUS   But what trade art thou? Answer me directly.

COBBLER   A trade, sir, that, I hope I may use with a safe conscience; which is, indeed, sir, a mender of bad soles . . .

FLAVIUS   Thou art a cobbler, art thou?

COBBLER   . . . I am, indeed, sir, a surgeon to old shoes: when they are in great danger, I recover them . . .

FLAVIUS   But wherefore art not in thy shop today?
Why dost thou lead these men about the streets?

COBBLER   Truly, sir, to wear out their shoes, to get myself into more work.

JULIUS CAESAR (1.1, 12–31)

Earlier, in our discussion of *King Richard II*, we noted the wisdom of the gardener and the servant who were commenting on Richard's inattention to his "garden," England. King Lear ignores the wisdom not only of the noble, Kent, but also of his Fool. Shakespeare chronicled what nobles, past and present, know instinctively but are often reluctant to acknowledge—that they need a court jester to tell them things that others are afraid to utter. Here is Lear's Fool remonstrating with his master, who, foolishly, has divided his kingdom in half and given it to two selfish daughters:

FOOL   That lord that counselled thee to give away thy land,
Come place him here by me; do thou for him stand.
The sweet and bitter fool will presently appear,
The one in motley here, the other found out there.

KING LEAR (1.4, 137–40)

My paternal grandfather was a scholar-philosopher and mathematician, and my maternal grandfather was a sharecropping cotton farmer in East Texas. Neither was a leader of a great enterprise— one was an "intellectual," the other worked with his hands—but both, and their ilk, had collective wit, wisdom, and intellect that far surpassed that of the "choice and master spirits of their age."

Hamlet nails it absolutely with his meditation on man:

> . . . What a piece of work is a man, how noble in reason, how infinite in faculties, in form and moving how express and admirable, in action how like an angel, in apprehension how like a god: the beauty of the world, the paragon of animals . . .
>
> HAMLET (2.2, 305–309)

Infinite is the key word for me in this passage. The permutation of the experience, ability, and information of humankind is indeed infinite and beyond control, no matter how wise and powerful the center might be.

But unfortunately, Lord Acton's timeworn phrase "Power tends to corrupt and absolute power corrupts absolutely" too often holds true. As leaders reinforce the doctrine of their own infallibility, they centralize power and decision making. Like the sun, they control the movement of everything in their orbit. That's fine for planets and moons, but a loser for human beings.

President Nixon's Folly

I'll never forget an evening in August 1971. We were hosting a lawn party for the visiting committee (comparable to a board of overseers) at the dean's house at the Harvard Business School. Just before dessert was served, one of our colleagues stepped out of the house to report on a phone call he had received. President Nixon had just announced price controls on selected commodities. The shock was palpable. Some of the world's most powerful business leaders and some reasonably good economists (faculty guests at the dinner) declined strawberries and ice cream to sort out the impact of Nixon's action. I was soon to experience the impact firsthand, for only a few months later, I left my post as associate dean to become president of Pathmark Supermarkets, headquartered in New Jersey. Nixon's price controls were a bureaucratic nightmare. We spent days in Washington listening to government staff members who were trying to explain the regulations. I remember one officious young man, in his late twenties, who was explaining the latest regulation on meat prices. As he talked, it began to dawn on us that he did not know the difference between pork and veal, yet his decisions would have enormous impact, not only on producers but also on consumers. I remember, also, listening to a cattle producer, who asked, "How can I control the price of beef when I have no control over my costs: the increasing price of land rental, corn, gasoline, and wages? It's like trying to hold the lid on a kettle of boiling water. Sooner or later, something will blow up." And, as we all know now, it did. The market system had been tampered with. Price controls were a disaster. Many years later, when I wrote *The Economics of Trust*, I wrote the sentence "The market system is more effective than any system designed by man." When my editor suggested that I meant "better than any *other* system designed by man," I replied firmly, "No, leave it the way it is and let's be sure also that some well-meaning copy editor doesn't stick in the word *other* while we're not looking." The point is this: the market system, which generally works best without central intervention, had been tampered with by a well-meaning president. I had voted for President Nixon, admired his foreign policy skills, was disgusted by Watergate, and was furious over his price controls. The price controls failure demonstrated again that large, complex governance systems designed and centrally administered by man will not solve Polonius's paradox. What might have been good for beef eaters was bad for consumers of other commodities. Producers and retailers had to raise prices on other products in order to stay in business. And because beef producers had reduced their herds, prices rose abnormally after controls were removed.

One person or one group of persons, brilliant as they might be, can never know enough about all human activities to centrally administer large systems. (Remember the bureaucrat who did not know the difference between veal and pork.)

Shakespeare: The Practical Economist

Economics, as a formal social science, did not exist in Elizabethan England, but Shakespeare commented pithily on a raging economic debate of the time: lending money at interest. At issue was central control. Charging interest on loans was illegal in pre-Elizabethan times; however, in 1575, the Privy Council allowed money to be lent at no more than 10 percent interest. (This was the law for which Shakespeare's father was fined.) Shakespeare's most famous comment on this controversy was, of course, in *The Merchant of Venice*. While Shylock demands no interest for the loan of three thousand ducats, there is a forfeit if it is not repaid on time: a pound of flesh. Is a pound of flesh more or less than 10 percent? That purveyor of bad advice, Polonius, weighed in on the issue also:

> Neither a borrower nor a lender be,
> For loan oft loses both itself and friend,
> And borrowing dulls the edge of husbandry.
>
> HAMLET (1.3, 75–77)

This advice would not only quash economic growth but would put business school professors on welfare and would turn New York City back into a bucolic farming community.

I have no idea whether President Nixon had read *The Merchant of Venice*, but if he had let the market correct itself—as it almost always does—he would not have exacerbated the situation with price controls that in the end cost the economy much more than a pound of flesh.

The Nonsolution Solution

It would be easier to spin straw into gold than it would be to phrase a simple, straightforward answer to Polonius's paradox. I am aware that I am following a time-honored scholarly tradition—taking liberty with the Bard's intentions or ascribing intentions he might never have had—but I like to think that he would agree that although there is no solution to the paradox, there is an approximation to a solution. If we take the best features of legal governance systems and the nonpolitical aspects of the great religious systems and mix them judiciously with the market system, we might gain some useful insights. The legal and religious systems prescribe a duty to your neighbors and community and proscribe certain antisocial and unethical behavior, while the market system allows us to choose our actions within those restraints. The recent resounding failures of collectivist systems that centralized power, abolished religion, limited choices, and ameliorated consequences for their citizens should convince us of what the classical economists have known all along: The system works best when man has freedom of choice as well as the freedom to accept the consequences, good or bad.

Now, old Polonius, rest in peace. Instead of Hamlet's epitaph, we should say thanks to the man whose bad example and foolish aphorism made us think more carefully about one of our greatest dilemmas, the reconciliation of Man Alone and Man in Society.

The Business Application

This chapter raises important questions for businessmen and -women. The overriding question is this: Is a business (which is a somewhat closed society) analogous to society as a whole; specifically, a society where people are relatively free to choose, where they are not conscripted or enslaved? Is freedom in business the same as freedom in society? The corollary questions are these: First, how much freedom to decide, then act, should individuals have within a business enterprise? Second, is the market system's process for measuring and then rewarding the activities of individuals—choices and consequences—also applicable to business enterprises?

Let's address the corollary questions first. How much freedom should individuals have within a business? I have found that the best performing businesses are those that not only give lip service to the concept of individual freedom but are headed by a leadership team capable of understanding the problems that arise from the tensions of organizing a group of independent thinkers. These leaders abjure the comfort of rigid command and control for the more demanding—and lively—task of encouraging creativity and commitment rather than conformity. The reason for this is straightforward: it encourages innovation. Innovation not only in a technical sense, but also in services, systems, and—equally important—finding new ways to respond to customers' wants and needs. Innovation was important in Shakespeare's day—witness the Golden Age—and is crucial today. And innovation often comes from people closest to the points of contact—closest to the customers and closest to the work being done. Senior leaders are often too far removed from the points of contact to initiate meaningful innovation.

Regarding the second question (is the measurement and reward system in business analogous to that of the market), the answer is yes! There is a counterpart to the market's system of measurement and reward in the business organization. (The answer would be a provisional no in a collectivist or totalitarian state and would have been a weak yes in medieval times, when people's choices were limited.) But in most of today's world—even in some collectivist societies—the market rewards the work. You are paid for what you do. If people feel that their efforts are measured improperly or their rewards are inappropriate, they can change jobs. I am not recommending quarterly or annual job changes. I *am* saying that the fact that people are free to choose their places of employment brings the market into play. Few companies can, for long, underreward their employees, either in monetary terms or in recognition and job satisfaction.

The answer to the overriding question "Is business analogous to society as a whole?" is also yes, with the caveats we have expressed. True to Polonius's paradox, there are always constraints, boundaries, and limits. Individuals in business, like people in society, need to act in support of the enterprise's values, mission, goals, and objectives. In society it means we need to think deeply about the education of our young—on every level of society—and how we handle the problems of the sick and the incapacitated. In business we need to think about the far-reaching effects of what we do, as well as short-term gains. We should all act within the framework of the enterprise's policies, practices, and procedures; and we must encourage improvement of policies, practices, and procedures when they are inappropriate or repressive.

The society, and the business, that performs best is populated by experienced, able, informed leaders who are willing to acknowledge that the collective experience, abilities, information, and understanding of those they lead far surpasses their own. That is the key to leading people in the market system.

9

The Choice and Master Deceivers of Their Age

What's Fair in Love, War, and Business

> Is he a lamb? His skin is surely lent him,
> For he's inclin'd as is the ravenous wolves.
> Who cannot steal a shape that means deceit?
> Queen Margaret in KING HENRY VI, PART 2 (3.1, 77–79)

> . . . one may smile, and smile, and be a villain—
> HAMLET (1.5, 108)

MARK Antony called Brutus and Cassius the "choice and master spirits of their age." But Brutus, Cassius, and Mark Antony were

212

all out to deceive, and they led Rome into chaos. Which are you? A firm spirit or a deceiver?

Deception is at the center of all of Shakespeare's tragedies. Without Iago's deceit, *Othello* would have been merely the story of an interracial marriage. Without the element of deceit in *King Lear,* literature would have missed out on one of its greatest villains—Edmund, Gloucester's bastard son, who convinces his father that his legitimate son, Edgar, is going to kill him. In *Hamlet,* Claudius deceives Hamlet, but so does Polonius. Even Ophelia deceives Hamlet, knowing that her father is spying on them. Macbeth deceives King Duncan, Cressida deceives Troilus, Richard III deceives just about everybody; so does Rosalind in *As You Like It.* And so it goes.

Shakespeare recognized the dramatic possibilities of deception, and in so doing forces us to think about its pragmatic and moral complexities in our own lives. Iago, Richard III, and Edmund are examples of people who use deception for purely evil purposes. Rosalind uses it for good and for love. Claudius deceives Hamlet with murderous intent, while Hamlet deceives Rosencrantz and Guildenstern, he feels, in self-defense and retribution. But what about Cleopatra when she turns her back on Antony in order to entice him? Is that kind of deception allowed? What about Prince John in *King Henry IV, Part 2,* who promises to redress "these griefs" of the rebel leaders, who thereupon disband their troops—and when they are without weapons and troops, John arrests them?

Deception seems acceptable sometimes, and not at others. What Shakespeare shows is the complexity of power and its necessities; sometimes, he seems to be saying, what might seem evil (that is, deceit) is necessary. It was an extraordinary—and shocking—insight for the Elizabethan era. In Shakespeare's day, most people were Christians and committed to the moral teachings of the church. While practical politicians, military men, or businesspeople understood that lying and deceit were a fact of life, most would have argued that such actions were wrong. Niccolò Machiavelli changed that. In *The Prince,* completed in 1517 and well known when Shakespeare wrote his first known play just seventy-six years later, Machiavelli argued that though the Christian ethic of "love thy neighbor" was supposed to dominate civilized behavior, in the real world those who "turned the other cheek" got conquered. His point: You could be a good Christian, but it was unlikely that in a world where the odds were in favor of the strong and self-interested, you would end up a Christian with power. The church was full of powerful men, but how many were true Christians? The "Machiavel" became a stock stage character in the morality plays that preceded Shakespeare, a purely evil character with no saving traits. (The future Richard III describes himself as a superior Machiavel:)

> Why, I can smile, and murder whiles I smile,
> And cry 'Content!' to that that grieves my heart,
> And wet my cheeks with artificial tears,
> And frame my face to all occasions . . .
> I can add colours to the chameleon,
> Change shapes with Proteus for advantages,
> And set the murderous Machiavel to school.
> Can I do this, and cannot get a crown?
> Tut! were it further off, I'll pluck it down.
>
> KING HENRY VI, PART 3 (3.2, 182–95)

Machiavelli might have proved to us that self-interest makes the world go round, but it was Shakespeare who advanced our understanding of evil by showing that villainy is more psychologically complex than previous writers knew. This insight into the motivation of powerful kings and others who wanted to be powerful kings better helps us understand how the quest for power and the use of deceit can lead us astray.

But how do you know when you've crossed the line? Shakespeare had no black-and-white rules. And neither do we. A thoughtful and ethically minded manager is likely to know when some deceit might be useful (and harmless) while another ploy crosses the line into unethical or even illegal business practices. One thing, however, Tina and I are sure about: a little deceit tends to open up the gates for more deceit. And while not all actions of deceit may be wrong, deceit will have its social costs. Trust vanishes, and the social consequences are large. As a playwright, Shakespeare avoids moralizing. "Shakespeare speaks for his characters," explains the Dartmouth scholar Peter Saccio, "but they do not speak for Shakespeare."

Yet in exploring the possibilities of deception, Shakespeare seems to come closest to giving us his moral opinion, if only by implication. The great deceivers in Shakespeare's plays tend to come to a bad end.

WHEN IS DECEPTION ACCEPTABLE? WHEN IS IT NOT?

Like Shakespeare, Tina and I are not going to give you definitive answers to this question, and, like Socrates, we will answer the question with a question—four questions, in fact. We are aware that Socrates, according to some traditional scholars, was forced to drink the cup of hemlock because he would never answer his own queries about virtue, goodness, and beauty except with a counter-query. We'll take our chances on the hemlock and ask you to ponder the following as you read this chapter:

- Is deception acceptable if it harms no one?
- Is deception acceptable if it does no harm to someone who trusts you?
- Is deception acceptable if it harms someone who intends to harm you?
- Is deception acceptable if it does not harm you or someone who trusts you?

Consider this dilemma: For the third time in two years, the product category that you manage has been outmaneuvered. You had a good product in your R&D pipeline, but you didn't push for it. The fact is, you knew that the cost of this product's introductory marketing would have put the profit plan for your product line at risk. However, as it turned out, the real risk was in not rushing the product into the marketplace. Your market share dropped from 10 to 7; the profit shortfall for the period was $5 million.

As you take the long walk to the corner office to explain what went wrong, you can't help thinking about the new house you bought last month and the college tuition for your two kids. But then you remember something: at the first quarterly review, the R&D director of your company was criticized because products were not moving out of the pipeline on time. As you approach your boss's office, you stop to consider three possible explanations you might offer: (1) You come clean and admit that you were outmaneuvered by the competition, and immediately outline your recovery plan; (2) You say that you didn't push the new product because R&D screwed up; (3) You come clean, but, as you're discussing your recovery plan, you drop an innuendo about the problems in R&D and also mention that pressure for short-term performance had caused several other product managers to delay the introduction of new products.

To deceive or not to deceive? It is a common dilemma for managers at every level. When I ask the participants in my executive seminars to vote for solution 1, 2, or 3 in this new product foul-up, most vote for 1. Coming clean, they explain, is, after all, the "manly" thing to do. I push them: "You wouldn't mention the R&D pipeline at all?" Some respond by asking me more questions about the R&D problems. Others inquire about the nature of the two preceding miscues in marketing. A few realists in the seminar ask about the job market for category managers. Others chime in with comments along the line of "I'll do whatever it takes to preserve my job. I won't take the rap for an inflexible budget system and a screwed-up R&D department. That's management's responsibility." When I point out that the job title "category manager" implies that *you* are part of management, the typical reply is "They make policy, we just follow it."

The proper answer to the category manager's problem is, in my opinion, 1. He could have worked with R&D to get the product out. If his efforts had failed, at least he tried. And the problems in R&D are already well known. There's no need for him to beat a sick horse.

Consider some other examples on the scale of deceit:

- Announcing plans for a new plant that you know will never be built. But you do know the announcement will dissuade competitors from adding to their capacity.
- Announcing a price increase that forces your competitors to follow with higher prices—and then you undercut their prices.
- In a turnaround, you assure customers, bankers, and employees that everything is going to be just fine when you yourself don't have a clue.
- A pharmaceutical company sells essentially the same drug as a competitor—except that the competitor's drug is better and they know it. Nevertheless, the company raises the sales manager's revenue target by 10 percent. If you're the sales manager, what do you do? What do you tell your sales team to do?

Moving down the continuum of deception a bit:

- You're in a job interview and you resist giving a balanced appraisal of your strengths and weaknesses.
- In a performance review, you do not inform an employee that he is on a path toward getting fired because, at the moment, you do not have anyone to fill his spot.
- Your advertising hypes a product's positive features but is silent about its negative ones.
- You create expensive packaging for a ho-hum product.

Finally, let's move to the ridiculous:

- Should women wear high heels, lipstick, and hair color to present themselves better in public?
- Should men use elevator shoes, suits with padded shoulders, and hair color to present themselves better in public?

There is deception, and there is deception. Absent all deceit, the spider could not trap a fly, the chameleon could not catch a bug, and the triggerfish would starve. Only in a utopia (Greek for "no place"), where there are no adversaries or unrequited love, could we live without some measure of deception. In some instances, deception is clearly acceptable. In others, it is wrong. And in many cases, reasonable (and ethical) people might disagree.

How do you know when you've crossed the line? Often only some hard analysis and thought will tell you, factoring in your company's goals, your values, and the standards of your business and times. Let's look at another example more closely.

"Everyone Does It"

You hate your job. You're working for a medium-sized high-tech company and don't get the recognition you think you deserve. More important, you believe that the CEO's use of other people's patents has bordered on the unethical (maybe even illegal). You've decided to leave to start your own firm. To make it work, you'll need the talents of five of your present colleagues. Your dilemma: *Do you recruit them before you quit and take the plunge into your new business, or do you take your chances and wait until after you resign?*

When I present this case to the participants in my executive seminars, the number of those who would recruit colleagues before resigning is shocking. Their various justifications:

- The CEO's not recognizing you for your good work and it's clear he doesn't trust you, so why should you do him any favors?
- There's no such thing as "loyalty" in corporations anymore. They get rid of good people for cynical reasons, so why should employees be loyal to the corporation?
- You could be fired at any moment, so you'd better make a move in your own self-interest.
- You suspect unethical behavior and therefore owe the company nothing.
- Everyone else does it.

The last excuse is particularly lame—but common. When I ask the members of the seminar how they would feel if an employee recruited the top aides for his new company under their noses, they reply that they would be furious and justifiably so. Why? Because they would not act that callously or dishonestly. My next question is "Should the boss pay you if he believes that you would do him harm?" A shrug is what I tend to get. Then I raise two more possibilities: "Don't you have to be absolutely sure the CEO has been dishonest or unethical?" "Shouldn't you have both sides of the story? Maybe there's a good reason this disgruntled employee has not been properly recognized." They tend to stumble a bit over those two points but usually remain firm in their opinion that the employee in this case would be acting properly if he recruited colleagues before quitting.

Then I pose another case—from Shakespeare's *Julius Caesar.* The play begins with the city of Rome in political turmoil. Caesar's various successes on the battlefield have made him without question the most powerful man in Rome. Before the action of the play, Caesar has solidified his political position by packing the Roman Senate with his supporters. The question is: How much power does Caesar want? His critics and enemies believe he wants to extend his power by restoring the monarchy with himself as king—a highly illegal move. Even Brutus, a close associate of Caesar, is profoundly concerned.

Ordinarily, Brutus might have raised the issue on the floor of the Roman Senate. But Cassius, motivated by his own deep and abiding dislike of Caesar, argues that this is a crisis situation, and Caesar must be destroyed swiftly before he destroys the Roman Republic. He needs Brutus's credibility on his side. To put a stop to Caesar's ambition, Cassius, ironically, appeals to Brutus's ambition:

> Men at some time are masters of their fates:
> The fault, dear Brutus, is not in our stars,
> But in ourselves, that we are underlings.
> Brutus and Caesar: what should be in that 'Caesar'?
> Why should that name be sounded more than yours?
>
> JULIUS CAESAR (1.2, 137–41)

You, too, can be a star! How many times have managers used words similar to Cassius's to lure someone to their company? Notice how much this appeal to Brutus also sounds like a pitch to a colleague to join him in a new venture that will dwarf the ungrateful company they're working for (or bury it). Cassius and his gang need the stature and credibility of a man like Brutus, who, as one conspirator notes,

> . . . sits high in all the people's hearts:
> And that which would appear offence in us,
> His countenance, like richest alchemy,
> Will change to virtue and to worthiness.
>
> JULIUS CAESAR (1.3, 157–60)

Equally important, Brutus has the republican spirit in his blood. Cassius cleverly brings up Brutus's ancestor, who ran the last king out of Rome almost five hundred years before:

> O, you and I have heard our fathers say,
> There was a Brutus once that would have brook'd
> Th'eternal devil to keep his state in Rome
> As easily as a king.
>
> JULIUS CAESAR (1.2, 156–59)

The fish eyes the hook. Brutus admits that he has had similar thoughts "of this and of these times." He says of himself that

> Brutus had rather be a villager
> Than to repute himself a son of Rome
> Under these hard conditions as this time
> Is like to lay upon us.
>
> JULIUS CAESAR (1.2, 170–73)

And so Brutus is ready to take the bait. Like the executive in the case I cited, he is unhappy with the state of the current leadership, and, like the participants in my executive seminars, Brutus is inclined to think more about himself than others. Do you hear in Brutus's words a hint of the modern refrain "Everyone does it"? Brutus, however, tells Cassius that he will think about his proposal.

Think about it he did! Indeed, in Brutus's soliloquy in his orchard, Shakespeare shows us how a man can justify murder with no evidence. (In a mere twenty-six lines!)

Brutus points out that he has no personal reason to kill Caesar, his friend:

> It must be by his death: and for my part,
> I know no personal cause to spurn at him,
> But for the general. He would be crown'd:
> How that might change his nature, there's the question.
>
> JULIUS CAESAR (2.1, 10–13)

So the justification comes down to the extent of Caesar's ambition. The crown, Brutus notes, "might change his nature." But he doesn't know that. It's mere speculation. Brutus has no hard evidence that Caesar intends to make himself king of Rome. It will take real imagination on Brutus's part to join a conspiracy to kill Caesar, and Brutus's imagination seems up to the task:

> It is the bright day that brings forth the adder,
> And that craves wary walking. Crown him?—that;—
> And then, I grant, we put a sting in him,
> That at his will he may do danger with.
>
> JULIUS CAESAR (2.1, 14–17)

Brutus thus convinces himself that while he has no evidence that Caesar is a snake, he is at least a potential snake—and Brutus is willing to appoint himself Rome's St. Patrick. He reinforces his resolve with these words:

> Th'abuse of greatness is when it disjoins
> Remorse from power.
>
> JULIUS CAESAR (2.1, 18–19)

This is a beautifully crafted and profound observation worthy of the good philosopher that Brutus was supposed to be. Unfortunately (and tragically), Brutus transmogrifies it into the central premise to justify Caesar's assassination. Without firm evidence, he persuades himself that Caesar "may do danger"; that Caesar "may" climb the ladder of ambition and turn his back on those who helped him make his ascent. In short, Caesar's ambition is bound to make him hateful and dangerous to the Roman Republic. Shakespeare sticks with the snake metaphor:

> And therefore think him as a serpent's egg,
> Which, hatch'd, would, as his kind, grow mischievous,
> And kill him in the shell.
>
> JULIUS CAESAR (2.1, 32–34)

Brutus has decided to join the conspiracy. He will deceive Caesar, a man who trusts him as a colleague and friend, *even though he has no hard evidence.* (In fact, as we saw in the previous chapter, there is hard evidence to the contrary: Caesar refused the offer of a crown three times in front of the Roman people.)

Now think back to the case of our disgruntled employee who decides to recruit colleagues for his new business before he tells his ungrateful and unethical boss to stick it. Is that boss really unethical? There is no hard evidence. And while this employee may think that he deserves more recognition, his boss may have a different take on his performance.

And what about secretly lining up fellow employees to join a new venture, deceiving a boss who trusts them?

Shakespeare would call that a *conspiracy.* And so would I. Conspiracy is not only illegal, it carries stiff penalties. A surprising number of students in my executive seminars don't seem to see the deceit of recruiting among colleagues before resigning to form another company as a conspiracy—until I point it out to them. When all those employees walk out the door to form their own company, their boss would not be out of line to say "Et tu, Brute!" And then get on the phone to the company lawyer.

DEFENSIVE DECEPTION

And what about Mark Antony's clear act of deception? Is that morally acceptable? Antony persuades Brutus to allow him to speak, claiming to have "come to bury Caesar, not to praise him." And then he proceeds to praise Caesar and do his best to bury Brutus and Cassius. After Caesar's assassination, he has good reason to fear for his life. Cassius wanted to kill Antony along with Caesar on the Ides of March, but Brutus argued that with Caesar out of the way, Antony would be harmless. Cassius acquiesces. But why on earth would Brutus and Cassius give Antony the podium after Caesar's death?

Immediately after Caesar has been killed, Antony sends a servant to Brutus with a message that is full of respect for Brutus, who is, says Antony, "noble, wise, valiant, and honest." Antony has told the servant to say "I love Brutus, and I honour him." And here's his deal:

> If Brutus will vouchsafe that Antony
> May safely come to him, and be resolv'd
> How Caesar hath deserv'd to lie in death,
> Mark Antony . . . will follow
> The fortunes and affairs of noble Brutus
> Thorough the hazards of this untrod state,
> With all true faith.

> JULIUS CAESAR (3.1, 130–37)

Cassius is nervous about Antony. But Brutus welcomes him because Antony has read Brutus correctly. He knows that above all Brutus wants to appear fair and honest. Antony uses Brutus's vanity. When Antony arrives at the scene of the crime, Caesar's body is still there. He knows it will undercut his credibility with the conspirators and the crowd if he tries to cover up his genuine horror and grief at seeing Caesar dead. His opening lines are addressed not to Brutus or Cassius but to the corpse of Caesar and paint a famous image of how easily death overwhelms glory:

> O mighty Caesar! dost thou lie so low?
> Are all thy conquests, glories, triumphs, spoils,
> Shrunk to this little measure?
>
> JULIUS CAESAR (3.1, 148–50)

When Antony finally turns to Brutus and Cassius, it is to offer his own life:

> No place will please me so, no mean of death,
> As here by Caesar, and by you cut off,
> The choice and master spirits of this age.
>
> JULIUS CAESAR (3.1, 161–63)

How about that scraping bow to Cassius and Brutus—"The choice and master spirits of this age"? It would be downright ungracious to kill a man who has described you so handsomely. Brutus, always the gull, replies:

> O Antony, beg not your death of us! . . .
> To you our swords have leaden points . . .
>
> JULIUS CAESAR (3.1, 164, 173)

Brutus and Cassius express their respect for Antony, who shakes "the bloody hand" of Brutus, Cassius, and the other conspirators. From the moment he arrives, Antony has been disarming—dissimulating, deceiving, and flattering—his adversaries, and should they now have second thoughts about Antony's battlefield conversion, he quickly confronts any doubts about his motivation head-on:

> Gentlemen all—alas, what shall I say?
> My credit now stands on such slippery ground,
> That one of two bad ways you must conceit me,
> Either a coward, or a flatterer.
>
> JULIUS CAESAR (3.1, 190–93)

Antony then launches into another paean to his dead friend, which understandably unsettles the conspirators. (Remember, all this is still happening in public, in the Roman Senate.) Cassius wonders whether Antony, with his allegiance to Caesar, can still be "a friend." Antony looks these murderers in the eye and says, "Friends am I with you all, and love you all" (*Julius Caesar* [3.1, 220]).

Antony's goal is the opportunity to speak at Caesar's funeral. Once he attains that goal, he becomes the conspirators' canniest enemy. He turns the crowd violently against Brutus and Cassius and passionately in support of him.

WHATEVER HAPPENED TO "TRUTH IN ADVERTISING"?

Shakespeare is forever proving to us that there is very little new in human nature—or business. In *Troilus and Cressida*, Hector, Troy's most revered warrior, issues a challenge to the Greeks that he will take on any one of their warriors in hand-to-hand combat. He expects Achilles, the preeminent fighter among the Greeks, to accept this challenge. Crafty Ulysses, who three years later would design the famous Trojan Horse, had a better idea: send out Ajax, Greece's lumbering giant. If Ajax can beat Hector, well and good. If not, the Greeks can trot out their number one contender, Achilles. Shakespeare has Ulysses explain his ploy in a way that would be easy for any modern businessperson to understand:

> . . . Let us like merchants
> First show foul wares, and think perchance they'll sell:
> If not,
> The lustre of the better shall exceed
> By showing the worse first.
>
> TROILUS AND CRESSIDA (1.3, 358–61)

Truth in advertising? There is no such thing—at least not the whole truth. When I was in the advertising business, we used to claim, "The purpose of advertising is to inform." I think we were being disingenuous. There were always limits to how much information about our products we were willing to give. Recently, I attended a board of directors meeting of a consumer products company. The company has an outstanding record and a deserved reputation for honesty. However, one of our products that was designed to be environmentally friendly is not as efficacious as a competitor's leading product. Will our advertising ever say, "Incidentally, this product is not as good as theirs"? I don't expect so. In fact, millions of customers already have figured this out on their own; they have elected protecting the environment over efficiency, and thus we are the number two brand in that category. Niche players can be successful in spoofing the shortcomings of their products while extolling their virtues. But anyone battling for market share with the proximate goal of creating value for shareholders cannot afford that risk.

Or can we? Each year, we, our competitors, and other advertisers have to spend more and more to move our products, even though we do engage in "legally" deceptive advertising. Deceptive advertising is big business, not only for the direct players but also for lawyers, government regulators, and copy acceptance departments at radio and television stations that have to answer the question: What is deceptive and what is not?

The fact is that customers have already taken their position on advertising: they don't trust advertisers to tell the truth, the whole truth, and nothing but the truth. And because consumers don't trust us, we have probably harmed ourselves and our shareholders by spending so much on advertising no one believes anymore. Three or four points shaved from our marketing costs would look very nice on the bottom line.

The Price of Deception

Why are the students in my seminars so willing to overlook a conspiracy? Why do we put up with so much deceptive advertising? "Everyone does it." And, sadly, almost everyone does. It's as if we've fallen into a nationwide pit of self-deception. We've convinced ourselves that all sorts of things on the borderline of the ethical and illegal are merely business as usual.

As general moral standards have fallen, so have our business ethics. And we pay a large social price. Because deception is so pervasive and because it comes in so many forms, we are conditioned to mistrust almost everything and everyone—politicians, journalists, business executives, union leaders, advertisers, salespeople, even the clerk at the checkout counter. The emotional burden of such widespread mistrust is bound to weigh us down. The machinery of living gets clogged up.

The economic cost is also substantial. My own studies of mistrust in organizations show that more than half of their activities—and thus the costs of those activities—are unnecessary, in part because of incompetence, but also because of fear of deception.[24] Witness expense accounts, insurance claims, time clocks, write-ups for screwups, and a host of other personnel-related activities. How much of our marketing costs are due to the fact that potential customers do not believe us anymore? Fear of deception prompts restrictive work rules, exhaustive checking of references for new hires, all that memo writing (particularly memos to file). Much of the regulatory reporting required by local, state, and federal agencies assumes that we are criminals, and to prove that we are not we must spend an enormous amount of time and money.

Worse still, deception and fear of it muddles our communications. Information needed for effective business operations is often masked, misrepresented, or garbled. When information is guarded or garbled, innovation is stifled. And without innovation, you are soon out of business.

THE FATAL FLAW: SELF-DECEPTION

Notice how Shakespeare's great practitioners of deception tend to deceive one person the most—themselves. Antony deceives himself into thinking he can simultaneously rule the Roman Empire and be ruled by his passion for Cleopatra. Brutus talks himself into believing that Cassius wants to assassinate Caesar for the good of

Rome and not for self-interest. He also deceives himself into thinking that Antony will not try to attack him in his funeral oration for Caesar. And Shakespeare's self-deceivers tend to play a terrible personal price: Hamlet, King Lear, Macbeth, Richard III, King John, Julius Caesar, Mark Antony. Brutus is the most tragic figure, in my opinion. He deceives himself into the notion that Caesar should die; he deceives himself that Antony will legitimize his conspiracy against Caesar. And Brutus also deceives himself into believing he is a great battle commander, ignoring Cassius's advice to dig in, stay put, and fight from a position of strength. Even Antony concedes at the end of *Julius Caesar* that Brutus intended to do the right thing. Brutus's tragedy was that he failed to grasp the fact that his co-conspirators had their own interests in mind and not Rome's. For this act of self-deception, Brutus died.

Again, Shakespeare seems to be warning us all, this time against self-deception. But who has not succumbed? Think back to the category manager deciding whether to come clean about missing his target or implicate his colleagues in R&D. Think about the person deciding whether or not to conspire against his boss by recruiting his associates before leaving to start his own business. Think of the times we have concocted excuses for being tardy. Even courteous white lies, when they become integral to our behavior, could cause us to become panderers or flatterers.

Tina and I said that we would not answer the four questions posed earlier, but we have given you some hints. Let's look first at questions two, three, and four.

Is deception acceptable if it does no harm to someone who trusts you?

This compound question might be as difficult as solving a simple equation with two variables. What is deception and what is harm? What if there are unforeseen and unintended consequences? On the one hand, Cleopatra's coquettishness with Antony seems harmless enough, as does the courteous white lie "John, you haven't aged a bit." If I were foolish enough to enter the New York Marathon based on that bit of flattery, I would probably deserve the consequences. What about Cassius's efforts to persuade Brutus to join the conspiracy? Did Cassius believe that he was deceiving Brutus? Did Cassius know that the conspiracy could kill them all?

Now for a larger issue: Does this question mean it's all right to deceive people who either do not trust you or have no cause to trust you? The CEO who announces a new facility that he does not intend to build to confuse competitors could pass this test. Does this mean, then, that it is all right to deceive adversaries, or does it also mean that deception *creates* adversaries?

Is deception acceptable if it harms someone who intends to harm you?

One further question might be "How do you know they intend to harm you?" A general on the battlefield can rest assured that the enemy intends serious harm. Obviously, deception is acceptable in this case. But what about the situation where the person is so conditioned by the deception in the world that he develops a case of permanent paranoia? Here again, the notion of adversaries, real or imagined, rears its ugly head. The question remains "Does deception protect you from adversaries, or does it create them?"

Is deception acceptable if it does not harm you or someone who trusts you?

Here, in Tina's and my view, is the central question. When we deceive others, do we deceive ourselves? I tell my MBA students and participants in executive seminars that the category manager whom we met earlier who thought about implicating his colleagues in R&D to cover up his own shortcomings is skating on thin ice. What if he gets away with it? Yes, he has harmed his colleagues, but, more important, he has harmed himself. Or the person who would recruit his colleagues before leaving the firm. She might deceive others—at least for a time—but she will carry the knowledge of her deception forever. Her future victories will be sullied by that knowledge. Her self-worth will be called into question time and time again. I am not preaching from an exalted pulpit. I, like you and most everyone, have succumbed to the temptation. I have deflected blame, taken unfair advantage of others' weaknesses, and been less than forthright in personnel reviews, surprising the person when later he was terminated for unsatisfactory performance and finding myself sobered for misleading him.

Now for the first question: Is deception acceptable if it harms no one?

By now, we realize that this is an oxymoron. To the extent that deception tends to make us lose touch with ourselves, to the extent that deception adds to the mistrust inherent in society, to the extent that it garbles communication and creates adversaries, it is harmful to someone—either ourselves or others. But we could not live without it. Shakespeare, the great philosopher, and life itself, make us confront it. When is it justified? When is it not? Because deception is so integral to our lives, our sensibilities are often dulled. Too often, we fall into the trap: "Everybody does it." Very few phrases disturb me as much as this one. I tell my students that if they want to be the genuine "choice and master spirits of this age" (not the conspirators whom Antony was flattering), they have the responsibility to lead us out of the deception trap. "Everybody does it" is for sheep, not for leaders.

10

Banish Not Your Jack Falstaff

The Value of Mavericks in Our Midst

The fool doth think he is wise, but the wiseman knows himself to be a fool.

AS YOU LIKE IT (5.1, 30–31)

No, my good lord; banish Peto, banish Bardolph, banish Poins—but for sweet Jack Falstaff, kind Jack Falstaff, true Jack Falstaff, valiant Jack Falstaff, and therefore more valiant, being as he is old Jack Falstaff, banish not him thy Harry's company, banish not him thy Harry's company, banish plump Jack, and banish all the world.

KING HENRY IV, PART 1 (2.4, 468–74)

Iғ George Taylor owned two ties, I only ever saw one. He wore white socks with a dark blue suit, and when he removed his jacket, his shirttail was hanging out of his pants. His face was constantly flushed, and his belly was round as a Buddha's. But George was a top research scientist for a large pharmaceutical company, a brilliant scientist who was able to take what others thought was an intractable problem, reframe it, and reveal the solution. More important (and more valuable) was his ability to stimulate other people to solve problems.

I met George Taylor (not his real name) when my colleague E. Kirby Warren and I were hired as consultants to help the pharmaceutical company shorten the time it took to get its new products to market. From the time of inception through all the internal scientific research, testing, and documentation plus the approval process at the federal Food and Drug Administration, the average time it takes to get a new drug on the shelves is 12.5 years. Our job was to analyze the product process within the company and see where we could speed things up. We began creating a timeline of how a product made its way through the company week by week, and quickly identified one relatively simple, but obvious, problem: a bottleneck in the printing department. Developing a new drug requires an enormous amount of research and testing, which must be documented and shared by in-house scientists in various specialties. The slowdown we detected in the dissemination of such printed materials was adding several weeks a year to the development of any given product. Company policy stipulated that all internal documentation must be printed in-house. But the facilities were grossly inadequate.

George had known this all along. In fact, he'd been trying to change the printing procedures for years, without any success. His last effort, just before my colleague and I were hired as consultants, had been rebuffed again: the budget, he was told, was set, and the policy could not be changed until the end of the fiscal year, if then. My colleague and I couldn't believe it: one of the company's top research scientists had pointed to a major glitch in the system, and no one had done anything about it! Our "cross-functional task force" reviewed the salaries and overhead for the twenty professionals working on the drug, and it came to about $14,000 a day. The cost to improve printing schedules would be less than $10,000 a year. The opportunity loss of another company beating us to market with a similar product was incalculable and enormous!

We vowed to get this problem solved immediately, and, as paid consultants, we had the clout to do it. When I pointed out to the brass that George had already alerted the company to the printing problems, I recall one particularly pompous executive trying to explain why he and his colleagues had ignored George: "He's always bugging us with maverick ideas."

What to do about "the maverick," the one person in the company or the department who's a little different—brilliant, to be sure, but a bit strange and maybe not so presentable, who threatens the status quo? During my fifty years in business, this has been one of the most difficult and complicated management problems I have faced, and executives I have taught or consulted for seem to agree. Does disorder have a place in corporate life? If so, how much? Shakespeare is a very good guide for dealing with the maverick in your midst. In fact, Shakespeare created one of the most engaging and controversial mavericks of all time, Sir John Falstaff, Prince Hal's drinking and carousing companion in the two *Henry IV* plays.

As usual, Shakespeare offers a complex perspective. His *Henry IV* plays, along with parts of *King Henry V,* provide a useful framework within which to examine the role of order and disorder in an enterprise. "Maverick thinking" is crucial to any enterprise that wants to grow and meet the challenges of the marketplace. Mavericks have founded some of the largest and most successful companies in America. Henry Ford was a maverick. So was Thomas Edison. Steve Jobs and Bill Gates were mavericks, kids, really, creating the computer revolution in their garages. John McGowan created a small telephone company that challenged in the courts AT&T's monopoly on phone service for eleven years—and won. His company, MCI, recently merged with WorldCom to become one of the world's largest (and best-run) communications companies.

Exceptional leaders not only know how to live and work with the

Falstaffs (and George Taylors) of their world, but they have also worked out ways to manage them and inject them into the give-and-take of corporate creativity. The sign of a great leader is to know how to learn from your mavericks, to know when to let your Falstaffs bloom and when to nip them in the bud.

"A Minion of the Moon"

The future Henry V hung out at the Boar's Head Tavern in London's seedy Eastcheap section, where the ingeniously entertaining Falstaff was king. With his friend Poins and Falstaff's cronies Pistol and Bardolph Prince Hal got an education in drinking and whoring; Hal even joined them in some highway robbery for the fun of it. (The prince returned the money the next day.) King Henry IV, like any responsible father, was not pleased. After all, he was the pragmatic Bolingbroke, who had usurped the crown from the extravagant Richard II. Was his own son a future "skipping king"? Moreover, the king had his hands full fighting rebels in the north and didn't need the distraction of a playboy son. Especially one whose best buddy was a fat, alcoholic, gourmandizing, womanizing, slothful, intellectually brilliant, funny maverick.

So who was Falstaff? As the great critic William Empson once said of Falstaff, "It's hard to get one's mind all around him." Harold Bloom, the unabashed "Bardolator" at Yale, reveres Falstaff almost as much as Shakespeare. For Bloom, Falstaff and Hamlet are "the most intelligent of Shakespeare's persons"; both characters are, according to Bloom, what Hegel said of the best characters in Shakespeare: "free artists of themselves." We watch Falstaff come to be and change before our very eyes. "Sir John is Shakespeare's Socrates," enthuses Bloom. He may look like your usual saloon blowhard, but Shakespeare's Falstaff is a philosopher, a teacher, and a skeptic. Above all, Sir Jack has a wicked, witty way with words. To Bloom, he is a "signature of Shakespeare's originality." Following that line, I see Falstaff as the embodiment of Shakespeare's commitment to the importance of originality—even when the source of that originality is hard for the authorities to take: like

Falstaff (and George Taylor). These are men who see the world differently from the rest of us.

When Prince Hal teases Falstaff about the fat knight's dissolute life, Falstaff points out that he is a man who, unlike ordinary men, is guided not by Phoebus, the sun, but by the moon:

> Marry then sweet wag, when thou art king let not us that are squires
> of the night's body be called thieves of the day's beauty: let us be
> Diana's foresters, gentlemen of the shade, minions of the moon;
> and let men say we be men of good government, being governed as
> the sea is, by our noble and chaste mistress the moon, under whose
> countenance we steal.
>
> KING HENRY IV, PART 1 (1.2, 23–29)

In short, Falstaff is a true lunatic (from the Latin for "moon-struck"), variable, not to be depended upon, different. When a writer pours so much of his own energy, wit, and wisdom into one character, surely it's evidence of how much he loves his creation (and his own best stuff). Shakespeare was, I think, as mesmerized as Harold Bloom by his wondrous Falstaff. But like any lover, Shakespeare is not inclined to judge his beloved. As we saw in the previous chapter, he keeps his opinions about politics, religion, and morality to himself. Shakespeare's take on life was not necessarily Falstaff's. The same writer who gave Falstaff that speech about change and stealing put in the mouth of Ulysses, a Greek commander in *Troilus and Cressida,* these words, from a speech we have examined before:

> The heavens themselves, the planets, and this centre
> Observe degree, priority, and place,
> Insisture, course, proportion, season, form,
> Office, and custom, in all line of order.
> And therefore is the glorious planet Sol
> In noble eminence enthron'd and spher'd
> Amidst the other; whose med'cinable eye
> Corrects the influence of evil planets . . .
>
> TROILUS AND CRESSIDA (1.3, 85–92)

This is straightforward commitment about proportion: there's a place for everything and everything in its place. Just as the bodies in the heavens must "observe degree, priority, and place," so must we on Earth. But what happens when something gets out of place?

> . . . O, when degree is shak'd,
> Which is the ladder of all high designs,
> Then enterprise is sick. How could communities,
> Degrees in schools, and brotherhoods in cities,
> Peaceful commerce from dividable shores,
> The primogenity and due of birth,
> Prerogative of age, crowns, sceptres, laurels,
> But by degree stand in authentic place?
> Take but degree away, untune that string,
> And hark what discord follows.
>
> TROILUS AND CRESSIDA (1.3, 101–10)

Comforting. The conventional wisdom of the world of business would certainly take Ulysses's side. Order is crucial, businesses are structured as hierarchies, and when the rules are broken, most CEOs would agree with Ulysses, the "enterprise is sick." But how dull is that? Where is the movement in Ulysses's world? Where is the impetus for innovation and change? Shakespeare, I believe, raises a big question for us all: If we agree with Falstaff, do we have to disagree with Ulysses? Or can we accommodate both order and disorder, predictability and innovation, stability and change?

ORDER AND DISORDER IN THE ELIZABETHAN WORLD

I have been fascinated by the role of disorder in society ever since I took Franklin Ikenberry's course "Shakespeare's History Plays" at the University of Tulsa so many years ago I don't want to count them. The great British Shakespeare scholar E. M. W. Tillyard had recently published *Shakespeare's History Plays,* in which he addressed order and disorder, a deep concern of Elizabethans. In the

century and a half before Elizabeth's coronation, six of her predecessors had been either deposed or killed. The Wars of the Roses
and ongoing civil strife had made what John of Gaunt had called
"this scepter'd isle" a dangerous place to live. Tillyard's first chapter traced these concerns by analyzing Ulysses's speech to
Agamemnon, portions of which we have just read. Scholars now
find Tillyard's approach somewhat too conservative, but it lit a fire
under me. I proceeded to write one of the world's worst epic
poems, about thirty pages long. I saw the relationship between
Henry IV and Prince Hal as the embodiment of the concern Elizabethans had for order, and which Tillyard wrote about. The place
of rebellion in life clearly struck a note in that young Oklahoman
struggling to grow up, and I've been thinking about the role of the
maverick ever since.

In *King Henry IV,* Shakespeare creates a double plot of disorder:
the rebellion in the north against the king stirred by Hotspur, and
the rebellion of spirit in Prince Hal stirred by his relationship to
Falstaff. Which worldview is Shakespeare's—that of Falstaff or
Ulysses? The little that we know about Shakespeare's life suggests
that the playwright shared his fellow Elizabethans' preference for
political order and stability. He certainly was interested in it
enough to chronicle the ups and downs of the English monarchy.
Even Elizabeth's forty-five-year reign was not without its share of
political and religious intrigue. Shakespeare's own patron, the
Earl of Southampton, was implicated in the Earl of Essex's rebellion against Elizabeth, for which Essex lost his head. In 1587, Elizabeth reluctantly agreed to execute her cousin Mary, Queen of
Scots, to put an end to the plots to assassinate Elizabeth. And don't
forget (because Shakespeare never could) that the playwright's
own colleagues in the theater, Christopher Marlowe and Thomas
Kyd, were both arrested for political reasons. Kyd was tortured on
the rack and died shortly after, his health broken. Marlowe's murder may have been politically motivated, rather than a simple bar-
room brawl, as alleged. Ben Jonson, Shakespeare's famous fellow
playwright, served time for killing a man.

It is no wonder that Shakespeare kept any overt political, moral,
and religious convictions away from his audience, and thus history.

He was brilliant artistically in part because he made his political and social insights general rather than specific. His observations and insights can apply to almost any situation in any country. The career choice of theater was a risky one for a young man in Elizabethan times. But Shakespeare proved to be a shrewd businessman, and while he took a few overt political risks in his plays, they were calculated ones, and he got away with them—and filled the seats of his theater and his coffers.

In short, Shakespeare, artist and businessman, found a perfect balance between innovation and the status quo, between order and disorder, between the views of Ulysses and those of Falstaff. This middle path, I too believe, is the best one to take. Companies that find that delicate balance between order and disorder tend to flourish.

THE FALSTAFF AMONG US

One of my prime tests for organizational effectiveness is how well a company integrates its Falstaffs (and George Taylors). Not only are they the sources of innovation and purveyors of common sense, they are also the teachers. Prince Hal's gift of lively, persuasive speech did not come from God or his father but from Falstaff. Riposting with the nimble-witted knight, young Hal sharpens his own wit and language skills. Shakespeare acknowledges the role of teacher when he has Falstaff say:

> Men of all sorts take a pride to gird at me. The brain of this foolish-compounded clay, man, is not able to invent anything that intends to laughter more than I invent, or is invented on me; *I am not only witty in myself, but the cause that wit is in other men* [emphasis added].
>
> KING HENRY IV, PART 2 (1.2, 6–10)

Among Falstaff and his Boar's Head Tavern cronies, Hal learns more of the world and the people he will govern than he could ever learn at court. And when Falstaff disparages Prince Hal's cold and calculating brother John, Duke of Lancaster, we are inclined to agree with Falstaff: "a man cannot make him laugh; but that's no marvel, he drinks no wine" (*King Henry IV, Part 2* [4.3, 87–89]).

Falstaff launches into his famous speech praising a good, strong sherry as the source of wit and courage. Who does not enjoy the company of a brilliantly entertaining character like Falstaff? As Tina points out:

> Falstaff is an incredible force of laughter. I think you always need that in any enterprise. Everybody loves laughter. It literally releases tension. Laughter provides relief. It is useful to have a figure like Falstaff around, someone who stands not for the rather Puritan virtues of discipline and order but for what are usually perceived as the "lowest things in mankind"—laughter, drinking, and sex. Falstaff's presence in *King Henry IV* offers Prince Hal the kind of companionship and education in the ways of the world that his father, the king, cannot. Falstaff loves Prince Hal for who he is, not for who he will (or must) be. As this kind of more accepting parental figure, Falstaff becomes a kind of maternal figure for the young prince. Mrs. Henry IV is nowhere to be found in the play. It's Falstaff who seems to play this female role, the parent who accepts the child no matter what. Compare Hal to his brother John of Lancaster, who is eager to be his father's son. How does he end up? John is a deceiver and a vicious killer who plays only to win.

Shakespeare's mavericks are also purveyors of good common sense. Falstaff speaks candidly to Prince Hal. Anticipating the king's anger over his son's drinking and whoring ways, Falstaff suggests that Hal rehearse with him before he appears before the king. Good advice. Of course, Falstaff cannot resist playing it for some laughs. He berates Hal for the company he keeps—except, he jokes, for that "goodly portly man . . . of a cheerful look, a pleasing eye, and a most noble carriage." Falstaff as king advises his son, "there is virtue in that Falstaff, him keep with, the rest banish" (*King Henry IV, Part I* [2.4, 416–24]). Every enterprise needs someone to inform the emperor when he is wearing no clothes—sometimes a dangerous job. As we saw earlier, the Earl of Kent was banished on pain of death when he publicly disagreed with Lear's decision to disinherit Cordelia. And the other maverick in Lear's entourage, "the Fool" or court jester, knows that even though it's his job to tease the king and speak his mind, "They'll have me whipped for speaking true."

At Pathmark, my Falstaff was Jay Toor, director of planning. (I hope Jay will not be offended by my saying that he even looks like Sir John.) He scoffed at the company's arcane policies and procedures. He was a classic iconoclast, which, in the eyes of some of his colleagues, was not a good thing. To others (me included), he was a near genius. Jay had one crazy idea after another, most of which worked. Some of his innovations were prescient. Jay suggested branch banking and optometrist shops in our largest stores long before they became commonplace in supermarkets. He supported the marketing director, Ken Peskin, and me when we decided to post prescription prices in our in-store pharmacies (a practice prohibited by law in the New York, New Jersey, Connecticut area) and expose some pharmacies that were overcharging for their products in poor neighborhoods. We mavericks thought that by challenging the law, we would not only get it changed, we'd also enhance our competitive position. Soon we were the largest dispenser of prescription drugs on the eastern seaboard. Moreover, the increased traffic in the stores upped our sales of health and beauty aids, all of which have gross margins much greater than the profits on canned peas. Because we were willing to tolerate our Falstaffs, our stores became more innovative. And more profitable.

In the late 1970s and early '80s, the top management at Texas Instruments were engineers preoccupied with cost control as a way to gain market share. In addition to this narrow focus, the people running the company were autocratic, a prescription for disaster. TI's slide was chronicled by my colleague Danny Miller (of Columbia Business School and the École des Hautes Études Commerciales) in his book *The Icarus Paradox:*

> This self-defeating obsession with cost even carried over into TI's consumer products, which were approached as though they were chips. The company assumed it could conquer markets by offering the most performance at the lowest price. It completely ignored

fashion and styling. Take the abortive digital watch effort. As one former member of the watch group recalled: "Fred [Bucy] and Mark [Shepherd], TI's two top executives, kept pushing to slash the price to $9.95. That meant having a plastic band. We kept telling them the consumer didn't want that, but they wouldn't listen." To them engineering and specifications and cost figures mattered, appearance and attractiveness did not. The watch bombed.

Texas Instruments ran into the same kind of consumer resistance when it tried to produce its own line of personal computers. "Again," writes Miller, "the narrow focus on cost and engineering compromised the saleability of products."

In 1983, TI folded its computer business, taking a $600 million write-down and reporting a net loss of $145 million for the year. The company had shown no innovation or even common sense. It was not because such qualities did not exist at Texas Instruments, which had its Falstaffs. Trouble was, those engineers in top management had either ignored them or squelched them.

I have nothing against engineers generally, or any other group, for that matter. But I do think that when everyone at the top looks, thinks, and acts the same, when the culture of an enterprise cannot tolerate diversity, let alone a wild card like Falstaff, the organization cannot be considered a healthy one. Because when trouble comes, when the bottom line goes south, those companies do not have the range of responses needed to think differently; they can't change course quickly to counteract negative trends. George Taylor, a research scientist, probably would have been squeezed out by the bureaucrats in that pharmaceutical company if he hadn't had a few protectors in management who thought he was a genius. In spite of his talent, George Taylor had never led a project. His wit and sharp tongue had made too many enemies at the top. Nevertheless, the teams George worked on always exceeded expectations. At a biotech start-up, George would have been the company icon, a legend in his own time. At this large buttoned-down pharmaceutical corporation, poor George was a sore to be hidden under a bandage. In my opinion, he should've been running the whole show.

THE MAVERICK WITHIN

The word *disorder* has pejorative connotations to most managers and kings. But disorder is the source of innovation. To create something new, you have to be dissatisfied with the old, the status quo, and shaking things up usually requires a nimble and inquiring mind.

I was fortunate to start my business career in advertising. By its nature, advertising is creative and always looking for something different to catch people's attention. The most creative people tend to see the world a bit differently and act accordingly. You cannot succeed in advertising without being something of a maverick or having mavericks on your staff. As I moved into my other businesses, I realized that the uses of disorder applied to them, too, and everywhere I've gone I've tried to identify the mavericks on my payroll and create an environment where what they have to say will be heard.

Sometimes that means revealing your own maverick streak. In some of the turnarounds I've attempted, I've arrived at the company to find a rigid set of policies and procedures. Worse, I quickly noticed that people were hiding behind these principles, not willing to confront issues, not willing to make decisions. They had a simple answer for everything: "It's company policy." Every company has to have policies and procedures. I'm not against that. What burns me up is how policies accrete over time. Something goes wrong, and some executive says, "That's never going to happen to me again." So he makes a policy. And thus the company "manual" gets thicker and thicker with everyone's policies and procedures. Nobody, however, is double-checking whether all these rules and regulations still make any sense.

This is how I've dealt with this problem (twice). I call a meeting—out in the parking lot. In front of the assembled employees, I take out the company manual and tell them that all the old policies and procedures are over. And to prove it, I set the sucker on fire. Burn it right there in the parking lot. "Let's create some new policies and procedures!" They love it. It's another example of leadership as theater. But by burning that manual in public, I'm also demonstrating that I'm something of a maverick who is putting the status quo on notice.

Polite society shuns mavericks, sometimes with good reason. Occasionally, however, mavericks represent our own repressed thoughts and actions. How often have you heard someone express an unpopular view, which you secretly shared but were reluctant to support for one reason or another? How often have you kicked yourself when that once unpopular view became the coin of the realm? (Emerson once said that "in every work of genius, we recognize our own rejected thoughts: they come back to us with a certain alienated majesty.") You could've gotten the credit for that innovation! But you were too scared to speak out, to be a maverick.

Of course, you cannot blurt out every maverick thought that crosses your consciousness; nor should you, willy-nilly, support every maverick notion that might seem attractive (at the time). But if you repress those thoughts and actions consistently, you will lock yourself into a set of responses that might be appropriate for today but disastrous for tomorrow. For some temporary comfort, you will be trading away your ability to cope with a changing marketplace.

In half a century of thinking about these issues, I've finally come to one clear conclusion: every organization must find a balance between Falstaff and Ulysses.

How Do You Balance Fat Jack and Wily Ulysses?

It's no easy task. When John Sculley stepped in at Apple in 1982, the company, according to one of its own executives, was "a zoo." There was incredible innovation and discipline in its new product development. But Apple's operations and marketing were out of control. Sculley, former president of PepsiCo, tried to blend in with Apple's casual, creative culture by wearing open shirts and loafers around the office. But when he tried to tame the zoo by imposing big-company discipline, he ended up killing the animals, or at least their energetic spirit. Apple lost its innovative edge; its market share plummeted, and so did its stock. The company almost went under. Founder Steve Jobs returned. Older and wiser, Jobs has found a balance between order and disorder, and, at this writing, the company is back on the road to corporate health. As I was writing this, Jobs introduced Apple's new, colorful, moderately priced computer, the iMac, and Apple's stock price was $99 a share, three times as high as its fifty-two-week low.

At Pathmark, I was acutely aware of the need for balance between order and disorder. To turn around any big company, you better not pretend that you're the only creative person in the room. Our twenty-four-hour-a-day campaign was a maverick idea that had all the classic problems: the company as a whole had misgivings, the logistical and marketing challenges of such a radical policy required outrageously innovative ideas; a can-do, "to hell with the rules" attitude had to win the day; we had to work together. Company morale was lousy, and it manifested itself as shrinkage.

Shrinkage—the difference between our theoretical and actual gross margin—was more than $30 million a year. Some of the loss was due to sloppy procedures; most of it was due to customer and employee theft. Our controls were poor. To make the company price-competitive again, we had to institute controls that would reduce shrinkage to no more than $7 million a year. So we had to revive esprit de corps, stop the stealing, keep the stores open, and make a profit. The maverick idea and commitment did that!

You need mavericks. Trouble is, mavericks aren't easy to have around. Shakespeare offers his own evidence on how hard it is to keep a Falstaff on the payroll.

THE CASE OF THE CENTURIES: HENRY V VERSUS JACK FALSTAFF

Falstaff is away from London when he hears of Henry IV's death. Certain that he and his friends from the bars and brothels of Eastcheap will receive lucrative appointments from their old friend the new king, Henry V, Falstaff rides all night to attend the coronation. Too late for the ceremony at Westminster Abbey, Falstaff stands among the crowd outside and shouts in glee as the new king and the lord chief justice, no fan of Falstaff, leave Westminster:

> God save thy Grace, King Hal, my royal Hal! . . .
> God save thee, my sweet boy!
>
> KING HENRY IV, PART 2 (5.5, 41–43)

The king does not acknowledge his old friend. Instead, he orders the chief justice to "speak to that vain man." The chief justice obeys: "Have you your wits?" he chastises Falstaff. "Know you what 'tis you speak?" Yet Falstaff cannot repress his exuberance (nor his expectations of the perks he believes Henry owes him). Finally, Henry V says to the man he drank and caroused with in Eastcheap, where the witnesses were many:

> I know thee not, old man. Fall to thy prayers.
> How ill white hairs becomes a fool and jester!
> I have long dreamt of such a kind of man,
> So surfeit-swell'd, so old, and so profane;
> But being awak'd I do despise my dream.
>
> KING HENRY IV, PART 2 (5.5, 47–51)

Not the kind of greeting Falstaff had ridden all night to London to hear from his old crony, Prince Hal. And if he thought he, too, was dreaming, King Hal sets him straight:

> Presume not that I am the thing I was;
> For God doth know, so shall the world perceive,
> That I have turn'd away my former self;
> So will I those that kept me company.
> When thou dost hear I am as I have been,
> Approach me, and thou shalt be as thou wast,
> The tutor and the feeder of my riots.
> Till then I banish thee, on pain of death,

As I have done the rest of my misleaders,
Not to come near our person by ten mile.

KING HENRY IV, PART 2 (5.5, 56–65)

A finer termination speech you will never hear. But neither the king nor Shakespeare can banish his affection for Jack Falstaff. Henry could have been a lot tougher on him. Instead, the king, in spite of his cool demeanor, offers Falstaff a pension, not exactly a golden parachute, not even brass. Of course, if it were left up to the chief justice, who suspects Falstaff to be a thief, a liar, and a coward, the only compensation Sir Jack would get would be a rope around his neck. So the king takes care of his old companion's corporeal needs:

For competence of life I will allow you,
That lack of means enforce you not to evils;
And as we hear you do reform yourselves,
We will, according to your strengths and qualities,
Give you advancement.

KING HENRY IV, PART 2 (5.5, 66–70)

Falstaff is incredulous and assures one of his cronies, Shallow, whom he owes a thousand pounds, that the king is only putting on a show and will call for him later, in private. Shallow no sooner expresses his doubt than they are interrupted by the chief justice and Hal's brother, the rigid John of Lancaster, who carts them off to prison to await their expulsion from London, as the king ordered. Lancaster is impressed with his brother's kingly response to his old friend. But the rest of us are not sure. Falstaff's banishment doesn't sit well, though what we would have done, we're not sure. And it turns out sadly. Like so many faithful employees who have been fired, food for the body is not enough. Falstaff, rejected, dies of a broken heart (reported in *King Henry V*).

SHOULD FALSTAFF HAVE BEEN FIRED?

Some critics are stunned by what they perceive as Henry's public humiliation of his old friend. What do you think? It's a question I put to my Columbia students and those who participate in my executive seminars. Some of them can be even tougher on "that sweet creature of bombast." I don't see how anyone could consider being tougher on Sir John. I know that the king was "making a statement" in his decision to publicly humiliate Sir John, but I can't ever forgive the king for his cruelty. However, sadly and with a heavy heart, I agree that Shakespeare's Jack Falstaff should be fired. He recklessly put himself in a situation that embarrassed Henry. But I would not want people in my organization to think that all Jack Falstaffs should be fired.

I have believed in and have written about the importance of trust in organizations, and I have written specifically that if anyone is caught lying, stealing, or cheating, he or she should be fired swiftly and summarily. Here's the case against Sir John:

Hard evidence abounds in the *Henry IV* plays that Falstaff is not the sort of maverick it's safe to keep around. He is a big man with big defects. He takes bribes to excuse recruits from military service; through his own poor leadership, he loses all but three of his 150 ragtag soldiers. When Hal raises an eyebrow over this dereliction of duty, Falstaff shows little remorse. The men were "food for powder, food for powder." Falstaff brags about his thievery and earlier in the play commits highway robbery at Gadshill. When Hal and Poins, for the hell of it, attack Falstaff's gang and steal the money they robbed from pilgrims going to Canterbury, Falstaff is such a coward that he is literally scared out of his boots. And when Hal asks him what happened, Falstaff lies (as Hal knew he would), saying that he and his three fellow thieves were attacked by "a hundred" men. Shakespeare exposes the man as a liar, a cheat, a thief. We also know that he is a whoremonger, a heavy drinker, and a lousy manager of money—hardly an appropriate job description in the "reform" administration that King Henry V envisioned.

Some people would banish Falstaff also because he is politically incorrect. I disagree. It is precisely this trait that endears him to me. Remember that I publicly burned the corporate policy manuals to make a statement about change and innovation. The medieval version of the corporate policy manual was the chivalric code, which was the linchpin of upper-crust society. The code of chivalry guaranteed, among other things, safe conduct for enemy emissaries; it prescribed the proper method for settling arguments among the nobility; and it specified the right and wrong reasons and methods for killing people. The measure of the good, the proper, and the noble was *honor.* Just as trust is said to be the lubricant of society today,[25] honor is what fueled the knights, nobles, and royals of the Middle Ages. The rebel Hotspur in *King Henry IV,* outnumbered and almost certain to lose the battle at Shrewsbury, spurs his soldiers on to their deaths with the words "Doomsday is near; die all, die merrily." What could be so merry about certain death? Dying for honor, that's what, and, according to the age-old code of the warrior, there is no better death. Even rebels like Hotspur played by the rules of honor. At Agincourt, as we have seen, Henry V urges his troops on in the cause of honor. "The fewer men, the greater share of honour," says Henry.

But Shakespeare, through Falstaff, grabs us by the scruff of the neck and shakes us into thinking more clearly about honor. On the one hand, it is the linchpin of society. On the other hand, it can cause us to do foolish things. Falstaff realizes that even though the chivalric code was medieval society's stabilizer, it caused a lot of needless killing.

In a gross violation of corporate policy, he trashes the central notion of chivalry. Shortly before the Battle of Shrewsbury, Falstaff has his qualms, confiding to Prince Hal, "I wish 'twere bed-time, Hal, and all well." Hal responds with a more traditional attitude toward battle. "Why," he says to Falstaff, "thou owest God a death." As soon as the prince leaves, Falstaff muses about death in his own unique, unknightly way:

'Tis not due yet, I would be loath to pay him before his day—what need I be so forward with him that calls not on me? Well, 'tis no matter; honour pricks me on. Yea, but how if honour prick me off when I come on, how then? Can honour set to a leg? No. Or an arm? No. Or take away the grief of a wound? No. Honour hath no skill in surgery then? No. What is honour? A word. What is in that word honour? What is that honour? Air. A trim reckoning! Who hath it? He that died a-Wednesday. Doth he feel it? No. Doth he hear it? No. 'Tis insensible, then. Yea, to the dead. But will it not live with the living? No. Why? Detraction will not suffer it. Therefore I'll none of it. Honour is a mere scutcheon [a shield carried in a funeral procession]—and so ends my catechism.

KING HENRY IV, PART 1 (5.1, 127–41)

I would not have given the sack to old "sack and sugar Jack" for this catechism, shocking as it was for medieval society. As I said before, I would have fired him for his actions, not his thoughts. Society needs, always, the guy who makes us think again and again about codes that might be outmoded and outworn. I personally believe, fervently, in honor, duty, and country; but I also believe that others in society should push me to be clear in what I believe—and why. Here is Tina Packer's view, which, to some extent, is different from mine:

Honor can be seen as a social construct—a way in which we have been persuaded to think about ourselves and our society and about how we must "protect" ourselves. To die for the sake of honor is one way of thinking about the world and war. And while we are inclined to think that honor is a good thing, because it is selfless and you need a lot of courage to act honorably, I would say that you could also argue that honor is a lie, as Falstaff does. Honor convinces a lot of people to march into battle without really knowing why, lose limbs or their lives and kill other people. For what? A king's or president's or prime minister's version of honor? Because you've been told this leader or that is dissing your country? Too many battles in history have been fought for evil reasons. Nazi and Japanese soldiers went to their deaths in World War II for "honor." Their "honor" was to us an evil. In fact, we know that when men are in the midst of the horror of battle, it is not honor that motivates them, by and large; it is the comradeship of their friends. The horror of battle exposes the lie of honor. The literature of World War I is full of examples of soldiers who return to the front not for the honor of country but because they cannot bear to leave their friends behind in danger in the trenches. Germany and England have butchered each other twice in this last century with 60 million dead—and for what? England and Germany are now both part of a united Europe. Could we have got to this collaboration without killing all those people for honor's sake?

I think it's in our blood to fight for our own honor, or for the honor of our family, or tribe, or community. But honor for a whole country—what does that mean? Do we all, no matter what our backgrounds, religious beliefs, or political prejudices, share the same definition of honor? In an America that is increasingly pluralistic, what is the definition of honor? To fight for love, that I would like. And that kind of fight takes just as much courage—because you have to give up your definition of yourself. All honor calls us to be bigger than we are. Could we have the "honor" of saying we are one world? Amazingly, Shakespeare was raising these questions through Falstaff's speech, through Hotspur's death and Hal's transformation.

Tina and I agree that people who do not deserve honor have used the concept of honor to persuade others to do their bidding—fighting an unjust war, for example. I have a slightly different view, however, of "honor and country." I enlisted on my seventeenth birthday, March 30, 1945. I had to go to reserve training for a year because I would not be allowed into active duty until I was eighteen. I didn't have any battlefield buddies because World War II ended five months after I enlisted. But I joined because of honor and country . . . and so did the others in my battalion. I believe that when the leadership is reasonably honest and the cause is reasonably just, even in a pluralistic society people will fight fiercely for country. After all, King Henry, at the gates of Harfleur, didn't call out, "for your countrymen." Instead, he urged, "God for Harry, England, and Saint George!" And here Tina's admiration of fat Jack comes back to where I stand: banish Jack, particularly if Henry V means what he says outside Westminster Abbey:

> Presume not that I am the thing I was;
> For God doth know, so shall the world perceive,
> That I have turn'd away my former self . . .
>
> KING HENRY IV, PART 2 (5.5, 56–58)

The king knows that Falstaff will not fit into his vision of England. And he is eager to shine up his own reputation. At the end of Act 4, as we mentioned earlier, his dying father advises him to divert potential rebellions against his rule in England with overseas wars. This strategy, the king points out, would provide the young king with another advantage: proving his valor and dissolving his reputation as an Eastcheap wastrel. The new king knows that the first and easiest way to improve his image is to distance himself from Falstaff. "I like this fair proceeding of the King's," says Hal's coolly calculating brother Lancaster.

Although I have agreed that Falstaff should be fired, I do not believe it was the "fair proceeding" that Lancaster describes. While Henry believed that he was trying to polish his image, I believe that he tarnished it.

Sometimes I have wished that Shakespeare would leave me alone . . . or, at least, give me some easy riddles to solve. But, as we will see when later we talk about having friends in business, there are precious few easy riddles. That's why Shakespeare lives today. Just look at Tina Packer and me. First, we like Falstaff; next, we're disgusted with him. Then we fight about him. Finally we agree that he should be fired. Tina sums it up well: "He's much too chaotic. If there were only Falstaffs in the world, it wouldn't work. Everything would devolve into pure chaos."

WOULD YOU WORK FOR HENRY V?

Yes—at least if you were an English subject in 1413, had been pressed into service, and wished to escape banishment or the gallows. But today, at the turn of the twenty-first century, you have a choice about the kind of leader you will work for. Typically, you want to choose a boss who will promise to advance your own economic interests; you also want to work for someone you trust. To be sure, flawed, even venal leaders, have been known to maintain a cadre of reasonably effective managers, as long as they keep the bonuses coming. Employees, however, who make self-interested economic decisions for the short term often pay an onerous price. Executives and managers who worked for Allegheny International during Robert Buckley's tenure as CEO had difficulty finding jobs after Allegheny went bankrupt. The same was true for managers at U.S. Surgical during its troubles—and dozens of other failed or troubled companies whose names would not look good on your résumé.

Leaders earn trust through their honesty and straightforward style, as well as for short- and long-term competence. Henry V, according to the *English Chronicles,* was "the perfect king." In my opinion, he got that reputation because there was so little to choose from. He was a brilliant military leader, to be sure, but, according to historians, he had more than his share of luck at Agincourt. Yes, he was a persuasive orator; he also had a newfound Christian piety and an intimate knowledge of his subjects, thanks to Falstaff. Henry was also a scheming, cynical, manipulative hypocrite. Our first evidence of Hal's propensity to turn everything to his advantage comes early in *King Henry IV, Part 1,* when Hal soliloquizes about his relationship with the gang at the Boar's Head. He says, "I know you all," and goes on to signal that he is using them for the time being and will dump them when the time comes. In the opening scene of *King Henry V,* we learn that Hal has made a deal with the Archbishop of Canterbury: if the archbishop will sanction his invasion of France, he will reduce taxes on church properties. When Henry calls on God, it is usually for help in pursuing his own self-interest. Why should God grant Henry His support at Agincourt? Henry lists his charitable acts since becoming king ("Five hundred poor I have in yearly pay . . ."). A truly religious man would not treat prayer as a kind of bill for his services. In his anger toward the French ambassadors, Henry claims to be acting "by God's grace . . . and in his name," while at the same time promising to avenge their petty insult of the tennis balls by creating among the French "many a thousand widows" and causing misery to those "yet ungotten and unborn"—hardly the message of the Christian saint Henry pretends to be. And while you cannot blame him for his retribution against the traitors Scroop, Cambridge, and Grey, the way Henry toys with them before he reveals that he knows they've been plotting a rebellion against him exposes a streak of cruelty in the king. More evidence comes at Harfleur, when Henry threatens the city with the sight of "naked infants spitted on pikes" unless the town fathers capitulate. And Henry doesn't flinch when he learns that Bardolph, one of his friends from the Eastcheap days, has been sentenced to hang for having stolen an item from a French church.

Whenever I have worked with business leaders who have made a decision to go ahead with actions that I find devious—even when the enterprise is bound to benefit—a chill comes over me. My commitment decreases, and my defenses are on alert. "Am I next? If not next, when?" No one expects leaders to be perfect, but they must work harder than the rest of us to try to be perfect. I do not see that in the new King Henry. I would not want to work for him, and if I did, I'd turn all my creative energy into my search for a new job. Tina Packer reminds me that Shakespeare's own verdict at the end of the play seems appropriately harsh (and ironic). The play ends with the triumphant Henry preparing to marry his trophy wife, Katherine, Princess of France. That hopeful note is blotted out in the Epilogue, informing the audience what most of them would already know, that Henry V, "this star of England," as Shakespeare calls him, had a "small time" on the throne. After a mere six years, he died and was replaced by his infant son, Henry VI, whose handlers were, according to the Epilogue, "so many . . . that they lost France and made his England bleed." So much for the triumph and loss of life at Agincourt.

SHOULD YOU HAVE FRIENDS IN YOUR COMPANY?

Certainly! Most of us spend our waking hours working and thinking about work. As we discussed in Chapter 3, it is best to balance friends on the inside with a confidant on the outside. Business can put unusual strains on otherwise congenial relationships within a business. What if one of you is promoted and the other is not? What if her bonus is bigger than yours? Or if you get the job that he wanted?

I had a close personal relationship with one of the executives of a privately held company over which I had voting control. We fished together and drank together, and he and his wife even vacationed with my wife and me. My friend had excellent leadership ability and was proficient in his specialty. I appointed him to the board of directors, where he was a wise counselor whose judgment I trusted. I tried my best to acknowledge his contribution further by giving him a piece of the action. But we did not always agree on the best course of action, and I felt I had to go the way I thought was correct. After all, I was "the boss." Once, after a particularly serious disagreement over strategy, he said, "I'm going to call a board of directors' meeting." "That's fine," I replied. "Then I'll call a shareholders' meeting." Our friendship cooled demonstrably after that.

When E. T. "Bud" Gravette, former CEO of Turner Construction, the world's largest commercial builder, on whose board I proudly serve, addressed one of my seminars not long after we had been discussing Falstaff, someone asked Bud, "Should you have friends in business?" He told them a story about an experience he had while he was chairman of a large bank in New York City. Off to work one morning, he asked his wife about her plans for the day. "I'm playing bridge with Gloria today," she said. "That's interesting," said Bud. "I'm planning to fire her husband this morning."

ORDER AND DISORDER — A PROPOSED RESOLUTION

The first requirement, of course, is that you have a stable, growing, profitable enterprise. (For nonprofits, the sine qua non is that you have money left over or the debt capacity to fund future activities and growth.) The role of business is to develop, finance, produce, sell, and collect for products and services that get and keep profitable customers. That sounds like a business professor talking. I plead guilty. At my age, GE's board is not about to make their first call to me when Jack Welch retires. (Under Welch's leadership they have developed hundreds of executives more qualified for the job.) Nevertheless, at the tender age of seventy-one, I occasionally think that I'd like one more shot at running a large enterprise—to correct the mistakes I made and build on those things that I have done well. I'd also like to augment my leadership with the experience and insights gained in the past fifteen years as teacher, writer, and consultant.

I've always found business life easier when the goals and values of the enterprise—the mission—are understood, believed in, and accepted eagerly by most of the people in that enterprise.[26] That sentence is easy to say but devilishly hard to achieve. When people don't know where they're going or how they'll get there, or even if they really want to go, there's no hope.

Once the mission is decided—and understood—strategy and tactics need to be developed. Too many businesses, perhaps influenced by monarchies of the past, try to develop strategy and tactics at the top, then administer them centrally. The best ideas often come from people who are closest to the points of contact, namely, the work to be done and the customers who purchase it. Typically, the senior managers haven't seen a customer or been down on the plant floor for a long time. You want those people who are in the field to be part of the brainstorming. Often, it is the maverick who can move you ahead, break new ground. Dissatisfied with the status quo, maybe even unhappy with his job, it's this kind of "troublemaker" who sees new relationships and new opportunities. In plotting strategy, mavericks can be a great asset, because they want something different, and they keep building on from what's there.

The next requirement is to have a permeable organization structure, that is, a company where managers can cross over to other departments—marketing talks to sales, sales talks to finance or production, and so on, without having to go through the big boss first. As important as hierarchy is to any enterprise, those "stovepipes" on the organizational chart are inimical to productiv-

ity and growth. It is still amazing to me how many companies refuse to let people in one department talk to their peers across the
hall. You need processes that are interactive across departments.

And for all of the above, you need a trusting environment. The
final decision, of course, rests with the leadership. But if you've
learned anything from our study of Shakespeare's kings—Richard
II, Henry IV, Henry V, even Lear—you've noticed how easy it was
for them to become isolated and vulnerable. A true monarchy is
unlikely to be as productive as a republic, where the distance between leaders and followers is a lot closer. Moreover, if you're in-
volving a number of people in your strategy sessions, you ought to
try to listen to what they have to say.

In an environment of trust, your mavericks will be willing to step
forward with their best and even wildest ideas. An open, trusting
workplace lets people concentrate on doing their jobs rather than
just trying to keep them. And with a solid mission in place, you can
play the role of facilitator, pressing them to be clearer, sharper,
more probing; you can ask the hard questions and send them back
to the drawing board. *(See box.)* And when somebody steps into
outer space or presses you with a genuinely nutty idea that is beyond the bounds of your corporate goals or values, all you have to
do is point to the mission. If it supports the mission, entertain the
idea. If it does not support the mission, your rejection of the idea
will not seem to be personal. The maverick might then be encouraged to come back with another "nutty" idea, one that works!

When the above requirements are met, you will have plenty of
room in your company for the Falstaffs; better still, the mavericks
will find profit in supporting the enterprise rather than rebelling
against it.

MANAGING YOUR MAVERICKS

• The creative process has two distinct phases: producing ideas, and then judging their merits. Both are important, but they should be done separately. Too many nascent good ideas are lost because the boss judges them too soon—before they can be fully developed and understood. To that end, listen to your Falstaffs and George Taylors. Don't interrupt. Let them talk right through to the end before you say a thing.

• Never throw cold water on their ideas in public.

• Probe their options. Use the phrases "what if" and "what else"—for example, "What if we did this or that?"—building on their initial statement. Or "What else could we do?" again building on the initial idea.

• Never listen and then say, "I'll get back to you." If you must think about it, indicate your seriousness by being specific: "I'll get back to you at ten o'clock Tuesday morning, and here's what we will do."

• Don't overcompensate either. Saying "It's a wonderful idea" when you think it's crazy will not work either. By trying to build up your maverick's credibility, you will lose your own.

• Judge the ideas, of course. No enterprise has the resources to take on every idea that comes along. But if you judge ideas in the context of a clearly understood mission and strategy, you run less chance of stopping the flow of future ideas.

• Always remember, in the arena of great and revolutionary ideas, you are a nut (or a nerd) until you are a genius. To wit: Henry Ford, the Wright Brothers, Edison, and the creator of the first $500 billion company, Bill Gates.

• Banish the Jack Falstaff of Henry IV, yes, but banish him with love, care, and caution. Otherwise, you will scare off other Jack Falstaffs who will help to make your enterprise rich, powerful, and famous.

11

To Be or Not to Be:
It's Up to You

Hamlet's Fatal Flaws

> . . . I do not know
> Why yet I live to say this thing's to do,
> Sith I have cause, and will, and strength, and means
> To do't.
>
> HAMLET (4.4, 43–46)

> The readiness is all.
>
> HAMLET (5.2, 221)

THE story of Prince Hamlet, one of the world's greatest works of dramatic poetry, is a great object lesson in strategy: how it can go awry, how people react when they make mistakes, and ultimately what actions you can take to minimize mistakes and mitigate consequences.

As the play begins, we learn that Hamlet's father, the warrior king of Denmark, has recently died and the king's brother, Claudius, has assumed the throne and married Gertrude, the king's widow and Hamlet's mother. King Claudius and Gertrude implore the young prince to put aside his mourning; they also ask him not to return to Germany, where he has been studying at the University of Wittenberg, but to remain in Denmark. Hamlet agrees, but in his first soliloquy, he expresses his state of mind and attitude toward the world:

> O that this too too sullied flesh would melt,
> Thaw and resolve itself into a dew . . .
> How weary, stale, flat, and unprofitable
> Seem to me all the uses of this world!
>
> HAMLET (1.2, 129–34)

Hamlet makes clear his distaste for his uncle ("My father's brother—but no more like my father than I to Hercules") and his anger over his mother's remarriage less than two months after Hamlet Senior's death ("O, most wicked speed! To post / With such dexterity to incestuous sheets!"). With characteristic Shakespearean understatement, he declares that the situation "is not, nor it cannot, come to good." Two short scenes later, the ghost of his father informs Hamlet that Claudius poisoned him in his sleep. The ghost orders Hamlet to revenge his father's death. The rest of the play deals with Hamlet's indecision and ineptness, and his rashness in carrying out this command—resulting in the deaths of eight people, including himself.

Those familiar with the play are likely to wonder what they can learn about strategy from Hamlet. "It's not so much that Hamlet had a flawed strategy," the objection goes, "but that he had no strategy at all." On the contrary, every individual, including Hamlet, as well as every enterprise, always has a strategy. It might change from moment to moment; it might be submerged in our subconscious; it might be self-contradictory; it might be fuzzy or just plain wrong. But a strategy, explicit or implicit, always directs our actions. Implicit strategies usually lead to more trouble than those that are clearly articulated.

Effective leaders always know what they are doing, and why. When a strategy is explicit, you, as well as those you wish to influence, will have a better chance, first, to understand it, then, if necessary, to modify it.

An effective strategy is grounded in a set of realistic beliefs and expectations about our external worlds that helps us know what to do and how to do it, while making certain that we have the resources and will to carry it out.

In this respect, strategy and its execution are symbiotic. And because one depends so much on the other, it is foolish to separate them. Moreover, our expectations cannot be realistic if our beliefs are clouded by evidence so contradictory that it produces crippling uncertainty. To complicate matters further, there may be several external worlds from which to choose.

As the play unfolds, we see that Hamlet fails our strategy test on all counts. First, he was confused about the external world. Indeed, he was bridging two worlds that had entirely different views of retribution. One world—the old world, the pagan world, the world of the Old Testament—demands revenge. "Revenge his foul and most unnatural murder," the ghost commands Hamlet. The son himself must slay his father's murderer. The other world—the world of Wittenberg University, which Martin Luther himself attended—is based in the Christian tradition and forbids personal retribution. Society's laws would right the wrong, or, eventually, God would. "Vengeance is mine; I will repay, saith the Lord" (Romans 12:19).

And Hamlet, like a business leader rushing into a risky venture, fails the test on another count. He does not have the resources he needs, no powerful friends on his side—only Horatio, who has no standing in the court. Most important, however, is that Hamlet lacks the will and the discipline to acquire the resources. As we will see later, resources were available, but because he chooses not to acquire them, he seals his doom. He cannot lead, manage, or follow. He throws away any chance he might have had to succeed to his murdered father's throne. His revenge plans constantly go awry; he cannot follow his father's clear and careful instructions, nor can he create an alternative strategy.

Hamlet's plight is similar to that of today's business leaders facing e-commerce, wild currency swings, and market values calculated as a multiple of next year's revenues instead of last year's earnings. What are business leaders to do when the Phillips curve no longer curves, when healthy economics no longer automatically triggers inflation, when technical wizardry is the primary drive of productivity increases, when price-earnings ratios are in the hundreds, when the Dow's average price-earnings ratio is in the twenties? No wonder some CEOs look forward to early retirement rather than tenure extensions.

Think of Hamlet as a young CEO of enormous potential: brilliant, perceptive, thoughtful, physically attractive, and an excellent communicator. A corporate recruiter visiting Wittenberg University would have courted him assiduously. Were he writing today, the Bard might have chosen James Robinson at American Express or John Akers at IBM as his subject. Or Bob Allen at AT&T, John Sculley at Apple Computer, or a host of other princes of American business whose worlds changed so profoundly that beliefs and expectations that once were realistic no longer applied. In this chapter, we will examine the strategies of these CEOs and why they went awry. We will also take a look at their reactions to mistakes and what could have been done to minimize them and mitigate their consequences. Finally, we will contrast their actions with those of the founder and CEO of one of today's great and incredible (the word does not seem out of place here) American companies, Amazon.com.[27]

In the meantime, we will hold all of the above up to Hamlet's mirror, always asking two questions: What went wrong with Hamlet? What can business leaders learn from Hamlet's failures?

WHY STRATEGIES GO AWRY

James D. Robinson, who had been chairman and CEO at American Express since 1977, also failed the strategy test. His dream of building a "global financial supermarket" ended on January 30, 1993, when his board of directors, goaded by angry stockholders, asked him to step down. Robinson wasn't prepared for the rough-and-tumble competition that came from almost every quarter. Shearson Lehman, his investment bank, was on the ropes, the famed American Express credit cards were losing out to Visa and other bank cards. Robinson's company did not have the financial or human resources to compete effectively on many fronts, and Robinson had squandered his own management resources trying to be a business statesman and a mover in New York society, as well as a CEO. His internal decision model of a clubby corporate world where charm and connections were the criteria for success was no longer useful. I believe watching *Hamlet* could have helped Jim Robinson reexamine his original beliefs and expectations and see that they could not bring him to his goals. The play helps me keep up with a changing business world. When I was in the publishing business, I believed for a while that in spite of cutbacks in federal funds for education, we could continue to produce and profitably sell curriculum materials to schools. I was wrong, but I didn't feign madness as Hamlet did (although such an escape seemed attractive when the outlook was gloomiest). I simply acknowledged that the world had changed and that I could not change it back. We repackaged our curriculum materials and a line of books that we had previously sold directly to schools. The repackaged products were marketed through regular bookstores.

Sometimes strategies go awry because of unresolved contradictions. Often, these are not based on evidence or rationality, but they have a profound effect on our actions. For example, while I could listen all day to a certain financial guru, I could not bring myself to pay 400 times earnings for a start-up Internet company he was touting.

The more profound contradiction Hamlet faces is his attitude to the ghost of his father. Ghosts were accepted phenomena in both medieval and Elizabethan times. The question was, were they agents of hell or heaven? Or were they agents of a pagan god? When Hamlet first saw the ghost, his reaction was decidedly Christian: "Angels and ministers of grace defend us!"

Then he mixed in terms from the supernatural:

> Be thou a spirit of health or goblin damn'd,
> Bring with thee airs from heaven or blasts from hell . . .
>
> HAMLET (1.4, 40–41)

Spirits and goblins. Heaven and hell. Hamlet seems further confounded when his father's ghost urges him to "revenge his foul and most unnatural murder,"—pure retribution and thus the pagan way of settling things—even though the ghost has revealed that he is

> Doom'd for a certain term to walk the night,
> And for the day confin'd to fast in fires,
> Till the foul crimes done in my days of nature
> Are burnt and purg'd away.
>
> HAMLET (1.5, 10–13)

That seems to be a description of what in Roman Catholic theology is known as "purgatory," a place where souls destined for heaven are cleansed or "purged" of all unrepented or unpunished sins. In spite of these pagan-Christian contradictions, the ghost wins the day for personal retribution. Hamlet vows:

> Yea, from the table of my memory
> I'll wipe away all trivial fond records . . .
> And thy commandment all alone shall live
> Within the book and volume of my brain . . .
>
> HAMLET (1.5, 98–103)

Hamlet's last words to the spirit of his father are a pledge of revenge: "I have sworn't" (*Hamlet* [1.5, 112]).

No ambivalence there. Hamlet commits himself absolutely to the world of personal retribution. Claudius, whom the ghost of King Hamlet has denounced as "that incestuous, that adulterate beast" (*Hamlet* [1.5, 42]), appears as good as dead.

Yet for most of the play, Claudius remains very much alive and very much in control. Hamlet does not keep his promise. Why?

What has happened to Hamlet's strategy to punish his uncle and give his beloved father's spirit eternal rest?

Even with the best of intentions, it would have been difficult for Hamlet to keep his promise and suffer no repercussions because he never truly understands all the implications. How many grandiose corporate initiatives have been announced and then dropped because the leader had not thought them through? John Akers, former CEO at IBM, was sure that "quality" would solve the troubled giant's problems. He announced a major initiative to make quality the watchword at IBM, but he did not see to it that his people had the information, the training, and the resources to do the job. Quality doesn't happen just because you want it to. Senior executives and the board of directors must understand how the company's current processes, practices, reward systems, and culture contribute to poor quality. Then the executives, from the top down, must be willing to change those things—even kill a few sacred cows—in order to improve quality.

During the early stages of IBM's quality efforts, my colleagues and I at Columbia were working with Dr. W. Edwards Deming, the man who helped turn around Japanese automobile companies in the 1950s and 1960s through improved quality, and who was currently working with both General Motors and Ford Motor Company. Because of our association with Dr. Deming, we were contacted by IBM executives asking for help. After some investigation, we concluded that there was no hope. IBM's senior leaders not only did not understand what quality was all about, they weren't about to change their current practices. Like Hamlet, they failed the strategy test. They did not understand the world of "quality"; consequently, they did not dedicate the resources required to produce real quality. Compare this with the successful quality initiatives that Larry Bossidy put into place at Allied Signal and that inspired Jack Welch at General Electric. Each began with massive training programs for everyone—including senior leaders. GE and Allied Signal changed procedures, installed measurement systems, and revised pay and bonus systems—all aimed at rewarding improvement in quality. Because they had thought the strategy through before they announced it, and because they had understood how improved quality increased not only sales and customer loyalty but productivity as well, they produced measurable results. Quality was more than a word; it was an integral part of their strategy.

Bossidy and Welch would have warned Hamlet of the consequences of announcing a strategy too soon. Hamlet's father's ghost might have won the day, but he did not win the month or year. Like many of us faced with difficult decisions and uncertain evidence, once he is over the emotional impact of encountering the ghost, Hamlet vacillates. Now he calls the ghost into question:

> . . . The spirit that I have seen
> May be a devil, and the devil hath power
> T' assume a pleasing shape, yea, and perhaps,
> Out of my weakness and my melancholy,
> As he is very potent with such spirits,
> Abuses me to damn me.
>
> HAMLET (2.2, 600–605)

The revenge strategy that was so clear earlier is now in doubt. Could Hamlet justify killing the lawful king of Denmark by saying, "A ghost made me do it"? We get even more evidence of Hamlet's indecision when he speaks to his friend Horatio, saying it is possible that

> It is a damned ghost that we have seen,
> And my imaginations are as foul
> As Vulcan's stithy [forge].
>
> HAMLET (3.2, 83–85)

Like Hamlet, the executives at Merrill Lynch faced two worlds, and they had considerable doubts about how to bridge them. And, as is usually the case when you are bridging two worlds, there will be unpleasant consequences no matter what you do. Merrill Lynch was a juggernaut in the traditional brokerage business, with more than 14,000 well-trained brokers worldwide. Then, almost overnight, online trading appeared on the scene. At first, a few small firms offered e-trade access; then Charles Schwab, once an upstart discount broker but now a powerful, innovative brokerage firm, entered the fray. Merrill Lynch was caught in a classic strategy quandary. On the one hand, it could adopt what was called a "straddle strategy." Michael Porter at Harvard and other business strategists, including me, have pointed out the dangers of straddling two worlds. However, the dangers of staying in one world (while it is shrinking) can be worse. After months of doubt and debate, Merrill Lynch decided to make the jump. Herbert Allison, president and COO of Merrill, made the tough and controversial decision to go online and to match Schwab's prices.

If you were a broker at Merrill Lynch, how would you have felt? *Betrayed* is the word. And the brokers fought back. Here is the rest of the story: while Merrill's decision came late, it was the right way to go, even though it meant enormous changes in the organization. And Allison was going to have to pay a price. Shortly after announcing the decision to go online, Allison announced his resignation. He had been informed that he would not be the successor when the present CEO retired. According to the business press, Allison had several strikes against him, one of which was a "buttoned-down" management style. He was not a "hail fellow well met" type, as brokers are wont to be, and, the business press suggested, the brokerage side of Merrill had mounted a campaign to oust the "traitor." So although he made the difficult decision, the troops managed to knock him off his throne. I'm sure that the "ousting" was a deep personal disappointment to Mr. Allison. But he has nothing to be ashamed of. He retained his dignity and the respect of many of his colleagues, as well as much of the investment community. In my view, he waited too long, but he made the right decision. He chose the dangerous straddle strategy. In this sense, his actions could have informed our young Prince Hamlet: there are precious few perfect strategies.

Indeed, in many instances, one must choose the best of several less-than-attractive options—then do one's best to make it better. There's no room at the top for a perfectionist in the fast-moving, rough-and-tumble business world. Hamlet was in a rough-and-tumble world, too. It is no light matter to kill a king. But Hamlet was a perfectionist and a philosopher, waiting for the perfect time and place to take his revenge, and always asking himself whether or not he should do it. While scholars ponder Hamlet's ethical problems, most businesspeople would probably opt for fast revenge. In which case, unlike Herbert Allison, Hamlet waited far too late. The world—and his opportunity—passed him by.

How People React When Strategy Goes Awry

The downsizing of the past two decades has thrust many brilliant, thoughtful, perceptive people into a strange world. No longer protected by the stability of corporate life, they have been forced to seek jobs with smaller companies. Many others are working from their homes, answering their own phones, sending faxes, sending invoices, then trying to collect payment in time to pay the rent. Many have made the transition; others, just as brilliant, thoughtful, and perceptive, have resorted to hand-wringing and breast-beating. A few dream of revenge. They have not been able to develop a realistic relationship with the new world they live in. Their beliefs and expectations have not changed as their world has changed. They do not know what to do, let alone how to do it.

In some cases, the decision to try to stay put and fight the good fight is appropriate. If the problem is not "what to do" but "how to do it" (the strategy is fine but the execution is flawed), the wise decision maker knows to stay the course, adjusting the tactics while reaffirming the strategy. In other instances, people have the common sense and courage to acknowledge that the strategy does not reflect a realistic perception of the external world and the resources actually available to them. Setting hubris and personal pride aside, they change the strategy.

And then there are those whose reactions are inappropriate. These include vacillation, paralysis, bravado, intransigence, impatience, hand-wringing, breast-beating, rage, withdrawal, and flight. Even though these reactions are inappropriate, they are understandable. It is perfectly normal to feel them, even to give in to them from time to time. They are dangerous, however, when they take control. The trick is to recognize them early enough to escape. (A wise friend of mine once said, "You can be forgiven for shooting yourself in the foot, but not if you reload.") Many of these destructive responses, if not caught in time, lead to rash behavior.

Here's what to be on guard for:

• *Vacillation.* When you try one thing after another, discard it, try something else, then go back to your original plan, you're probably guilty of vacillation. As we have seen, Hamlet is an expert in this manifestation of strategy gone awry. The ghost is real, then it is not; he stages a play to trap the king, traps him, then, when the opportunity presents itself, lets the king escape when he easily could have killed him. His soliloquies are masterpieces of vacillation. He even thinks about how he is thinking:

> . . . Now whether it be
> Bestial oblivion, or some craven scruple
> Of thinking too precisely on th'event—
> A thought which, quarter'd, hath but one part wisdom
> And ever three parts coward—I do not know
> Why yet I live to say this thing's to do . . .
>
> HAMLET (4.4, 39–44)

Bob Allen, the CEO of AT&T, wanted to be in the computer business, then he didn't. He bought NCR and, several billion dollars later, abandoned it. He wanted an integrated company—but then he spun off Lucent Technology. Goaded by his board to name a successor, he chose John Walter; nine months later, he gave Walter $25.8 million to leave. No one can accuse Mr. Allen of inaction, but he is definitely guilty of vacillation.

• *Paralysis.* This is sometimes confused with vacillation because the result is similar: no forward motion. I once had a client who was paralyzed by his vivid imagination. Too educated for his own good, he would contemplate one elaborate scenario after the other, unable to evaluate the merits of one over another. He drove us wild with his indecision. I should have been forewarned at our first meeting: he could not decide what to order for lunch. I ordered for him. In business schools, we call this analysis-paralysis. I have seen corporate chieftains who refuse to acknowledge the new reality—that their cash is disappearing, their customers and employees deserting. They just keep doing the same thing, only harder, longer, and sometimes louder. I ask these foolishly brave leaders if they know the Theory of Holes. "No, John, what is the Theory of Holes?" they ask. My answer: "If you want to get out, stop digging."

• *Bravado.* Hamlet exhibits this trait when he leaps into Ophelia's open grave to struggle with Laertes, her bereaved brother. He rejected her while she was alive; his behavior contributed to her madness, yet when she's dead, he shouts

> I lov'd Ophelia. Forty thousand brothers
> Could not with all their quantity of love
> Make up my sum. What wilt thou do for her? . . .
> Woo't weep, woo't fight, woo't fast, woo't tear thyself . . .
> I'll do't.

HAMLET (5.1, 269–77)

It can work the reverse way, too. I have known territory managers in a construction company who felt that their manhood would be in question if they admitted uncertainty about whether a problem existed or if they admitted that they didn't know how to solve it by themselves. Manfully, they kept marching along until, finally, the project came crashing down on their heads.

• *Intransigence.* Some people stubbornly refuse to accept new information even when concerned and trusted colleagues present it. A former colleague of mine in the oil business refused to believe that oil would ever sell for less than $35 a barrel. He kept drilling shallow wells in worn-out oil plays where the lifting costs were higher than the price of oil. In another venture he drilled a $3 million dry hole, wearing out ninety-three drill bits in 16,000 feet of rock, refusing to believe the well logs that clearly showed that there was no hope for a commercial well.

• *Impatience.* Sometimes this can be a virtue. Doing something, even if it is wrong can, on occasion, be better than paralysis, particularly if the decision maker is able to recognize mistakes and willing to correct them. Unbridled impatience, however, can lead to disaster. Al Dunlap, whose aggressive cut-and-slash turnaround style earned him the nickname "Chainsaw Al," once wrote, "A business that can't be turned around in a year can't be turned around at all." When his turnarounds fell behind schedule, his impatience usually created another round of draconian, sometimes mindless, job cuts, unrealistic sales projections, and unbelievable (in the pejorative sense) financial statements.

Dunlap's brand of impatience would have wrecked two turnaround companies on whose boards of directors I serve. The leaders of those companies carefully developed turnaround strategies. Both were dramatically successful. Neither was accomplished in less than thirty months.

• *Hand-wringing, breast-beating, and rage.* We have all exhibited these behaviors and felt their underlying emotions at one time or another. Let's ask Prince Hamlet to demonstrate how these reactions can overtake us when they get out of control. Distraught over his indecision, Hamlet soliloquizes:

> O what a rogue and peasant slave am I! . . .
> A dull and muddy-mettled rascal, peak
> Like John-a-dreams, unpregnant of my cause,
> And can say nothing—no, not for a king,
> Upon whose property and most dear life
> A damn'd defeat was made. Am I a coward?
>
> HAMLET (2.2, 550, 568–72)

Then from hand-wringing he shifts to breast-beating:

> But I am pigeon-liver'd and lack gall
> To make oppression bitter, or ere this
> I should ha' fatted all the region kites
> With this slave's offal. Bloody, bawdy villain!
> Remorseless, treacherous, lecherous, kindless villain!
> O, vengeance! [28]
>
> HAMLET (2.2, 579–83)

(John Barrymore was said to have run the entire length of the stage, shouting those last two words: "O, vengeance," dramatizing how, in today's lexicon, Hamlet had "lost it.") Exhausted by this outburst, Hamlet calms down, still self-critical, still beating his breast:

> Why, what an ass am I! This is most brave,
> That I, the son of a dear father murder'd,
> Prompted to my revenge by heaven and hell,
> Must like a whore unpack my heart with words
> And fall a-cursing, like a very drab,
> A scullion! Fie upon't! Foh!
>
> HAMLET (2.2, 584–89)

And after all the hand-wringing and breast-beating, he still does nothing.

• *Withdrawal and flight.* These are two of the most distressing reactions. I have consulted with or assumed leadership of companies where all the doors in the executive suite are closed. Everyone is hiding in his or her hole, staring at the wall or papers on the desk. To make matters worse, travel has been curtailed to save money at the precise time when executives should be visible to employees, suppliers, customers, and bankers. Perhaps they are rehearsing Hamlet's lines:

> . . . To die—to sleep,
> No more; and by a sleep to say we end
> The heart-ache and the thousand natural shocks
> That flesh is heir to: 'tis a consummation
> Devoutly to be wish'd.
>
> HAMLET (3.1, 60–64)

Flight is also a siren song that beckons many corporate souls. Rather than "take arms against a sea of troubles and by opposing end them," they seek solace in outside activities. I have known executives who have flown from troubles at the office to accept prestigious government appointments or who have tried to become business statesmen. Realizing that they couldn't solve their company's problems, they addressed the problems of the world. They seemed to embrace high-profile debates where accountability was absent. Hamlet's flight was to assume madness while figuring out what to do and how to do it. My hunch is that he became too comfortable with his escape, losing touch with the real world that he lived in.

All of the above reactions, if left unchecked, lead to rash behavior. As a board member, I am suspicious of ambitious programs proposed by a CEO almost ready to retire whose earlier strategies have not worked out. After all, this is an executive who has not yet left his mark on the corporate world. The risks he is willing to take might be ill considered and dangerous to the enterprise. Leaders of seriously troubled companies often announce projects without the proper resources in hand or even the hope of finding them. I am not against looking for creative, sometimes risky, solutions. What I am counseling is extreme care in assessing your resources and your resolve, as well as the resolve of those who will carry out the project.

John Sculley, after a great start at Apple Computer, became so frustrated about the company's not bringing to market anything better than the Macintosh that he created a revolving door for his technology chiefs. In apparent desperation, he named himself technology chief, a position for which he was decidedly unqualified. While the company was burning up cash and credibility, he fiddled around with Newton, a handheld device whose performance was questionable and for which the market potential was underwhelming.

When the late, lamented Allegheny International was awash in red ink and drowning in debt, CEO Robert Buckley decided to build a fancy office building in Pittsburgh. When Buckley's critics called it his "Taj Mahal," they were right, because the building soon became a mausoleum—for Buckley and Allegheny International.

Shakespeare spotlighted rash behavior throughout his plays. What could be more dramatic (or ironic or absurd) than a character acting decisively—and catastrophically? Hamlet thrusts his sword into the drapery, thinking that the hated Claudius is eavesdropping on him and his mother—and kills Polonius! He sends his hapless university friends Rosencrantz and Guildenstern to their deaths, even though they were unknowing pawns in Claudius's plot to have Hamlet executed. Surprised to learn that his onetime sweetheart Ophelia has the leading role in the funeral he happens upon, Hamlet leaps into her open grave and struggles with her bereaved brother, Laertes. Hamlet accepts Claudius's request that he fight a duel with Laertes—a match in which the prince has nothing to gain and his life to lose.

In every instance, Hamlet could have acted otherwise: more sanely, less rashly. He is brilliant and he is stuck—because he cannot align his thought, his desire, and his action.

MINIMIZE MISTAKES, MITIGATE
THEIR CONSEQUENCES

You cannot eliminate mistakes, but you can reduce their number and mitigate their consequences if you align (or realign) your strategies with your external worlds. But you will also need the resources and the will to carry out these strategies.

To demonstrate how Prince Hamlet's failures can instruct us in what not to do, we will pair him with a company facing even more complex issues, albeit with less severe consequences. (Debt is preferable to death.) In 1994, Jeff Bezos, who was working as a vice president for a hedge fund company in Manhattan, had a wonderful new idea for selling an old product—books. Eschewing the bricks and mortar of retail stores, Bezos began selling books via the Internet. He called his virtual bookstore Amazon.com.

Jeff Bezos lives in at least five worlds, facing major uncertainties in each of them. To concentrate all his energy on Internet marketing, Bezos outsourced the management of his inventory and shipping to third parties. The almost immediate success of Amazon.com captured the imagination of the financial world, which flooded Bezos's cyberspace bookstore with equity, convertible debentures, and other forms of debt so he could rush to preempt market share—a classic strategy for burgeoning markets. The outsourcing costs, along with tremendous marketing and technical expense, far exceeded the company's gross margins. Profits were not possible, but, as is typical of Internet start-ups, profits were not Amazon.com's primary concern for the first couple of years. Business writers and investors, however, were wondering whether they were dealing with the old supermarket excuse: "Sure, we lose money on everything we sell, but we'll make it up on the volume."

So Jeff Bezos entered two new worlds: production (including order handling) and operating finance (including inventory management). Amazon opened warehouse and distribution centers across the country. Then Bezos entered yet another world: if he could sell books on the Internet, he could sell CDs. The hope was that the incremental gross margins from CDs would help cover the fixed costs from the new distribution system. Still no profits. In fact, losses more than doubled. Not to worry. Market dominance is still the name of the game. In many respects, Bezos's market dominance strategy was confirmed. Barnes & Noble, the $3 billion bricks-and-mortar bookstore chain founded in 1873 that, like Shakespeare's Julius Caesar, "doth bestride the narrow world like a Colossus," was late to the Internet party. Bezos had not sent an invitation, but Barnes & Noble's ambitious CEO, Leonard Riggio, apparently thinking, better late than never, crashed the gate anyhow, taking his company online in 1997. Although a bit late to this party, Riggio is a worthy adversary.

Riggio dropped out of New York University in 1965 to open his own bookstore, SBX, around the corner from the college bookstore where he had worked as a clerk. Six years later, he had five college bookstores. Today he has 350. He bought Barnes & Noble in 1971, introduced steep discounting on remaindered books, and then bought his main discount competitor, including its mail-order operations. Using junk bonds for his next move, Riggio bought the B. Dalton chain of 800 bookstores in 1986. In the early 1990s, he realized that a major competitor, Borders, had hit on a new idea: the superstore concept. Riggio redirected his strategy, adopted the superstore model, and opened several hundred. He raised his share of the U.S. book market from 7 percent to 15 percent in six years. Today Barnes & Noble has more than 1,000 book-stores, and Riggio is again rethinking his strategy.

Barnes & Noble introduced Bezos to another new world: com-petition. Resourceful as ever, Bezos priced *The New York Times'* best-sellers for 50 percent off list, tarnishing Barnesandnoble.com's 1999 initial public offering (IPO), which climbed only 27 percent on its first day of trading—much less than Barnes & Noble had hoped—and Wall Street yawned. But, as we say in retailing, "Com-petitors don't bring you any business." As a result of B & N's entry into the online bookstore business, Amazon.com lost some of its glamour, prompting investors to wonder whether Bezos's business model would ever make a profit. As great at marketing as he has proved to be, his marketing costs are rising at a faster rate than his revenue.

The question remained: Is Amazon.com a good investment? On December 16, 1998, analysts raised their target price for Ama-zon.com from $150 a share to $400 a share. That day its market value rose 20 percent, to $15 billion. Bezos's personal net worth climbed from $914 million to $5.7 billion. Within two months, the market had taken all of that back. The stock then went on another tear, doubling to 221¼ shortly before Barnesandnoble.com's IPO. Again, the market took back the gain before 1999 was half over.

Did Bezos, like Hamlet, vacillate, become paralyzed, show bravado, intransigence, or impatience, wring his hands, beat his breast, rant and rave, withdraw, or flee? Hardly. Bezos used the money that people had given him for bookselling and became a venture capitalist—preempting the role that his investors had thought they were playing. Betting that e-commerce someday, somehow, will pay off, Bezos is using Amazon's marketing clout and its access to Internet customers to invest in joint ventures with companies selling CDs, pet food, groceries, and even prescription drugs.

Will Amazon.com make it? The jury is out. Bookselling has not been a growth industry in the 1990s. Would Tina Packer and I in-vest in it? Not on your life. But the suspense and excitement of the drama are spellbinding. Has Jeff Bezos made a contribution to the economic world? Absolutely. He has energetically entered brand-new worlds, has adjusted his tactics and strategies to meet exigencies. The complexities he has faced are of a magnitude as great as those facing Prince Hamlet. Hamlet's decisions affect the country, the army, the succession, his family life, his love life, and his friends. Jeff Bezos may not affect the country, army, and succession, but his decisions do affect an enormous number of investors and a hell of a lot of money, and all the ramifications thereof.

Now let's hold Shakespeare's mirror up to Prince Hamlet and Jeff Bezos and, while we're at it, take a glance at ourselves. Perhaps we can gain some insights that will help us when we face problems similar to theirs.

UNCERTAINTY AND RISK— MAKE THEM YOUR FRIENDS

Uncertainty is existential, inescapable. Those with an inordinate fear of uncertainty are not only incapable of action but are usually unhappy, even miserable. The antidote to uncertainty is improved information gained through planned action. My late mentor and colleague W. Edwards Deming's "PDSA cycle" (Plan, Do, Study, Act) revolutionized the way we deal with uncertainty: make a plan, implement it on a small scale, study the results, and act on what you have learned. Then start the process all over again. Never stop; continually learn and improve.

Hamlet fails Deming's test, too. Perhaps he thinks he has a plan when he feigns madness and when he stages the play before the king and queen with a scene similar to his father's murder, hoping to get Claudius to respond guiltily and thus to, as Hamlet puts it, "catch the conscience of a king." But these were half plans, not fully thought through. Although Hamlet does follow steps two and three of the PDSA cycle—he stages the play and studies the reaction of King Claudius—he never acts on what he has learned.

Jeff Bezos's actions were better framed. Back in 1994, working for a hedge fund company, he prepared the business model for his new idea for a bookstore that would exploit the growth of Internet usage and circumvent the costs of bricks and mortar by outsourcing shipping and inventory. When his employer turned down the proposal, Bezos resigned and stepped out on his own. He carried out his initial plan and studied the outcomes. Then he acted to modify and improve. He saw that outsourcing was too costly, so he began developing his own distribution and inventory management systems. At every step of the way, he has erased old uncertainties and faced up to new ones. The process is continuous, vibrant, creative, alive. (Yes, you should gain information through research and study, but without action and feedback the information tends to be sterile.)

Uncertainty has another important property: it is not yours alone. Too often we forget that our adversaries and competitors face uncertainties, also. If I deal better than they with uncertainty, I have a better chance of success. I wrote in an earlier book: "The successful entrepreneur, then, learns to live with uncertainty. He is like the marathoner who is certain that pain is coming. He doesn't know when or where, but when it does come, he tips his hat as to an old friend, then runs along with it—and sometimes through it." [29]

Risk is related to uncertainty, but the two are not synonymous. For example, the nature and magnitude of the risk are sometimes well known, and then deemed worth taking or not. However, risk is similar to uncertainty in that as information is gained, both risk and uncertainty are reduced. The most useful information comes from action and feedback. And, like uncertainty, risk is a fact of life, especially in business situations that are zero-sum (having winners or losers only)—as opposed to non-zero-sum, games, in which everyone can win. The zero-sum idea introduces a serious misconception about risk that should be put to rest. Some people believe that reward is a function of risk; in other words, that the greatest rewards come from taking the greatest risks. Nonsense: the greatest rewards usually come from doing more of what you already do well. Sure, there's always the possibility that something will go wrong, but your knowledge of the territory usually enables you to manage that risk. However, if you don't know the territory, you could be in trouble. For example, the rewards from day trading on the Web might (potentially) be astronomical, but for me, the risk would be prohibitive. I am sure I would run out of cash before I hit the jackpot.

Which brings us to another concept of risk management: Risk is reduced by the intellectual and financial resources held in reserve. Even though he was in new territory, Jeff Bezos started out carefully; then, as successes came, he managed the upside of risk. He went to the financial markets at the right time and raised an enormous amount of cash. He could afford to make some mistakes. He did not view risk as a fearsome adversary. He managed risk, not only by facing it squarely, but by welcoming it as an old friend.

Hamlet was no shrinking violet when it came to risk, but he did not seem to understand its implications, and thus he managed it miserably. When King Claudius proposes the duel between Hamlet and Laertes, Hamlet accepts; but, had he thought it through, he would have realized that he had nothing to gain and everything to lose. Even if the game had not been "fixed" (Laertes poisoned the tip of his rapier), and even if Hamlet had won fair and square, he would not have enhanced his resources to deal with Claudius.

REFRAME AND REDISCOVER

Sometimes after I have taken the red-eye from coast to coast and taught two three-hour seminars the same day, I have said to myself and regretfully to others, "I am dog tired. I don't know how I can take another step or sit on another airplane." What if I were to say, "My body is telling me to take a rest, slow down a bit, regroup so I can have the fun of consulting on another business problem and the exhilaration of exchanging ideas with a classroom full of brilliant, energetic students"?

That's called reframing. (I feel better already.) Think of the possibilities that Hamlet threw away by not reframing the ghost's admonition to "revenge his foul and most unnatural murder." It's not inconceivable that Hamlet could have deposed Claudius and assumed the throne. Shakespeare makes it plain that Hamlet was well liked. Given time and a plan, he might have begun building support, looking for other opportunities to throw suspicion on the king. Instead of moping around in "sables and weeds," he could have dressed in "light and careless livery" as Claudius suggested. He could have further allayed Claudius's suspicions by assuming a happy countenance, attending to his duties at the palace—and waiting for his opportunity. Then he could have staged his play, trapped Claudius with his poisoning scene, and won the hearts and minds of the other nobles at court when the king fled and they realized that Hamlet knew his uncle, Claudius, had killed his father. Or he could have waited for the opportunity to repay Claudius in kind, surreptitiously poisoning him without directing suspicion on himself. Instead, Hamlet squandered any chance he might have had at the throne by acting rashly and killing foolish old Polonius, ensuring that he would be sent out of the country.

Jeff Bezos certainly knows how to reframe. He did not go down for the count when it took longer than expected to sell books at a profit. He reframed the issue—and bought some time—by trying to cover his fixed costs by selling CDs and other merchandise. When that didn't work as quickly as it should have, he reframed again by recognizing that e-commerce was going to be big. He had the resources to invest in other e-commerce ventures. As I said before, the jury is still out. Perhaps Amazon.com won't make it. But you've got to give credit to Bezos. He's creative, and he knows how to reframe.

DON'T WALK ALONE

When Tina Packer compares the resourceful Rosalind from *As You Like It* with Desdemona, the doomed bride of Othello, she shows how Rosalind, time and time again, enlists the support of others. Hamlet also fails this test. He has one friend, Horatio, but he shuts himself off from anyone else who might be of help. For example: What if Hamlet had the insight and skill to turn his college friends, Rosencrantz and Guildenstern, into double agents, spying on the king for him? Instead, when, at the king's request, they come to recover Polonius's body, Hamlet makes fun of them, toys with them. To whom would you be loyal—Hamlet or the king? Laertes, too, could have been a stalwart friend, but Hamlet throws that chance away by driving Ophelia, Laertes's sister, into insanity. Hamlet would not confide in Marcellus and Bernardo, two of the king's army officers, who also saw the ghost. It is conceivable that they could have helped him gain the support of Denmark's army.

Without help from others, there was no hope for Hamlet. He reminds me of executives at troubled companies that I have consulted with or whose jobs I have assumed. As troubles mounted, they became reclusive. Perhaps they were embarrassed as well as confused, but all too often their response was to close their office doors and try to figure out all the answers by themselves. The next time you feel pressured, put on a happy face, go out into the world, and exchange ideas with others. It's amazing how many people really want to help—if you let them, and if you show respect for their ideas.

I don't know anything about Jeff Bezos's management style, but I do know that he doesn't walk alone. When selling books and CDs did not turn a profit as quickly as he had hoped, he entered into joint ventures with other firms in the Internet world.

LIVE IN AT LEAST THREE WORLDS

At a minimum, you need to know your own company (its products, services, personnel, policies, practices, and procedures); you need to know your markets as they exist today; and you need also to be able to predict the future. Three different worlds.

Predicting the future is the most difficult, so let's address it first. The higher the position you hold on the corporate ladder, the more you should pay attention to the future. (That's why we have ladders—so you can stand on the top rung and peer great distances.) Leaders and managers should have in place the policies, practices, and procedures to take care of the present. But today was yesterday's tomorrow. The world moves on, and if you're not ready, it will pass you by.

Should you be able to predict the future with certainty? Impossible! But being alert, thoughtful, and nimble will enhance your chances of success.

It might seem counterintuitive, but the most effective futurists (not dreamers) are the ones who know their present markets. When you are attuned to your customers, you can pick up signals that will not only help you serve them better today, but will also provide signposts for the road ahead.

Of course, you cannot serve your markets well if you are not aware of the strengths, weaknesses, and nuances of your own operation. The best proof of this is the salesman who knows his products and services so well that he can recommend new applications or procedures to his customers. We're not trying to tell you what you already know, but to warn you of the dangers of overspecialization. Certainly, if your job is production, then you need to know that job very well, but you can always perform it better if you understand the markets you're producing for. Similarly, if your job is marketing, you can perform it better if you know your production capabilities. And if your job is planning for the future, you need to understand both—your present operations and marketing: there is no future if there is no today.

Jeff Bezos lives in all three of those worlds, and more. He might not have conquered them yet, but he gives signs that he acknowledges their presence. Jack Welch lives in twenty or more worlds. Although he cannot know each of his businesses intimately, he knows the people running them; and he has to know enough to say yes or no to important acquisitions and other capital expenditure decisions.

Hamlet was confused. He did not know his company well. The policies, practices, procedures, and politics at Elsinore did not seem to appeal to him. If he wished to justify his actions, his market was the nobles at court and the people of Denmark. Although it appears that he was well liked as a young prince, we have no evidence that he cared about either the people or the nobles. And he seemed oblivious to the future, never giving a serious thought to the consequences of his actions or, more important, his inaction.

TAKE CHARGE

Alan Kay of Xerox PARC crafted the phrase "The best way to predict the future is to create it." You can't create the future just by reacting, as important as it is to react as feedback comes in. Admittedly, you're sometimes trapped in the reaction mode. In some turnarounds that I have done, there were so many fires to put out that, indeed, the first few weeks were spent in firefighting—reacting.

In the Pathmark turnaround, I was more fortunate. We opened all 125 stores twenty-four hours a day within one week after my arrival. The fires we put out were the logistical ones that we had started. But we were again in charge—moving ahead, not reacting to another chain's price cuts and promotions.

With some notable exceptions, I have found that the leaders and managers who take charge, energetically and forcefully, are the ones who make fewer mistakes. And when they do make a mistake, the "take charge" leaders are better able to mitigate the consequences. Counterpunching is an acceptable and necessary tactic, but when you take the fight to your adversary, you are setting the pace—*your* pace—which might not be theirs. (The "notable exceptions" that I refer to are those leaders who seem to take charge by making rash decisions, then thrash about wildly, with no plan and no assessment of the market or the competition.)

Some scholars argue that Hamlet finally took charge after he learned of Claudius's plot on his life and after his resourceful escape with the pirates who attacked the ship carrying him to his death in England. Yes, it was in many ways a different Hamlet who returned to Denmark, no longer contemplative and paralyzed. Still, most of his actions were reactions. He disses Laertes in Ophelia's grave. He lets Claudius call the tune in setting up the duel with Laertes. He lashes out when he discovers the foils are poisoned. Yes, Claudius dies in the aftermath, but where is the profit? Hamlet dies also, as do Laertes and the queen; and the kingdom is turned over to the aggressive outsider Fortinbras, a

Norwegian who is returning from a victory over some poor farmers in Poland. He acts immediately:

> . . . I embrace my fortune.
> I have some rights of memory in this kingdom,
> Which now to claim my vantage doth invite me.
>
> HAMLET (5.2, 395–97)

Jeff Bezos, too, knows how to take charge. Whether or not Amazon.com will eventually lose (under his direction) is not the main issue. He has built a stupendous business, not by waiting to see what was going to happen, but by making it happen.

The next time you notice that you are spending most of your time counterpunching, reframe, as we have suggested above. Don't meet the adversary head-on, outflank him. If that doesn't work, you can always go back to counterpunching. At least you tried. But when you take charge, the odds usually shift to your side.

THE WILL TO BE

It saddens me to have been so harsh with the young Prince of Denmark. He had such promise. Every time I read one of his soliloquies or notice one of his brilliant verbal ripostes, I learn more about myself, more about others, and more about the world. For these reasons, I admire Hamlet enormously.

I get angry with him primarily because he confronts me with so many of my own shortcomings. Too many times, I have lapsed into reacting rather than acting. Too many times, I have succumbed to various forms of hand-wringing, breast-beating, rage, intransigence, and impatience. Too many times, I have been unable to reframe an issue, or to know which world I was living in, let alone to understand it. But my impatience with Hamlet is also my debt to him. There have been those times, also, when he gave me fair warning. Through his and Shakespeare's mirror I have seen myself; and although it is not a property of mirrors, I have been able

283

to look ahead, to steer out of harm's way, to take charge, and, unlike the unfortunate Dane, to create my own destiny.

We began this chapter with a concept of strategy:

> An effective strategy is grounded in a set of realistic beliefs and expectations about our external worlds that helps us know what to do and how to do it, while making certain that we have the resources and will to carry it out.

Realistic beliefs and expectations about our external worlds are important, as are the resources necessary to carry out our plans. But without the *will*, these are hollow concepts. Jeff Bezos could not truly have had realistic beliefs and expectations when he began Amazon.com. He was soon able to develop realistic beliefs and expectations because he had the *will* to do so. Bezos certainly did not have the resources when he began, but he had the *will* to get them.

Prince Hamlet might have had the desire to rid Denmark of Claudius and assume the government himself, but he did not have the *will* to do it. He might have avenged his father's death, but he did not have the *will* to do it. He might have loved Ophelia, but he didn't have the *will* to build the relationship. He might have been king, but he didn't have the *will*. The tragedy is wrapped in his famous phrase before the duel with Laertes: "The readiness is all." What a difference if the readiness had been to live, rather than to die.

> To be, or not to be, that is the question:
> Whether 'tis nobler in the mind to suffer
> The slings and arrows of outrageous fortune,
> Or to take arms against a sea of troubles
> And by opposing end them. To die—to sleep,
> No more; and by a sleep to say we end
> The heart-ache and the thousand natural shocks
> That flesh is heir to: 'tis a consummation
> Devoutly to be wish'd. To die, to sleep;
> To sleep, perchance to dream—ay, there's the rub:
> For in that sleep of death what dreams may come,

When we have shuffled off this mortal coil,
Must give us pause—there's the respect
That makes calamity of so long life.
For who would bear the whips and scorns of time,
Th'oppressor's wrong, the proud man's contumely,
The pangs of dispriz'd love, the law's delay,
The insolence of office, and the spurns
That patient merit of th'unworthy takes,
When he himself might his quietus make
With a bare bodkin? Who would fardels bear,
To grunt and sweat under a weary life,
But that the dread of something after death,
The undiscover'd country, from whose bourn
No traveller returns, puzzles the will,
And makes us rather bear those ills we have
Than fly to others that we know not of?
Thus conscience does make cowards of us all,
And thus the native hue of resolution
Is sicklied o'er with the pale cast of thought,
And enterprises of great pitch and moment
With this regard their currents turn awry
And lose the name of action.

HAMLET (3.1, 56–88)

Epilogue: A Woman

As Rosalind says at the end of *As You Like It*, "It is not the fashion to see the lady the epilogue; but it is no more unhandsome than to see the lord the prologue." Perhaps as women are moving into positions of overt power, it is appropriate that Tina write the epilogue and speak for both of us:

I—Tina, now—find myself interested in the changing power plays that are emerging in the corporate and business world.

If we accept the idea that Shakespeare's plays are reflections of his most serious thinking—and that he has had a momentous effect on the way we all think, whether we know it or not—do we have something new to learn about relationships and management systems from his late plays? These plays he wrote at the end of his life, after he had proved his point, made all the money he needed, had one of the best houses in Stratford, was the chief shareholder in a thriving theater company. The late plays (or romances, as they are often called, a name that doesn't really acknowledge their subterranean power) seem to have been written when Shakespeare was back living in Stratford and returning to London only occasionally, instead of the reverse, his habit of the previous twenty years. These plays are *Pericles, Cymbeline, The Winter's Tale, The Tempest,* and *King Henry VIII* (often performed under its second title, *All Is True*).

After the violence of the *King Henry IV*s and *King Henry V*, the annihilation of nations in *King Richard III* and *Macbeth*, the indecision of *Hamlet*, the tenacious, loyal service of the Earl of Kent, Flavius, and Philip the Bastard, the deliberate deception of Iago, the self-deception of Brutus—all ways of power we recognize both inside and out of the corporation—then come the late plays, which change the story. These plays contain the same commitment to life as it is as all the earlier plays, yet end up with a sense of redemption, a sense of new growth, a sense of collaboration, with the distinction between leaders and followers becoming blurred.

Let me tell you the stories of four of these late plays.

Pericles: The man who discovers the secret of the evil empire (the perversion of innocent love: in this case, incest) chooses not to confront or do battle, but flees. He deserts his own country and embarks on a long journey. He falls in love with a woman who also chooses him, but in a huge tempest loses his wife and leaves behind his daughter. After many years, when he believes he has lost everything that was dear to him, he becomes a stone incapable of feeling. Eventually he is restored to life by the creativity of his lost daughter, and through his dream is reunited with his wife.

Cymbeline: A king, dominated by the old rules and a wicked wife, loses his daughter (having lost his sons years earlier). The daughter is betrayed by her husband, whom she married in secret, and is pursued by the brute her parents want her to marry. Disguised as a man, the daughter, through her allies, destroys a monster and returns the kingdom to its sanity, is reunited with father and husband, and returns the lost sons to their rightful place. The kingdom regains its peace and makes a new treaty with Rome.

The Winter's Tale: A king is jealous of his best friend and believes he's having an affair with his wife. Not heeding the voices of his counselors and then the Higher Power, the king destroys his wife and son and loses his daughter. The tale can be completed only through the collaboration of several people: a witch; a young man who stands with love instead of kingdoms; and the daughter whose return brings the mother back to life.

The Tempest: A leader, who neglected his dominion and pursued knowledge without care for consequences, is banished to a lonely island with only his daughter and his books, the tools of his creative power. He lives between two worlds, trying to control the forces of darkness and yet still being able to create whatever he wants. In the end he chooses love over revenge, acknowledges the thing of darkness as his own, turns the creative spirit free, and returns to the mundane task of daily living and leading, with the daughter who is able to embrace the "brave new world, that has such people in't!"

In all these stories, the person who has the power does not have balance in his life; consequently, his power becomes a destructive force when he makes mistaken choices, and it wreaks havoc on everyone around him. Then, as now, those with power hold that power in part because of the work and collaboration of others. Virginia Woolf, a great voice of the twentieth century, expressed it this way: "Masterpieces are not single and solitary births; they are the outcome of many years of thinking in common, in thinking by the body of people, so that the experience of the mass is behind a single voice." [30]

I like to think of the well-run corporation as a masterpiece: a place that comes out of and gives life, strength, and a sense of recognition to the people who work there or receive benefits from it. Jack Welch or someone from R&D might be the acknowledged genius—but the work is dependent on everyone at GE, including those who no longer work for the corporation. In my own small way, I have fought to build an organization that supports the creativity of all the members—for, indeed, in the business of producing plays, the product *is* creativity, six days a week, for an audience of thousands, who will go home filled, we trust, with new creative energy, refreshed and ready to encounter the problems of the next day with alacrity and verve. It is a tremendous challenge to keep a group of people at optimum creativity, to give all members of the group a voice, to keep the mission of the company firmly in the forefront of everyone's focus, to act as a whole while allowing for individual creativity, and to keep the leadership as democratic as possible. It is the challenge we have given ourselves, and one I hope we are meeting.

An organization that is concerned with the humanity of human beings as well as the bottom line is, surely, a model for the future. The model we have been using for the past two thousand years— the model best exemplified by the army, the church, and the state, of ever mounting hierarchical chains of command—has always been dependent on control of knowledge. The person higher up the food chain has had more knowledge than the one below and therefore, in theory, was more capable of making the superior decision.

Few leaders give up power willingly. And there is a quick efficiency that comes from a "Do it because I say so" type of organization. (And in wartime we are grateful for the fast action that comes out of direct command.) But that kind of command doesn't encourage original thinking—and original thinking is necessary for the modern world. So the tide is turning, especially in some of the extraordinarily successful small and medium-size firms. The rapidity of change and the access to information at all levels are so great that there is no longer time for elaborate hierarchical structures. Economic forces require a flatter organization with fewer levels of management and a broader sharing of leadership, which in turn are encouraging a greater sense of commitment to the enterprise, an ethos that respects caring and fundamental human values. These values are reflected in the stated views of many notable corporate leaders as varied as Visa's Dee Hock, Monsanto's Bob Shapiro, and GE's Jack Welch. They are being field-tested with strong bottom-line results at places like the Lincoln Continental division of Ford and Dataquest, the computer industry analyst.

Competitive companies today are collaborating with others. In fact, by pooling resources, forming alliances, and sharing back-office services, companies are becoming more efficient *and* more collegial. So we see a trend toward forming alliances that exploit new opportunities, pooling resources to achieve mutual ends, and forming coalitions to achieve economies of scale. Such blurred boundaries are true even of such business giants as IBM, Ford Motor Company, and General Electric.

In America we are committed to the idea that we all have equal rights—no matter how far we fall short of the ideal—and we know from our experience of encountering the challenges of disaster, nature, or war, that the group that can work together, think creatively and collaboratively, and stay engaged in the problem is the group that will survive. Any woman or man who has brought up a child on her or his own knows it's much easier to do if there is extended family around, and better yet if, yes, there is a village willing to participate. It is to collaboration and celebration rather than competition and exclusion that Shakespeare points in his late plays.

There are generative principles (those key points that have to be struggled with, or new life will not come forth) that are common to all the plays. I am going to list them and then point to what I think the modern corporate equivalent is:

1. There is something that has been lost and must be found.

2. Inert life can be changed to joy and laughter by letting go of previously firmly held beliefs.

3. Creativity lives in everyone and must be given expression one way or another.

4. Riding the tempest is part of life and cannot be avoided.

5. Real satisfaction comes out of relationships, and power without relationship leads to disaster for everyone.

6. While we inherit the world with its beliefs and structures from those who have gone before us, we are giving the world to those we give birth to, and we will not like ourselves, nor they us, if we hand off something of which we are not proud!

7. The idea of the individual hero is only the first step of the journey; for the world to really work, many people must work together in collaboration and creativity over many years.

To put this in terms of the corporation:

1. The thing being made or the service being offered must have real value and bring with it a sense of recognition. The workplace must offer a sense of satisfaction; it must be possible after many struggles to develop a rightness and fullness about the job, no matter what the job is. There has to be a place for the soul.

2. A miserable workplace can be altered by inviting all the participants to think creatively about how their lives can be ordered and by allowing them to invest in the gains and losses; people perform better when they organize themselves than when others force them into regimented patterns.

3. Once technical skills are acquired (and all creativity comes out of first gaining mastery in the necessary techniques or disciplines) and have become second nature, then the real fun begins: creativity can be launched. This can be as simple as the way the re-

ceptionist decorates the reception area, the way the VP rewards her team, the way information flows through an organization, the way the workweek is organized. But every act can be an encouragement of energy bursting forth, a fresh way of seeing the world. Inventive mistakes will be rewarded, not penalized!

4. The organization will change; the ways of working will change; there is form in chaos, and the one constant is change. This is a reflection of nature. Satisfaction comes from letting go, from looking out, from having confidence that your colleagues will help you and you will help them, and from enjoying the discovery of new worlds.

5. If the thing you make or the knowledge you control has a destructive component, sooner or later that destruction will be visited on the world. Are you willing to be responsible for that destruction? Power has far-reaching effects; can you encompass both the good and the evil? Are you willing to think about these things? If what you want to do is to contribute to life—to the life of your spouse, your children, your workmates, your community— are you doing the things that will allow you to deepen those relationships?

6. What are the consequences of your work? Every action you take creates a reality; that reality in turn defines you: you must re-create out of that reality—and so it goes. Is this reality that you are creating the one you want your children or your community to inherit? Are they responding well to it? If not, can you think more deeply about it, shift some things that will make the whole function better? Whom can you ask? Which way can you look?

7. The old story—John Wayne taking on the bad guys alone, Charles Bronson cleaning up New York crime single-handedly, Oedipus being thrown out on the hillside, Alexander conquering Asia Minor from Athens to Egypt to India—these are examples from the first chapter in the development of human consciousness. They are not the whole story. The rugged individual standing up for his rights in the face of enormous odds (it is usually a man: women are organizing the kids, the parents, the friends, and so don't put so much emphasis on this first story) does not, by himself, get the world where it wants to go. It wants to go toward col-

laboration rather than opposition, toward win/win rather than win/lose, toward getting to "yes" instead of "me yes, you no." The secret is to be able to recognize others without losing your self, to have a sense of self-worth, even when you lose the game. The secret is loving celebration more than competition and using competition to celebrate, rather than celebrating competition as an end in itself. The secret is creating a story to live out of that will enable the individual and the group to live a full life, a creative life, a life well acknowledged.

Where are these things happening? In Shakespeare's late plays and in organizations, businesses, town councils, relief organizations, pop groups, high-tech start-ups, PTAs, unions, churches, *Fortune* 500 spin-offs. The new ways of working are creating a desire to revise the story, challenge the way we look at life. It is a huge change, not just in business, but in the world, the place in which we all live. This kind of paradigm shift is the world Shakespeare wrote about in his late plays, *King Henry VIII* in particular.

The very last play Shakespeare wrote was, we think, *King Henry VIII*, often called *All Is True*. And yes, he collaborated on it. He collaborated with John Fletcher—as he probably did with *Two Noble Kinsmen*. And this is the play that burned the Globe down—at least, the cannon from the play did—creating change in the life of the King's Men. And we will finish with a statement from *All Is True*. The play returns to the world of the all-dominating patriarch whose rule Shakespeare's generation inherited: we see that the great struggles for spiritual enlightenment (the Reformation) had more to do with the economic strife and personality differences of various individuals at the top than a search for truth; we see that the symbol of spiritual authority is a flawed man, like others; and finally that the power will pass to the feminine spirit—and, don't forget, the feminine spirit is the creative spirit in both men and women—in the form of the baby Elizabeth:

> . . . good grows with her;
> In her days every man shall eat in safety
> Under his own vine what he plants, and sing

The merry songs of peace to all his neighbours.
God shall be truly known, and those about her
From her shall read the perfect ways of honour,
And by those claim their greatness, not by blood.

KING HENRY VIII (5.4, 32–38)

I doubt we'll ever be that perfect, but it's an inspiring aspiration.

Notes

1. All quotations are in accordance with *The Arden Shakespeare Complete Works,* 3rd ed. (Surrey, U.K.: 1998).
2. Speech to the Electors of Bristol, November 3, 1774.
3. Discovered—on behalf of Europe: Native Americans and explorers from Iceland had, of course, long before "discovered" America.
4. One of the more irritating qualities of English monarchy is their propensity for having the same Christian names: Harry or Henry, Richard, and Edward, with an occasional Charles, James, or George thrown in. I suppose we have our share of Jacks, Johns, Garys, and Freds—but somehow they are not so confusing.
5. John Byrne, *The Whiz Kids* (New York: Currency, 1993), Chapter 21.
6. John O. Whitney, *The Economics of Trust* (New York: McGraw-Hill, 1996), Chapter 7.
7. Kenneth J. Arrow, *The Limits of Organization* (New York: W. W. Norton, 1974), 23.
8. I know it's not that easy for men either—but the odds are not anywhere near as long as they were for Oprah.
9. Statistics from *Women in Corporate Leadership: Progress and Prospects* (New York: Catalyst, 1996).
10. Ibid.
11. Katharine Graham, *Personal History* (New York: Knopf, 1997), 418–19.
12. *Women in Corporate Leadership.*
13. Ibid.
14. Over the years, the massive number of lines a Shakespearean actor in repertory must have in reserve has created some amusing mix-ups. One of Tina's favorites is the story of Frank Benson, who ran the company at Stratford-on-Avon in the early part of the last century. Benson also played all the leads. The company was financially poor and had to use the same stage sets for different plays. For example, the wall that Henry V's troops scale at the Battle of Harfleur was the same wall used for the Rialto in *The Merchant of Venice.* Playing Henry V, Benson would pole-vault over this wall, urging his troops to follow. During

one performance of *The Merchant of Venice,* the merchants of the Rialto (and the audience at Stratford) were astounded to see Shylock fly over the wall, yelling, "Once more unto the breach, dear friends, once more!"

15. Anthony Burgess, *Shakespeare* (Chicago: Ivan R. Dee, 1970).

16. This is Shakespeare's gloss on his rival Christopher Marlowe's description of Helen as "the face that launched a thousand ships and burnt the topless towers of Ilium." Moviegoers who saw *Shakespeare in Love* will recognize the lines from the hilarious scene where Shakespeare holds auditions for his new play and one actor after another recites this line from Marlowe, much to the competitive young Shakespeare's chagrin.

17. There is no evidence that *Troilus and Cressida* was ever performed in public. Some scholars believe that it might have been put on for a private, more politically sophisticated audience. The day before Essex's uprising, his followers had hired Shakespeare's players, The Lord Chamberlain's Men, to stage a performance of *King Richard II,* apparently hoping that his depiction of the deposition of the "skipping king" might turn the city against Elizabeth. The queen was not amused, and, doubtless, Shakespeare was not going to press his luck and give her the chance to see treason in *Troilus and Cressida.*

18. "My Way": words by Paul Anka, music by J. Revaux and C. François.

19. Donald E. Petersen and John Hillkirk, *A Better Idea* (Boston: Houghton Mifflin, 1991), 21–22.

20. Daniel 5:27. *Tekel:* "Thou art weighed in the balances, and art found wanting." (Part of the writing on the wall at Belshazzar's feast, as interpreted by the prophet Daniel. He correctly divined that Belshazzar's kingdom would come to an end and be handed to the Medes and the Persians—which prophecy was imminently fulfilled when Belshazzar was murdered that same night, with King Darius of the Medes taking over the kingdom.)

21. These emerging economic concepts and business practices were spread by Dutch traders to London and by Dutch colonists to New Amsterdam (founded in 1625), both centers of world capitalism today. Simon Schama, *The Embarrassment of Riches: An Interpretation of Dutch Culture in the Golden Age* (New York: Knopf, 1987).

22. Beginning with Edward II (died 1327), six monarchs were deposed: Edward II, Richard II, Henry VI, Edward V (one of the princes in the Tower), and Lady Jane Grey; Richard III died in battle fighting his de-

poser. Only four, Henry V, Henry VIII, Edward VI, and Elizabeth, were neither deposed nor involved in a deposition.

23. To be sure, he also had to please the queen's censors. He nearly paid the ultimate price for his deposition scene in *Richard II* when that play was linked to the Essex rebellion.
24. Whitney, *The Economics of Trust.*
25. Arrow, *The Limits of Organization,* 23.
26. Whitney, *The Economics of Trust.*
27. We are not touting Amazon.com's stock. It still isn't clear to us that Jeff Bezos will succeed in the long run, but so far, he's done amazingly well. We admire his intellect, his business sense, and his guts. Our chapter was written in the summer of 1999, six months before *Time* magazine named Bezos "Man of the Year."
28. This last line, from the First Folio, is not found in the Arden edition.
29. John O. Whitney, *Taking Charge* (Dow Jones–Irwin, 1987; republished by Beard Books, Washington, D.C., 1999).
30. *A Room of One's Own,* first American ed. (New York: Harcourt, Brace, 1938).

Acknowledgments

Writers are at once free spirits and captives. Free spirits because we are the ones who decide which ideas to advance, which word to use. Captives because we owe so much to others. Whether it be a chance remark by a friend, a reasoned argument by a colleague, a memorable piece of writing by a master, or an insight triggered almost accidentally by contemplation of an unrelated issue, there is precious little we can call our own.

The hero of this book, William Shakespeare, is testament to this verity. None of his plots is original; he, like his friends and his colleagues, is a product of his times; but the insights and words he chose were his. In this spirit, Tina Packer and I accept full responsibility for this work—its useful insights as well as its errors and omissions—but like all writers, we have a heavy debt to others.

Acknowledgments usually end with accolades for the writer's assistant followed by the obligatory gratefulness to spouse and family. I prefer to begin with thanks to my wife, Marcia, not only for her faith and encouragement but also for her patient prodding. She kept me on schedule. Joy Glazener has been my assistant at Columbia for the past ten years. Her knowledge of Greek, Roman, medieval, and Renaissance history and literature provided important insights into Shakespeare and the people he wrote about. Moreover, she turned my handwritten pages and Tina's emendations into finished manuscript. Another associate, Kenneth Craddock, a fine historian and devoted student of management theory, filled in the blanks on many of the book's business cases and historical anecdotes. When my course "In Search of the Perfect Prince" was announced at Columbia Business School, one of the first calls I received was from Wendy Kritzer, wife of one of our MBA candidates and a Shakespeare teacher in Boston. She helped design the course, wrote the teacher's manual, organized the readings, and, in the process, made a significant contribution to the book.

Two of my Columbia colleagues have been faithful, stalwart critics. Robert Lear, retired executive-in-residence, chairman of the advisory board of *CEO* magazine, and successful CEO of business turnarounds, read many of the chapters and provided both support and insight. John O'Shaughnessy, of Cambridge University, provided helpful comments, but, more important, our spirited discussions on life, literature, and philosophy were stimuli to ideas in several of the chapters.

I also acknowledge Peter Saccio at Dartmouth College for his superb audio lectures on Shakespeare and his plays. Although Harold Bloom probably would not agree with some of the ideas presented here, nonetheless his monumental book *Shakespeare: The Invention of the Human* was an enormous help. Earlier scholars, notably A. L. Rowse and E. M. W. Tillyard, have influenced my views on Shakespeare and his plays and my views on his times. Thanks also to Dr. Don B. Bane, whose spirited discussions of Roman, medieval, and Renaissance history also contributed to my understanding.

E. T. "Bud" Gravette, retired chairman of the Turner Corporation, on whose board I serve, addressed my classes at Columbia on several management issues relating to Shakespeare's plays, but, more important, his masterful turnaround at Turner reinforced many of my beliefs about management theory. My thanks, also, to Heidi Fiske, who arranged for some of my first seminars on Shakespeare and leadership with practicing business executives. Hubert Herring, editor at *The New York Times,* sat in on my *Coriolanus* class and interviewed many of the students. His article on December 6, 1998, triggered phone calls from eight literary agents and ten publishers. Thanks, Hubert.

The agent I selected, James Levine, has been a superb professional and a good friend. His thoughtful guidance, augmented by his education in the classics, contributed to both style and substance. When Fred Hills, editor at Simon & Schuster, interviewed me in February 1999, I commented that I favored a tough editor. Fred didn't let me down. I worked for three days on the introduction to one of the chapters. Fred took three minutes to say, "John, that might be good prose, but it doesn't support the theme of the chapter." He was right. Fred's other editorial comments were always on target. He's a real pro and a pleasure to work with.

When time was pressing in upon us, and as Tina and I were often at opposite ends of the earth, we asked Ed Tivnan to coordinate and reorder some of the material. He not only did that, but his classical training and interest in the subject resulted in additional insights, which delighted us and added to the finished manuscript.

I have been fortunate the past fifteen years to teach at Columbia Business School, where the stimulus provided by my colleagues and students has pressed me to do my very best. Professor Meyer Feldberg, dean of the school, has been unusually supportive, providing encouragement, resources, and time to write.

Two professors at Florida Atlantic University whose seminars I attended recently also were helpful. Marshall L. DeRosa provided a useful perspective on Shakespeare's Greek and Roman tragedies. Michael Guastella, a gifted actor and teacher, on the one hand questioned the wisdom of commandering Shakespeare into a management book, but his analysis of Richard II, "A man who cannot rule himself cannot rule others," seemed to belie his words. Whether or not we are in agreement, I acknowledge his comments on the *Hamlet* chapter and thank him for being an exciting teacher.

Both Tina Packer and I pay special tribute to Jane Polin, one of my former students who went on to an important role at the General Electric Fund. In that capacity she came to support Tina's work and, knowing of my interest in Shakespeare and the literary arts, arranged for us to meet.

And that leads to a special acknowledgment. Those who know Tina Packer agree that she is a joy to be around. Her enthusiasm, her laughter, her encyclopedic knowledge of Shakespeare's plays, and her organizational skills helped to make her the perfect collaborator.

—John O. Whitney
New York City and Palm Beach Gardens, Florida

As John ended with me, I will start with him. Through him, I have found my fascination with management structures has grown exponentially, making it almost as good as directing or acting in a play. His courtesy, elegance, and down-to-earth qualities have made the collaboration a delight, and his passion for the workplace has had extraordinarily beneficial effects on my own company, which (inevitably) has been undergoing its largest transition ever during the writing of this book. I want to acknowledge the management team and board of trustees of Shakespeare & Company, who have absorbed my writing absences and my teaching at Columbia in their stride. Their patience and enthusiasm as I insist on management structures that combine artists' creativity with a pursuit of ongoing managerial excellence have been thrilling. Michael Miller as board chairman and Chris Sink as managing director are in the pivotal leadership roles that absorb and expedite this tension, and I thank them from the bottom of my heart. And I think the artist managers of Shakespeare & Company will change the world.

My executive assistant, Michael Hammond, has been key in all the negotiations between myself and John, Fred Hills, James Levine, and the Columbia School of Business. Michael's insight is terrific, his humor necessary. What would I do without him?

I deeply join with John in his acknowledgment of Fred Hills and the team at Simon & Schuster, James Levine and his terrific colleagues, and the absolutely indispensable Joy Glazener and Ken Craddock. Our mutual delight in Jane Polin is ongoing; however, for me, Jane Polin has also been a tower of support in aligning Shakespeare & Company with GE, for both financial and management support. Clifford Smith, Maura Touhey, Bob Fines, Bob Hess, and now Duron Grossman have all contributed to our success, and so to this book.

Walter Campbell went through the book, aligning all the spelling and punctuation with the Arden edition. He insists his love of Shakespeare made it an easy task—but I am so grateful I did not have to do it. Ann St. Clair did an enormous amount of work on the manuscript from my end, and again when time was running out, Gail Molari and her staff, Tricia and Aimée, went into emergency overtime typing the rewrites.

Through the years I have had philosophic discussions with Mitch Berenson, a waterfront union leader turned real estate developer and founding chairman of the board of Shakespeare & Company, on the ways of power. He's an inspiration. Neil Colvin, founder of Phoenix Technologies, was the first corporate leader who loved the theater and Shakespeare with whom I became a close friend. And I have enjoyed walking in the woods with Torrey Harder, venture capitalist extraordinaire, discussing Thoreau, new capital, Shakespeare, and the excitement of business. Anything I do is deeply influenced one way or another by my son, Jason, and colleagues Normi Noel, Carol and Jim Gilligan, Kristin Linklater, Kevin Coleman, and all the core members of the Shakespeare & Company team.

Finally, of course, I acknowledge my husband, Dennis Krausnick. He not only proofed the manuscript and made emendations, but he has worked through the night with me on many occasions and never wavers in his support. We have now been discussing William Shakespeare for a quarter of a century, and may it long continue!

—Tina Packer
Stockbridge, Massachusetts

7

Index